Confucian Propriety
and Ritual Learning

SUNY series in Chinese Philosophy and Culture
―――――――
Roger T. Ames, editor

Confucian Propriety and Ritual Learning

A Philosophical Interpretation

Geir Sigurðsson

Published by State University of New York Press, Albany

© 2015 State University of New York

All rights reserved

Printed in the United States of America

No part of this book may be used or reproduced in any manner whatsoever without written permission. No part of this book may be stored in a retrieval system or transmitted in any form or by any means including electronic, electrostatic, magnetic tape, mechanical, photocopying, recording, or otherwise without the prior permission in writing of the publisher.

For information, contact State University of New York Press, Albany, NY
www.sunypress.edu

Production, Eileen Nizer
Marketing, Anne M. Valentine

Library of Congress Cataloging-in-Publication Data

Geir Sigurðsson, date.
 Confucian propriety and ritual learning : a philosophical interpretation / Geir Sigurðsson.
    pages cm. — (SUNY series in Chinese philosophy and culture)
 Includes bibliographical references and index.
 ISBN 978-1-4384-5441-2 (hardcover : alk. paper)
 ISBN 978-1-4384-5442-9 (ebook)
 1. Philosophy, Confucian. 2. Tradition (Philosophy). 3. Ritual—China. 4. Education—China. I. Title.

B127.C65G45 2015
181'.112—dc23   2014006585

10 9 8 7 6 5 4 3 2 1

Contents

Acknowledgments	vii
Introduction	1
Interpretive Viewpoints and Prejudgments	1
Subjective Objectivity and Hermeneutic Productivity of Cultural Distance	5
Chinese Culture, Ritual Propriety, and the Importance of Learning	10
The Modern Opprobrium of Ritual and the Confucian Tradition	13
1. First Assemblage: Tradition and Timeliness	19
From Aversion to Rehabilitation: The Modern Discourse on Tradition	20
Tradition as *Dao* 道: The Early Confucian Approach to Tradition	26
The Temporal Sequence of Practice and the Chinese Notion of Time	31
Hitting the Mark: *Zhong* 中, *Shizhong* 時中, and *Zhongyong* 中庸	38
2. Second Assemblage: From Reason to Intelligence	49
Education and/or Indoctrination: A Borderless Distinction	50
Reason I: Max Weber's Paradox	55
Reason II: The Quest for Reason in China	59
Reason III: Reasonable Alternatives	63
Reason IV: The Interplay of *Li* 禮, *Yi* 義, and *Li* 理	70
3. Third Assemblage: Education as Humanization	81
Education through Experience: Reconciling Tradition and Reason	82

Aesthetic Consciousness and Ritual Knowledge	91
Internalization and Efficacy: *Li* 禮, *Yue* 樂, *De* 德, and *Ren* 仁	100
Education as Exhortation and Personal Cultivation	111
Concluding Remarks	119
Notes	133
Literature Cited	161
Index	169

Acknowledgments

One who is not a sage is incapable of carrying through a major project without involving a few other persons, and a true sage would surely involve many more. While I of course assume the sole responsibility for the shortcomings of this work, it would not have been brought to conclusion without the direct and indirect help from others.

First of all, I want to convey my thanks to my former teachers in the Department of Philosophy at University of Hawai'i at Manoa, in particular Roger T. Ames, Thomas E. Jackson, and Graham Parkes (now at University College Cork, Ireland), who have generously shared with me, through words and deeds, their insights into and visions of the possibility of a better humanity.

The final phase of research for this book was undertaken at the Nordic Centre, Fudan University, Shanghai, and at the Asia Research Institute, National University of Singapore, while I was on sabbatical leave from the University of Iceland in 2012. I am grateful to all parties for having made these fruitful and savory visits possible.

While I was preparing the manuscript for publication, Neal O'Donoghue smoothed out rough edges in the text and made a number of ingenious philosophical suggestions to clarify its arguments.

Last but not least, I owe much gratitude to my wonderful family, Vilma Kinderyte, Viktoría and Emilía, for their patience and loving support. This book is for them.

Introduction

Interpretive Viewpoints and Prejudgments

Most serious students of philosophy in the contemporary West have surely felt themselves confronted with the following dilemma: on the one hand, one needs to undergo the immensely time-consuming process of adequately familiarizing oneself with a philosophical tradition spanning over two and a half millennia. Some of the more richly insightful philosophers and philosophical schools of the past appear to be virtually inexhaustible sources, and thus to merit a lifetime of study as such. On the other hand, philosophers are increasingly being expected, not least in their own camp, to make meaningful contributions to seminal issues and toward finding solutions to the more acute problems of the present. The continuously evolving puzzles arising in all areas of human existence require an ability to come up with fresh approaches and perspectives that would seem to leave little room for a focused concentration on bygone philosophical ventures.

This has brought many philosophers to refrain for the most part from considering the second task and to focus exclusively on the first. Albert Camus described the situation most poignantly when he wrote that "the age of philosophers concerned with philosophy was followed by the age of professors of philosophy concerned with philosophers."[1]

Further exploration of this "dilemma," however, reveals that it is overstated, resting upon the misconception that the two tasks are clearly distinguishable. It is assumed, in the first case, that we are able to engage in some kind of "pure" philosophy detached from and independent of tradition, culture and historical circumstances; and, in the second case, that further analysis of past philosophies will automatically lead to a better understanding of them. The latter belief presupposes that the scholarship of philosophical interpretation evolves in a qualitatively linear fashion. Certainly, misunderstandings occur, and they will often be revealed and corrected through further investigation. But the "better" understanding we obtain of past ideas will for the most part be better in the sense of being more appropriate to the paradigms of understanding and value within which we ourselves operate. In fact, in both of the above-mentioned tasks, we make past philosophies relevant, with varying degrees of success, to our present circumstances and issues. The difference between nuanced interpretations is predominantly a difference of emphasis and focus, depending on different intentionalities and attitudes of the diversely situated interpreters.

However, because we tend to underestimate the role of our own creativity in our hermeneutical ventures, the application of the philosophy in question tends to result in a detailed discussion and controversy over the "correctness" of its interpretation. And since the detailed interpretations of a particular thinker or school are almost as many as there are specialists, we get stuck again in concentrating on the first task—that of enhancing our understanding of past philosophies.

The present work certainly contains an implicit claim to a reconstruction of meaning. But it is a reconstruction that takes into account the situatedness of the reconstructing agent—namely, in this case, me and the projected audience. Hence, although the main source of this work is the Confucian philosophy of the Warring States period in ancient China, there will be no pretension toward a reconstruction of the "original" meaning of that philosophy. There is, in any case, no available "neutral" standard by which to appraise such a meaning.

It is a commonplace of philosophy and cultural studies to observe that whatever we approach, we always approach from some point of view. There is, as Thomas Nagel pointed out, no such thing as a view from nowhere. Evidently, such perspectivism applies not least to texts. When reading a text, we cannot but approach it from the point of view of the expectations we have of it, however vague they may be. One might object that in some cases we know nothing about the text before picking it up and therefore have no expectations at all. Nevertheless, as soon as we start deciphering it, we are bound to form some. We try to place the text (by language, period, genre, etc.), and as soon as we have made some preliminary categorizations, we have "pre-judgments" about it.

The notion of "pre-judgment" is borrowed from the late Hans-Georg Gadamer, whose hermeneutic philosophy serves as an important inspiration for the approach taken to the topic at hand. Pre-judgment (*Vor-urteil*), a rehabilitation of the more pejorative notion of "prejudice"

(*Vorurteil*), refers to the culturally and personally conditioned categories that enable us to meaningfully conceptualize and contextualize the objects of our attention, whereby we begin our journey on the path towards understanding them. Our understanding of things is therefore bound to be conditioned, not only by our particular cultural heritage, language, and environment, but also by our own education, experience, and personality. As Gadamer has written,

> [e]very age has to understand a transmitted text in its own way, for the text is a part of the whole of the tradition in which the age takes an objective interest and in which it seeks to understand itself. The real meaning of a text, as it speaks to the interpreter, does not depend on the contingencies of the author and whom he originally wrote for. It is at least not exhausted by them, for it is partly determined also by the historical situation of the interpreter and hence by the totality of the objective course of history.[2]

Without wanting to overstate the innumerable factors that contribute to a relativization or subjectivization of understanding, I suggest that even our best interpretation of a text would surely appear foreign to the temporally and spatially distant authors of that very same text. This applies even more so to texts such as the ancient Chinese ones, handed over in a linguistic medium so different from the one of the present work, and produced in a time and cultural environment so distant from the twenty-first century. These two—the ancient Chinese texts and the temporal and cultural setting of the present interpreter—are literally worlds apart. Gadamer, in the passage above, is referring chiefly to the interpretation of texts written within a chronologically distant but culturally related milieu such as the interpretation of ancient Greek or Roman texts in the contemporary West. He thus considers the assumed stance of interpreters of the texts to be one in which they attempt to come to a better understanding of their own culture. This is doubtless rarely the case when Westerners attempt to interpret writings that belong to a distant culture. In such endeavors, they take the stance of the Sinologist, the Japanologist, the Indologist, for example, and the dominant drive will be toward understanding the texts themselves on the basis of their own linguistic abilities and previously acquired knowledge of the culture in which these texts originate. It is perhaps only in the last instance, through mostly implicit, even unconscious, comparisons, that such an understanding helps to enhance Westerners' understanding of their own culture.

It is not my intention to criticize such approaches. In fact, the contemporary penchant to restrict the analysis of "exotic" cultural products to the sphere of that very culture or neighboring cultures is an important corrective to the earlier anthropological and ethnological practice of reinforcing the Westerner's self-satisfaction by posing questions merely within the paradigm of some dubious version of social Darwinism. An exclusively internal analysis of a culture not only signifies respect for that culture—its various aspects are taken on its own terms—but such an analysis is also more likely to yield better and more accurate results.

In the present work, however, I will be crossing the borders between East and West in a more conspicuous manner. Because this is not a work in Sinology but in philosophy, I shall permit myself to regard the Confucian insights primarily as philosophical and only secondarily as specifically ancient Chinese ideas. It goes without saying that these two viewpoints are not always clearly separable and that a provisional focus on the second is often necessary in order to even begin considering the first. Although there is a tempting truth contained in Roland Barthes's claim of the death of the author, it is difficult to conceive of the death of the entire culture within which a text is produced. An attempt to interpret a text while at the same time disregarding its underlying cultural factors may be, for literary-analytical as for other such purposes, an interesting experiment or an amusing game. Such an enterprise, however, seems fruitless when one is engaging in a critical philosophical inquiry that also needs to take heed of underlying cultural assumptions. There can be no philosophy independent of culture. At least this much we should have learned from thinkers such as Karl Marx and Friedrich Nietzsche.

To regard Confucian insights, then, primarily from a philosophical point of view does not at all mean to disregard the culture in which these insights came into existence. A sincere attempt to understand, interpret, and apply Chinese philosophy requires considerable Sinological detours. Nevertheless, cultivating the philosophical view still allows me some leeway to concentrate on the above-mentioned task of contributing to seminal philosophical issues of the present. Such a task requires, of course, that the Confucian philosophy be brought into interplay with some Western ideas that deal directly with these issues. How can such a move be justified? Are these worlds of thought not too diverse to allow for direct comparisons, let alone cooperation, between ideas?

We may think of this problem in modified Gadamerian terms. Gadamer suggests that temporal distance is not necessarily an obstacle for understanding a text. Through the advantage of having an overview of the history that has elapsed since the composition of the text, prejudices inherent in it and hidden from its contemporaries can be revealed and brought to light. The different perspectives and approaches of the variously historically situated interpreters thus enable new and divergent aspects of a text's meaning to be disclosed. Prejudices, commitments, and values that are obscured from one point of view can be illuminated by another, and the reading of a text can as a result be even more "objective" at a later time.[3] Hence, far from being a "gaping ravine," Gadamer says, we ought to "recognize temporal distance as a positive and productive opportunity for understanding."[4] We may follow Georgia Warnke, a commentator on Gadamer's philosophy, in referring to this opportunity as "the hermeneutic productivity of temporal distance."[5]

Subjective Objectivity and Hermeneutic Productivity of Cultural Distance

Gadamer assigns the normative power of judgment to "effective history" (*Wirkungsgeschichte*), which refers to the operating force of tradition over those belonging to it. Thus, his somewhat Hegel-inspired concept of "objectivity" has been subject to much criticism, for it would seem to entail the danger of justifying narrow or irrational ideological elements that may dominate the tradition at a particular time. While Gadamer denies that this is the case, this complicated and inconclusive discussion can be left aside on this occasion, for there is no need to subscribe to Gadamer's notion of objectivity. Instead, I want to pursue one of Nietzsche's observations in order to formulate a notion of "objectivity" that would seem to better serve the purposes of this work. In his *Genealogy of Morality*, Nietzsche introduces a perspectivistic approach that calls for as many viewpoints as possible to illuminate a given subject matter. As he says, "There is *only* a perspectivistic view of things, *only* a perspectivistic 'knowledge,' and *the more* emotions we let express themselves about a certain subject, *the more* eyes, different eyes, behold that very same subject, the more perfect becomes our 'concept,' our 'objectivity' of it."[6]

This statement requires some elaboration, for Nietzsche's thought and philosophy, for all its inspiring brilliance, has proven, to say the least, somewhat difficult to apply. Nietzsche's concept of "objectivity" is an attempt to break away from the traditional concept as referring to the "correctness" of a single interpretation of a certain subject matter. There is, in any case, no such interpretation. The closest we can get to "objectivity," according to Nietzsche, is by accumulating the maximally wide range of meaningful interpretations, or of viewpoints joined in forming an interpretation, of the subject matter. Nietzsche, no less than Gadamer, was of course fully aware of the personal and cultural import that comes with every conceptualization of the world or any of its parts, which implies that a wide range of vastly different interpretations of the same thing may be justifiable depending on the origin of each. We may disagree on an interpretation, and it can, indeed, *should*, be discussed and argued for and against, but in the last instance, its "correctness," or rather, "appropriateness," will to a significant extent depend on where it came from and what role it was meant to play.

An adequate treatment of Nietzsche's argument for the attainment of objectivity through an accumulation of perspectives must proceed through two levels. First, as regards the individual person, Nietzsche maintains that every person, whether consciously apprehended or not, simultaneously holds a multiplicity of different viewpoints and perspectives. The ego in Nietzsche's understanding is a collection of drives that are often in conflict with one another, and therefore it will depend, at a particular moment, on which drives are dominant what kind of perspective will be brought to bear upon the situation.[7] A maximally "objective" concept or knowledge of anything at all, then, requires the ability to bring to one's awareness all the different drives that give rise to the multiplicity of perspectives. Even a single individual is thus able to provide a variety of different interpretations of the same thing. This insight can then be carried further to the second level, the communal one. For, obviously, a single interpreter is unable to gather all possible viewpoints when conducting research. It is then that the accumulation of viewpoints takes place within the scientific community as a whole. The task and responsibility of the single interpreter, then, is to find new points of view to illuminate the subject matter, while being fully aware that the approaches and emphases of the research are individual choices made from a vast number of possibilities and on the basis of his or her personal and/or cultural values. This is the meaning of "perspective": an emotion expressing itself about a certain subject. As Alfred North Whitehead has put it, "perspective is gradation of relevance; that is to say, it is gradation of importance."[8] Whitehead, in fact, elucidates a position which is quite Nietzschean and even anticipates Gadamer's concept of prejudgment. He says that

> [w]e may well ask whether the doctrine of perspective is not an endeavour to reduce the concept of importance to mere matter-of-fact devoid of intrinsic interest. Of course, such reduction is impossible. But it is true to say that perspective is the dead abstraction of mere fact from the living importance of things felt. The concrete truth is the variation of interest; the abstraction is the universe in perspective; the consequent science is the scheme of physical laws which, with unexpressed presuppositions, expresses the patterns of perspective as observed by average human beings.[9]

Max Weber, one of Nietzsche's more consistent (and thus complex) disciples, argued that every theory and explanation about the world is value-laden in the sense that valuation is always prior to description. One cannot but notice the origin of this argument in Nietzsche's notion of affective drives giving rise to a perspective. According to Weber, a prerequisite for an explanation or description to emerge is the choice of those aspects of reality that are of value and interest to the observer. While this is pertinent to the truth-claim of all scientific disciplines, it has particularly acute effects on the human or cultural sciences. Arguing against the application of methods in the humanities along the lines of the methods in the natural sciences, Weber says that

> [w]e have portrayed the "cultural sciences" as scientific disciplines striving to understand the manifestations of life with regard to their cultural meaning. The *meaning* that the emergence of such a manifestation has in the cultural sphere and the *reasons* for that meaning can never be derived from, based on and made comprehensible with even the most perfect system of concepts of law, for the condition for that meaning is that it be related to *value ideas*. The concept of culture is a *value concept*. The empirical reality is to us "culture" because and insofar as we relate it to value ideas. It comprises those and *only* those parts of reality that become *meaningful* for us by virtue of this relation.[10]

Thus, only by relating the cultural reality to one's own valuations can one hope to make a meaningful contribution to the human sciences. Since something is of value only if there is someone who actually values it, it is the subjective values of the researcher, made clear and explicit before research is conducted, that warrant the possibility of meaningfulness by lending the research a perspective through which certain aspects are singled out as being of value or importance. This prejudgmental approach moreover implies that it is through the most conscious and explicit form of subjectivity that one makes a contribution to objectivity—namely, the widest possible range of perspectives.[11] However, as soon as one takes one's subjective point of view as *the* objective point of view, as "exhausting the whole meaning of importance,"[12] as Whitehead puts it, one paradoxically blocks the way toward objectivity by imposing a closure on the subject matter.

An encounter with a culture, in particular one unfamiliar to us, almost automatically activates our mechanism of understanding. We search for concepts that can help us consolidate our observations of the countless factors belonging to that culture so that we can, to a certain extent, systematize them. System facilitates understanding. Not only does it gather together into a consistent whole all the vague and indistinct impressions that may have disoriented us at the beginning, but it also assimilates new and hitherto nonexperienced elements to the system. System, however, can also be an obstacle to understanding. For it demands a certain degree of rigor whereby it restricts flexibility, at least to the point of ensuring its own self-preservation, and this can in turn result in the formation of explanations of a Procrustean nature.

For a study of culture, this vast and continuously changing conglomeration of human coexistence, a certain degree of systematization is indeed essential if such a study is to be comprehensible at all. Such a study, however, should be open-ended, at best in the form of a long sequence of smaller systems, each sufficiently open to allow for interaction between their various components.

Whitehead has argued that philosophy should never start from systematization. Since, as he says, "every finite set of premises must indicate notions which are excluded from its direct purview," a philosophy that starts by systematizing runs the risk of an a priori exclusion of some components of its subject matter. Instead, he suggests, it should begin with what he calls "assemblage": "Such a process is, of course, unending. All that can be achieved is the emphasis on a few large scale notions, together with the attention to the variety of other ideas which arise in the display of those chosen for primary emphasis."[13]

Whitehead's notion of assemblage is particularly germane to the Nietzschean-Weberian view of the value-laden perspectives consciously chosen by the subjective researcher. It moreover sums up my desired approach rather neatly. I shall, therefore, call my sections "assemblages."

With each assemblage, I aim at a certain level of systematization on the basis of some carefully chosen concepts but avoid, to the best of my ability, bringing the systems to closure in order to allow for their mutual interaction and the maximally widest possibility of their further elaboration.

The notions of each assemblage are chosen not only with regard to their relevance to the specific topic of this work, but also on the basis of their philosophical significance in contemporary discourse. Thus, there is a deliberate Western perspective at play in the discussion, both in order to make it relevant to contemporary issues and to illuminate and elaborate on the topic as such. To clarify the meaning of this statement, I would like to suggest a parallel notion to Gadamer's "productivity of temporal distance"—namely, the "productivity of *cultural* distance." This notion, in fact, considerably counteracts Gadamer's reliance on "objective history" as the normative force of interpretation.

Ideas or texts that have been produced at an early stage in a culture's history, but that still play an important and ongoing role in it, tend, through time, toward a fairly coherent consensus as to their interpretation. That is to say, there will, eventually, be something of an "orthodox" understanding of them.[14] This understanding is informed, reinforced, and, in more unfortunate cases, dogmatized by previously expressed understandings, by perceived or real historical significance and impact of ideas, by ideology, and, of course, by the generally accepted view, to name but a few factors. Now when these ideas are approached from a different cultural point of view, there is a degree to which we are liberated from the cultural baggage that they carry in the culture to which they belong. Such an approach obviously runs the danger of a catastrophic misunderstanding in which we simply approach them as if they belonged to our own tradition and were based on the particular presuppositions of our culture. Nevertheless, given our awareness of such a danger, and without the pretension of providing an elucidation of their "real" meaning, we may bring them into interplay with ideas from our own culture that to some significant extent resonate with them. As long as we recognize the different identities of both, this interplay, I believe, can be productive. For thereby we are sometimes able to tease out hidden possibilities inherent in the ideas that have been inhibited by the discourse and phenomenal structures of reality in which they have been placed in their own culture. We may reach "objectivity" in the Chinese meaning of the word: the "guest's eye view," *keguan* 客觀. As long as we, as (hopefully *informed*) guests, constantly keep in mind and respect

Chinese Culture, Ritual Propriety, and the Importance of Learning

In the ancient Daoist classic, the *Zhuangzi* 莊子, we read about the sages who preserve their own "constancy" within the flow of things by changing along with them in their continuous flux.[15] Being "constant" in this sense does not imply being static or stagnant; in fact, it means quite the contrary. By continually reconfiguring their stance vis-à-vis previously unencountered circumstances, the sages are capable of handling them in a productive and successful manner. Conversely, one who is stagnant does not change with things, does not adapt to new circumstances, but instead clings to some rigid principles, even when these are not effective or productive any more. On the other end of the scale, one can certainly change with the flow of things without preserving one's constancy. In such a case, one submits unconditionally to change and becomes its slave.

The Daoist orientation toward harmonious coexistence with nature, therefore, is no mere adaptability or submission to its forces. It is no Stoic adoption of inner passionlessness or apathy toward the events of our surroundings. It is rather a movement toward understanding the process of nature in its entirety, its internal interconnections, and the mutual influences of human beings and their environment. And for such a movement, experience is vital. The content of new experiences is processed within the content of previous experiences and thus absorbed into already grounded approaches to reality. Thus, while the world is in a certain sense "new" in every moment, it is not, from one moment to the next, so radically new that the present entirely outstrips or transcends the past. There is certainly continuity within time. The present always retains something from the past, and thus, fortunately, we do not need to start from scratch every time.

Despite the general Daoist preference for concentrating on the natural world, there is no need to limit our understanding of the "flow of things" to the operation of the forces of nature. Society is no less than nature subject to constant change. Thus, to successfully take one's bearings in the "jungle" of society requires, among other things, broadness of vision, adaptability, the ability to recognize features of the novel that may be informed by the old, as well as sufficient creativity and personal assertion to reinterpret and readapt these features to the situation at hand.

In this work, I want to suggest, as a basic prejudgment, that the classical Confucian approach to human culture is on a par with the Daoist approach to the natural world as distinct from the social. Thus, I would argue, whether speaking of Confucian or Daoist sensibilities, that the general orientation of ancient Chinese philosophical thought can be characterized as seeking harmony in a world, whether natural or social, of continuous change.

Such harmony, however, can never be conceived as being attained once and for all. Since the "ten thousand things" (*wanwu* 萬物), the ancient Chinese characterization of the world, persist in the form of a continuous process of an emerging order, human beings, constituting a part of those things, are required to participate in the process itself by configuring and reconfiguring their position within the whole. In a world characterized by change, there can be no pretension toward a permanent and "perfect" order.

In the culturally oriented Confucian philosophy, the main element of human existence preserving the continuity between the present and the past consists in the traditional customs of interaction. In this respect, interaction relates not only to interpersonal (and autopersonal) behavior and symbolic interaction between individuals and society as a whole, but also to people's interaction with the spirits of deceased ancestors and, more extensively, with the cosmos itself in all its manifestations. Thus, these customs encompass a vast range of symbolic and decorous acts, ranging from the formal to the informal, and include social etiquette and manners, forms of personal interaction, rites of passage, funeral rites, and various kinds of ceremony and ritual with more cosmological implications. This entire range of actions is all contained in the notion of *li* 禮.

The Chinese li certainly defies translation, and Western commentators never tire to point out that there is no succinct Western notion that has the semantic richness to grasp all that it encompasses. To illustrate its expressive abundance, I follow James Legge by quoting the words of the nineteenth-century French scholar J. M. Callery on the extensive semantic range of li. As Legge obviously recognized as well, the nature of the quotation is such that it must be presented in its original French:

> Autant que possible, j'ai traduit Li par le mot Rite, dont le sens est susceptible à une grande étendue; mais il faut convenir que, suivant les circonstances où il est employé, il peut

signifier—Cérémonial, Cérémonies, Pratiques cérémoniales, L'étiquette, Politesse, Urbanité, Courtoisie, Honnêteté, Bonnes manières, Égards, Bonne éducation, Bienséance, Les formes, Les convenances, Savoir-vivre, Décorum, Décence, Dignité personnelle, Moralité de conduite, Ordre Social, Devoirs de Société, Lois Sociales, Devoirs, Droit, Morale, Lois hiérarchiques, Offrande, Usages, Costumes.[16]

Whether all these possible meanings are strictly applicable or appropriate shall not be evaluated here. But it is at least beyond doubt that the semantic field of li cannot be grasped by any single Western notion. As we shall see, the common English translations of li as "rites" or "rituals," while certainly in some cases applicable, can be misleading and are without any doubt far too narrow. Roger T. Ames has argued that "achieving propriety in one's roles and relations does not reduce to generic, formally prescribed 'rites' or 'rituals' performed at stipulated times to announce status and to punctuate the seasons of one's life. The li—the expression of propriety through one's roles and relations—is more, much more."[17] While Ames opts for referring to li as "propriety in one's roles and relations," I have decided to leave it for the most part in its original Chinese, though on occasion I shall speak of "propriety" or "ritual propriety."

Li is one of Confucius's most discussed notions and an integral component of the entire Confucian tradition. However, the term li does not owe its origins to the Confucians. Initially, it belonged to no particular school of thought and is by convention believed to signify ritual actions enacted by royal families during the first three Chinese dynasties of Xia, Shang, and Zhou in order to please the spirits.[18] During this course of these dynasties, the notion gradually received a much wider reference, and has since then been expanded, deepened, and modified in a multiplicity of ways by Confucius and his followers and commentators up until the present day.

In the *Shuowen jiezi* 說文解字, a lexicon composed by Xu Shen 許慎 in the first century CE, which explains the meaning of characters by associating them with other semantically and/or phonetically related characters, li 禮 is associated with its homophone, li 履 (normally pronounced *lü*), "footwear," thus to "tread" or "perform," "carry out." It further provides a gloss in which li is explained as "a way in which to serve the spirits in order to receive good fortune," which accords with its probable application in its earliest days. Different commentators draw slightly different inferences from the character-association provided by the *Shuowen*. Thus, David Hall and Roger Ames emphasize the verbal meaning of li (*lü*), claiming that it emphasizes "the necessity of enacting and ultimately embodying the cultural tradition that is captured in ritual action."[19] Léon Vandermeersch, on the other hand, focuses on the meaning of "footwear," which, he suggests, indicates that the "steps" taken on the level of moral action are no less in need of support than the feet when physically walking.[20] He quotes, among others, Duan Yucai 段玉裁, a well-known commentator on the *Shuowen*, who says the following about the passage on li: "Footwear is that which the feet take for their support (by wearing them). By extension, everything that one takes for one's support (by wearing it) is called 'footwear,' simply on the basis of the rule of borrowing one word for another. The boots are footwear, the rites are footwear: in both cases, one behaves according to that which one wears, only in two different senses."[21] Vandermeersch thus takes li to imply a protective means that prevents one from "spraining" oneself when entering the moral sphere. In other words, it is a guideline for proper behavior. By taking these insights together, li comes through as a heuristic model for acquiring the skill of successfully realizing the (moral) values of the cultural tradition, and thus for finding one's place and identity within it. Li is in this sense an educative notion, one that in all its expansiveness enables socialization and thus, from the Confucian point of view, humanization.

The Modern Opprobrium of Ritual and the Confucian Tradition

It is to be expected that many Westerners will find the notion of "ritual propriety" rather unattractive, hinting as it does at formal, stagnant, predetermined behavior.[22] The present distaste for the idea of ritual in the West is without doubt a cultural product of the political and social upheavals of the last few centuries: the Enlightenment, the rise of democracy, industrial capitalism and individualism, and the subsequent decline of the Christian religion. During this process, ritual came to be viewed more and more as representing the "old order," the "traditional" (discussed in more detail in the following section), and the "antiprogressive." Such deprecatory associations can be found among numerous intellectuals during the modernist era. Herbert Spencer, for instance, formulated an evolutionary opposition between the industrialization of modern culture and the rituals of tribal or feudal cultures. At the beginning of the twentieth century, Max Weber associated ritual with magic, with which he contrasted the rationalism and "disenchantment" of Western culture.[23] According to the historian Peter Burke, the tendency to oppose ritual and reason can be traced back to the ethos of the Reformation, in which ritual was generally seen as artifice and mystification in contrast to the virtues of sincerity, simplicity, and directness. He argues that ritual was associated "with the shadow rather than the substance, the letter rather than the spirit, the outer husk rather than the inner kernel."[24] The late anthropologist Catherine Bell explains that within the field of comparative religion, the perceived contrast between ritual and reason resulted in an elevation of "the ethical Protestant-like religions in contrast to the magical ritualism of primitive, Catholic-like religions."[25] But she also points out that in the last decades there have been radical changes with regard to the evaluation of ritual, as many Western scholars have argued that modernization has in fact not resulted in the obliteration, but instead in the emergence of a variety of new forms of ritual. This has led to the Weber-influenced view that ritual is in fact an essential component of human society, providing meaning and significance to human life in the rationalized, disenchanted industrial world.[26] Bell argues, however, that such a view still rests upon an opposition between ritual and reason and implies that it therefore does not signify a fundamental change of attitude with regard to ritual, but that it does with regard to reason.[27]

This argument would certainly seem to contain an element of truth, but it is important to take into consideration the radical differences between the Enlightenment enthronement of reason as a near divine establisher of ends (for example in Kant and Hegel) and its Weberian instrumentalization as a mere means to an arbitrarily determined end. These contrasts must be carefully distinguished. The Weberian concession of reason as merely instrumental is far from being generally accepted, perhaps especially among philosophers.[28] Moreover, while social scientists tend to concentrate on the many undesirable side effects of modernization, the dominant orientation of thought in the West is still characterized by the will to progress, both scientific, implying more advanced and accessible technology, and social, implying further individual liberties, and with these ritual seems incompatible or at the very least unhelpful. The belief in the benign powers of reason is still strong, and the word "ritual," I believe, still generally leaves a bad aftertaste in the Western mouth.

Despite this opprobrium, or even because of it, I have no intention to overly deemphasize the ritualistic element in the notion of li. While li, as already pointed out, encompasses a much wider range of meaning than what is usually understood as ritual, it does entail a sufficient degree of formality to count as being significantly "ritualized" on all levels of enactment—hence the notion "ritual propriety."[29] Li, however, differs significantly from most other combinations of ritual, not least because of its being embedded in a Chinese cosmological sensibility of constant change in time. For instance, invariance is more often than not associated with ritual and even singled out as its defining characteristic.[30] However, being "ritualized" in a Confucian framework does not necessarily imply rigorous repetition and unchangeability. Further, a careful analysis of the function of the more ritualized element of li in the early Confucian conception of education and self-cultivation brings to light how li serves to enable students to enhance their performative creativity in the social and ethical sphere. Thus, to the extent that the present discussion focuses on ritual, the emphasis is on the ritual element in the Confucian tradition, and while li includes ritual, and may have something to say about ritual in general, I shall not venture to make universal claims. Such claims would in any case require an unthinkably vast investigation into the role and performance of ritual in other cultures.

For Confucius and his immediate followers, li is undoubtedly the strongest representative for cultural continuity. There are certainly others. There is, for instance, music (*yue* 樂), and the close association held by ancient Confucian philosophers to obtain between music and ritual propriety will not escape the attention of anyone who engages in a careful study of their writings. There are the verses and poems of the early Zhou dynasty, contained in the *Book of Odes* (*Shijing* 詩經), which, in the early Confucian writings, notably the *Lunyu* 論語 (*Analects of Confucius*) and some of the writings ascribed to Confucius's grandson, Zisizi 子思子, play a tremendously important role as a gateway to the experience and wisdom of the cultural tradition. There is the chronicle of past rulers of the Shang and Zhou dynasties and their proclamations, recorded in the *Book of Documents* (*Shujing* 書經), which is an endless source of models and antimodels of behavior for Confucius, and perhaps even more so for Mencius (*Mengzi* 孟子).

Although the focus of the present work is on ritual propriety, some consideration of the other cultural factors cannot be avoided. Among these factors, music is arguably the most significant one. In the writings of Confucius and his immediate followers, music has an explicit and intimate relationship with ritual propriety. In the *Lunyu*, Confucius often refers to ritual propriety and music simultaneously as *liyue* 禮樂. The same applies to the *Book of Rites* (*Liji* 禮記), which, although not put together until the latter part of the Western Han dynasty, is composed of writings that mostly date back to the Warring States period. In both the *Lunyu* and the *Book of Rites*, the importance ascribed to music is beyond question. Not only is music an indispensable element in formal ceremonies; it is also conceived as reflecting the moral and political condition of the state and as having a profound influence on the moral sentiments of the individual. Hence the Confucian vision of music as a crucial element for personal cultivation (*xiushen* 修身). Some of the recently excavated manuscripts at Mawangdui 馬王堆 and Guodian 郭店 help to reinforce the envisioned relationship of music with emotions, and thus with personal cultivation.

Confucianism has been a pervasive philosophical and ideological force in China and in other parts of East Asia during the last two and more millennia. Such omnipresence in almost all aspects of culture and society during such an extensive period has inevitably resulted in the absorption of originally non-Confucian thought processes and their adaptation to the already present Confucian culture. Thus, many of the ideas that over time became labeled "Confucian" are actually later modifications and appropriations of ideas from other sources and have little in common with the original ideas of Confucius himself and his followers. It has to be taken into account that actual applications of ideas are always particular interpretations, adjusted to the specific conditions of those times and places and sometimes even misappropriated to serve some narrow interests of certain privileged groups or individuals. Moreover, those applications are not only interpretations by virtue of being applications, but also interpretations based on other interpretations. Thus, the original teachings of the Confucian school have undergone vast transformations in the minds of people, and, since their beginnings, coalesced with other strands of Chinese culture. Even the unitary label "Confucianism" may be questionable. Peter Bol has asserted, for instance, that the notion is created in the West to define and discuss a phenomenon that existed in the past in China and is far from being synonymous with Chinese culture.[31] Although I would tend to disagree with Bol that "Confucianism" is a Western notion—in China one speaks readily of *rujia* 儒家 in much the same way as we do of Confucianism—it is true that its long history, cultural assimilation, and the general Chinese tendency toward syncretism have resulted in a certain confusion as to how to characterize Confucianism in general without specifying particular perspectives, periods, or even thinkers. For this reason, I shall by and large ignore the way in which Confucianism has been applied in actual social reality and focus almost exclusively on the ideas as they appear in texts produced during and immediately after the Warring States period.

The other side of the Confucian omnipresence, however, is its cultural resilience. Confucianism is a "living philosophy" that has, in one form or another, been a visibly influential cultural, social, and political factor in societies such as Hong Kong, Singapore, Taiwan, South Korea, and Japan up to the present day and has certainly been latently present in societies where it has been officially outlawed, such as in the People's Republic of China.[32] Following the de facto disintegration of the Maoist ideology in the latter, Confucianism has been gaining ground among Chinese intellectuals and others as a possible cultural and moral source for the new Chinese society in its rapid process of modernization—a source that is not only indigenous but has proven to be extremely productive and adaptable during the last two and a half millennia as well. The growing acknowledgment of this fact among the "cultural carriers" in the rapidly evolving Chinese society of the twenty-first century will without doubt bring about more concrete manifestations of Confucian values, perspectives, and policies in the People's Republic of China of the future.

Such manifestations, however, if they are to be effective, call for elaborate investigations of the ancient Confucian philosophy with regard to its relevance to and practicality in the present. This is precisely what the present work aims to do—namely, to serve as a modest contribution to the ongoing reinterpretation of Confucianism today by presenting a creative interpretation of the Confucian li and its role for learning and education with an eye to working out its possible meaning and applicability in the twenty-first century. To consider li from this point of view is in a sense to test the weakest link in the Confucian chain. Li is, for the most part, in both Asian and non-Asian eyes, viewed with skepticism and suspicion as belonging to the archaic order of the past. This work intends to mollify such skepticism by demonstrating, first, that even a "postmodern" version of Confucianism cannot afford to dispense with li, and, second, that li, functioning within the overall Confucian philosophy of education and culture, offers a process of socialization and humanization of which our world is presently in dire need.

CHAPTER ONE

First Assemblage

Tradition and Timeliness

In the first section of this chapter, I shall discuss the problematic notion of tradition in somewhat general terms and then indirectly infer its status and role in the Confucian philosophy with regard to li. Since there is no explicit general notion of tradition that emerges, say, through an opposition to reason, some Sinological detours will be required to detect its status in the Confucian discourse. Ritual propriety being a certain kind of practice, I shall complement the discussion of tradition by correlating it with a general discussion of practice.

By practice, I intend any kind of human action that is considered meaningful by a certain group of people, whose meaning is roughly shared by the members of that group and that therefore has become an established action within it. That the action is established does not mean that it is necessarily of a formal repetitive kind, but rather that it can be rendered symbolically or immediately meaningful on the basis of the interplay between the situation and the cultural milieu in which it is performed. I believe that such a wide definition is both sufficient and necessary to encompass everything that can belong to li.

In the latter half of the section, I shall turn to the role of time in ancient Chinese and, in particular, Confucian thought. Time is another semiveiled concept in the ancient Chinese tradition that has to be extrapolated by means of other concepts and issues. I first discuss the general conception of time in Chinese thought and then move to a more concentrated discussion of the concept of *zhong* 中, "focus," or, as I prefer translating it, "hitting the mark." Zhong sheds an illuminating light on the ways in which time affects the conception of li. Finally, I shall bring together the results of the section as a whole and show that through the medium of the Confucian notion of correct timing, ritual propriety appears not only as a transmitter of cultural tradition, but also as the most creative and innovative means for broadening it.

From Aversion to Rehabilitation: The Modern Discourse on Tradition

The notion of tradition is important to my analysis for two reasons: the first rests upon the thorough integration of li as a practice and the Chinese cultural tradition. For the former is not merely a product of the latter. Operating on all levels of human interaction, from the most mundane to the most formal, ritual propriety embodies the Chinese tradition in its most extensive manifestation.[1] It is moreover questionable whether the more extensive notion of practice can be made sense of in isolation from tradition, and vice versa. Some light may be shed on this claim through a brief etymological analysis.

The English word "tradition" is derived from the Latin verb *tradere*, "to hand down" or "to transmit." It refers to the continuous act of handing down to posterity what are believed to be the intrinsic features of a particular culture whereby that culture is maintained. The etymology of the modern Chinese word for tradition, *chuantong* 傳統, is similar. *Chuan* 傳 originally means "to transmit" or "to deliver" and is consistently used in this meaning in classical literature. *Tong* 統 refers to the main threads in a silk weave and has the further implication of "the essentials." Thus, chuantong could be understood as the "handing down of the essentials (of a culture) to posterity."

There are, of course, many things that are "handed down" from generation to generation; there are many "traditional" things. But the main purport of that which is handed down, "the essentials" of a tradition, consist in practices. We could say that practices "articulate" traditions. It would in any case be hard to make sense of traditions without them. However, whereas there may seem to be many practices that are not, strictly speaking, traditional, I argue that all practices derive their meaning from some tradition or another. Some practices could be, on the surface, based on a "private tradition," for example in the sense of a personal habit. However, as long as they are to be considered in any way meaningful, they can only be so within or vis-à-vis the broader context of a communal tradition. If they were not, they would suffer from the kind of inconsistency that Ludwig Wittgenstein found with the notion of private language. A practice is ultimately always, be it in the most remote sense, communal.

The other reason for concentrating on tradition concerns the present status and appraisal of tradition both in the West and in the People's Republic of China. Political and social events in both places have rendered the concept of tradition highly suspect: more often than not, it is now taken to signify a reactionary force hampering both scientific and social progress. While the actual events that have led to and enforced this view have been specific to each culture and location, the philosophical streams of thought that kindled them essentially share the same source. This source is the European philosophy of the Enlightenment.

The Enlightenment was characterized by a belief in progress on the basis of an independent and individual use of reason, and the renunciation of traditionalism and authoritarianism, which included the rejection of ritual practice. In 1784, when Immanuel Kant wrote in his celebrated "What Is Enlightenment?" that the advent of this movement of thought signifies "the human being's mental emancipation from self-incurred immaturity,"[2] he set the tone for a mode of thought that since then has by and large dominated the Euro-American political and intellectual scene. This is not to say that such a tension between reason and tradition in the West began with the Enlightenment. It has been present in European culture at least since Plato. However, it undoubtedly found its full force during the Enlightenment and the subsequent period known as modernity. Since then, and until fairly recently, the tendency within philosophy has been toward a prima facie rejection of any appeal to the authority of tradition as a sort of irrational parochialism or obscurantism. This applies not least to the philosophy of Marxism, an offspring of the Enlightenment mentality combined with the effects of the social conditions in the early phases of industrial capitalism in Europe. In *The Eighteenth Brumaire of Louis Bonaparte*, Karl Marx makes the following remarks on tradition:

> The tradition of all dead generations weighs like a nightmare on the brains of the living. And it is precisely in periods of revolutionary crises, when they seem to be occupied with revolutionizing themselves and their surroundings, with creating something unprecedented, that they panickly summon up the spirits of the past, borrowing their names, marching orders, outfits, in order to enact a new scene in world history, but with this time-honoured guise and this borrowed language.[3]

As we all know, Marxism has been a most influential force in shaping the contemporary Chinese outlook on tradition, sometimes with devastating consequences.[4]

Few extremes, however, persist without generating resistance to them, and alongside the modernist glorification of progress other philosophical and cultural streams developed, the most radical of which rejected reason and embraced tradition as the supreme moral authority. These streams, many of which were actually quite diverse, are often fit together under the heading of "romanticism." It is not necessary to enter the details of the romantic critique of the Enlightenment here. Suffice it to say that these opposite modes of thought have created a certain synthesis that is brought to expression by a number of twentieth-century thinkers. This synthesis consists in a reevaluation of the negative attitude to tradition and of the sharp contrast drawn between reified forms of tradition and reason. Subsequently, the antitraditionalism of modernity has increasingly been subject to various kinds of criticism. Many authors have seen it as insensitive to, if not downright naïve about, the important role that tradition plays for the integration and the sustention of the human community. Conversely, they have viewed the idea that reason alone can serve as the foundation of social and ethical values with growing suspicion. Critical scrutiny reveals that even the supposedly most theoretical forms of constructive ethics are essentially rationalizations of the cultural or personal values of the authors themselves, but hardly ever derivations from "pure" reason.[5]

Ironically, this contemporary suspicious attitude to the claim and authority of reason can at least in part be traced to the Enlightenment itself. For by undermining the authority of tradition, which in the West strongly involved undermining the truth claims of the Christian religion, the "critical" spirit of the Enlightenment also inadvertently contributed to the collapse of traditional metaphysics and thus to the collapse of the supposedly independent grounds of reason.

It seems appropriate, then, to provide some theoretical considerations about the extent to which tradition ought to, and, indeed, *does*, relate to human beings' modes of relating to themselves, to each other, and to society at large. In the following, I shall briefly elucidate some seminal attempts to rehabilitate the notion of tradition which all have in common a certain acknowledgment of its inescapable role in forming the human habitat. As is to be expected, I shall be highly selective in my discussion and focus especially on accounts that I believe may provide me with helpful perspectives from which to approach the notion of li. While focusing here on the more positive appraisals of tradition, I shall, in a later section, partly join forces with the Enlightenment spirit by considering the dangers of traditionalism with a special regard to ritual propriety.[6]

Many modern philosophers have concentrated on the situation of the human being as being, by birth, "cast into" a predominantly social environment. Such a situation has been variously termed as "situatedness," "embeddedness," or "facticity." Seeking to rehabilitate the notion of "habit," to which I shall turn later in more detail, John Dewey wrote already in 1922: "If an individual were alone in the world, he would form his habits (assuming the impossible, namely, that he would be able to form them) in a moral vacuum. They would belong to him alone, or to him only in reference to physical forces. Responsibility and virtue would be his alone. But since habits involve the support of environing conditions, a society or some specific group of fellowmen, is always accessory before and after the fact."[7] We can of course find statements with similar tones much earlier in Western intellectual history. In the *Politics*, Aristotle states that "man is more of a political animal than bees or any other gregarious animals" and that "a social instinct is implanted in all men by nature."[8] But there is an important difference between these claims. Dewey stresses the actual situatedness of human beings in societies as a necessary starting point for a science seeking to understand and to improve the human condition. It is precisely this social situatedness, according to Dewey, that constitutes the peculiarity of what it means to be human. Aristotle, on the other hand, speaks from a metaphysically teleological point of view as if nature had "intended" for human beings to fully realize their potentialities within society.

Many recent ethical thinkers have, knowingly or unknowingly, shared Dewey's social-philosophical approach. Alasdair MacIntyre, for instance, has pointed out that the only way to come to an understanding of an action or a practice is to view it from within some kind of narrative, which, again, receives its meaning from the larger tradition to which it owes its existence: "[T]he narrative phenomenon of embedding is crucial: the history of a practice in our time is generally and characteristically embedded in and made intelligible in terms of the larger and longer history of the tradition through which the practice in its present form was conveyed to us; the history of each of our own lives is generally and characteristically embedded in and made intelligible in terms of the larger and longer histories of a number of traditions."[9] Considering the context, it may seem peculiar to refer to MacIntyre, an outspoken Aristotelian striving to revive the concept of virtue as a central notion of ethics. But MacIntyre is a good case in point, because while being an Aristotelian, he does not seem to subscribe to Aristotle's metaphysics of natural or cosmic teleology, according to which society is the human being's "preordained" place. By focusing on the goods internal to practices in every tradition, he seems, instead, to share the view with many modern thinkers that it is the culture to which we belong that provides us with meaning and value. Despite the vast difference between Dewey and MacIntyre, these thinkers would probably both be in agreement that the possibility of meaning can only arise within an interacting community of individuals that have a shared sense of history and tradition.

Perhaps the most explicit attempt in modern times to rehabilitate the notion of tradition, however, can be found in the hermeneutical philosophy of Hans-Georg Gadamer. Gadamer denies that there is any sharp contrast between tradition and reason. He argues, first of all, that the Enlightenment critique of authority involved a too narrow concept of authority, because true authority, that is, one recognized or accepted as being legitimate, is not founded upon a mere act of submission, but on one of acknowledgment and realization: "That is, the realization that the other's judgment is superior to one's own, and that therefore his judgment comes first, that is, has priority over one's own judgment. It is for this reason that authority cannot simply be conferred on to someone—it is earned, and it has to be earned if that someone wants to claim it. It rests upon acknowledgment and upon an act of reason insofar as it, conscious of its own limits, trusts that others may have better insights."[10] Gadamer elucidates this different meaning of authority because he believes it approximates the way in which the romantics understood the concept when they argued for the authority of tradition. In his view, then, the romantic critique was an important corrective to the Enlightenment by pointing out that, for example, our mores as a matter of fact do and will largely retain their validity simply by virtue of being handed down to us from the past: "They are freely adopted, but their creation or the justification of their validity does not at all derive from free understanding. On the contrary, this is precisely what we call tradition: to be valid without rational justification."[11]

The fact that we often, indeed, every day, submit de facto to the authority of convention and tradition when making up our minds on various issues demonstrates our situatedness within the inescapable frameworks of our culture and its traditions. Without it, we would not be able to orient ourselves within society among other people. An adequate appropriation of tradition provides us with a sense of the more appropriate ways of interacting with others that also facilitates the efficiency of those of our actions that to some degree depend on the reactions of others.[12]

But does this establish the full authority of tradition to which we must submit blindly and unconditionally? Certainly not. Gadamer argues that one of the problems with the Enlightenment-romantic controversy over tradition was that the concept as such was understood too narrowly. It was considered as being contrary to rational freedom and thus identified as a historically given object comparable with nature, from which the Enlightenment and the romantic thinkers then drew contradictory conclusions. While both parties contrasted tradition and reason, the first identified reason with progress and tradition with regress, and the second identified reason with conflict and tradition with stability.[13] Such a sharp contrast between reason and tradition, however, is misleading. For even the most solid tradition does not maintain itself merely by virtue of some kind of natural inertia, but requires affirmation, apprehension, and nurture. Tradition is certainly a preservation of a kind:

> Preservation, however, is an achievement of reason, while admittedly one characterized by inconspicuousness. It is due to this that innovation, the pre-planned, purports to be the only act and achievement of reason. But this is mere appearance. Even when life finds itself in tumultuous changes, as during revolutionary periods, much more of the old preserves itself in the ostensible transformation of all things than anyone can ever know, and merges with the new to acquire new functions. At any rate, preservation is no less an attitude based on freedom than overthrow and innovation.[14]

Gadamer attempts to raise to consciousness the power that tradition, willy-nilly, exercises in our daily lives. Without knowing the extent of this power, reason has no means to appraise it and, consequently, no means to seek to either circumscribe or preserve it. One cannot confront an invisible or unknown challenge. It may therefore be appropriate to speak of tradition as a "carrier" or "bearer" of reason, for reasoning always takes place in a discourse belonging to some traditional mode of thought. Reason and tradition are thus far from being opponents in the world of action—they complement each other. In fact, it is questionable whether one could really exist without the other. It is tempting, in this respect, to modify a dictum from Kant and say that tradition without reason would be blind, and reason without tradition would be empty.

Tradition as *Dao* 道:
The Early Confucian Approach to Tradition

In the *Lunyu*, Confucius expresses a thought quite similar to the modified Kantian dictum above: "Learning without reflection results in confusion, reflection without learning results in peril."[15] One important implication of learning (xue 學) is the appropriation and transmission of the cultural tradition, which, I believe, is the dominant meaning of xue in this passage.[16] If we consider, then, for the moment, only its second part, Confucius is arguing that mere reflecting (here the functional equivalent of reasoning) without regard for cultural tradition will have as a consequence that one fails to grasp the appropriate ways of dealing with situations and will therefore endanger oneself and/or others. What sort of endangerment could he have in mind? According to Zhang Weizhong 張衛中, it consists in uncertainty or doubt, or the inability to establish anything at all,[17] and can thus be understood as losing one's foothold in reality, a reality that can only be adequately apprehended through the categories shared by one's culture. From this perspective, then, such endangerment is tantamount to a form of alienation in which the endangered subject loses itself in skepticism, in an evacuation of meaning, in a Durkheimian form of *anomie*, or, to use the words of MacIntyre, in an inability to "grasp . . . those future possibilities which the past has made available to the present."[18]

As many commentators have observed, Confucius clearly considered it to be his personal mission to transmit the Zhou dynasty culture, which in turn, as Confucius states himself, was a continuation of the tradition derived from the Xia and Shang dynasties.[19] This may seem a trivial point, considering that few, if any, would hold that Confucius did not endorse a form of traditionalism. However, it becomes less trivial as soon as we see that his particular kind of traditionalism rests upon a realization of the profound function that a cultural tradition has for human understanding, identity, integration, and orientation, a realization that has been emerging on a global scale in the last few decades. To Confucius and his followers, however, this function of tradition seems evident, even "common sense."

It is illuminating, in this respect, as Benjamin Schwartz has pointed out, that the classical Chinese language did not have a general word for "tradition" as we understand it today, and that chuantong, which I have discussed above, while Chinese in origin, is in fact a much later neologism taken from modern Japanese.[20] What does such a lack suggest?

It clearly does not suggest that the Chinese were unaware of tradition. In fact, the contrary is more likely to be true, that their life-world was so pervaded by tradition that a general word would have been inapplicable. Such lack may in fact be comparable with the lack of general words for "snow" or "ice" in some Inuit languages, which instead have a number of words to describe various formations and manifestations of snow and ice.[21]

An important reason not to be forgotten is, as many have pointed out, that the classical Chinese language is generally characterized by a relative absence of abstractness.[22] This does not mean that general terms cannot be formed, but it is not dualistically influenced in such a way that a metaphysical opposition has formed between the universal and the particular. Classical Chinese does not, as is the tendency among Indo-European languages, depend on a superordinated class to which referents are held to belong by virtue of their fulfilling the conditions of the formal definition of the class itself. Thus, there are no proper "universals" that can be used to convey abstractness. Instead, the meaning of words is mainly established in one of two interrelated ways: contextually, through the interplay between words in a text, and correlatively, through the dynamics of discourse. These linguistic-hermeneutic features also shed light on the ambiguity and allusiveness of the language as such. It is important to note that the discourse takes place either internally in the text itself or externally between the text and the reader, which accounts, at least in part, for the particular Chinese scholarly tradition of writing commentaries to canonical texts. For the commentaries do not merely attempt to explain the original text, which would normally be considered the proper aim of Western commentaries, but continue the dialogue in the hermeneutical sense that the ideas expressed in the texts evoke the commentators' own ideas and inspire them to elaborate them further.[23] In the *Lunyu*, however, we have a particularly conspicuous case of internal discourse, where vague comments and statements are complemented and enriched through the given response.[24] It seems, therefore, that Hall and Ames's description of the language of Confucius as "deferential," whereby "meaning is disclosed and/or created by virtue of a recognition of mutual resonance among instances of communicative activity," is most appropriate.[25]

Given that there is no general term for tradition in classical Chinese, and that tradition is nevertheless a pervasive element in the ancient Chinese, or at least the Confucian, world, one would expect to find numerous terms alluding to the different aspects of tradition in much the same way as the Inuit languages have many words for different manifestations of ice and snow. This is certainly the case, but not merely in the straightforward sense that there are specific terms that refer to tradition and others that do not. It is rather in the *mode* of discourse that the shades or tonalities of tradition are brought to expression. More specifically, when discourse becomes prescriptive, it enjoys its prescriptiveness largely by virtue of its (mostly implicit) allusion to the authority of tradition. For example, a character such as zheng 政, "to govern," "government," takes in certain contexts the meaning of "proper governing," or "appropriate governing," in which case it alludes to the model government of the early Zhou emperors.[26]

The core of this prescriptive mode is contained in Confucius's idea of zhengming 正名, which is usually rendered in English as "rectification of names." The final and hence most disastrous consequence of not using names correctly, Confucius says on one occasion, is that people will not know what to do with themselves; they will literally "not know where to place their hands and feet."[27] Such dismay or disorientation is another formulation of the alienation or the state of *anomie* in the above-mentioned endangered subject, a situation where norms are unstable or ineffective and which arises as a consequence of "reflection without learning."

The classical understanding of Confucius's proposal of zhengming is that the names of social posts and familial relations should call for the implied duties and responsibilities that were ostensibly contained in those names during the glorified Western Zhou dynasty. Such interpretations have portrayed the thought of Confucius as unfairly conservative and reactionary. In Ren Jiyu's 任繼愈 *History of Chinese Philosophy* from 1966, it says that "Confucius believed that 'reality' [shi] ought not to have changed, and intends to make use of 'names' [*ming* 名] (stipulations of Zhou rituals) in order to correct aspects of 'reality' that have already changed or are in a process of change."[28]

Apparently, this outlook has not changed to a significant degree, at least not in the People's Republic. In a recent study on the concepts of Chinese philosophy, Ge Rongjin 葛榮晉 says that with his theory of zhengming, Confucius "attempts to correct actual situations that have undergone changes by means of old names."[29]

These interpretations are problematic in two ways. First, the idea of zhengming, as Confucius presents it, is here understood in light of Xunzi's 荀子 elaborations on this idea. As John Knoblock points out, however, Xunzi took many ideas from the sophisticated linguistic and logical inquiries of the later Mohist 墨家 school and the Jixia Academy 稷下學宮, both of which did not arise until the fourth century BCE, or almost two centuries after Confucius.[30] Ren Jiyu and Ge Rongjin both interpret Confucius's demand for zhengming on the basis of the much later theory of the relationship between names (ming 名) and actuality (shi 實), and therefore come to the conclusion that by rehabilitating the old sense of certain words, Confucius's intention is to recreate a former state of things.

Second, the interpretations confuse consequences with intentions. Ge Rongjin, in fact, reveals this confusion when he adds to the passage quoted above as if to explain what role zhengming was always meant to play: "This single idea of 'zhengming' was later to serve the feudal rulers for a long time, applying it as they did as a prime tool of the system in order to strengthen the feudal ethical code and hierarchy."[31]

It is certainly true that zhengming models itself on the Zhou dynasty. But the idea is not a call for a simple return to the previous use of these names: it is rather an attempt to revive the *mode of thinking* that Confucius believes characterized the Western Zhou dynasty. Such a mode of thinking takes language seriously by seeing words not merely as labels, but as containing profoundly prescriptive elements. It is this cultural *tradition*, proceeding from the Zhou emperors, which he wants to carry on. Thus, it seems more apposite to say that Confucius wanted to return to the *path* initiated by the Zhou emperors.

We may, in light of this Confucian vision, describe tradition as the path on which the present arrived from the past, and which, provided we attend to its maintenance by constantly adapting it to new situations, will lead the present into the future. Such a description is in fact most appropriate. For I suggest that the word in classical Chinese that comes closest to the general English term "tradition" is dao 道, which is most often translated as "way" or "path." I argued in the introduction that the Daoist conception of nature as an ever flowing process is comparable to the Confucian approach to society. If we understand the Daoist use of the word dao as signifying the overall process of our natural environment, or, even more generally, like François Jullien, as "the course of things,"[32] then dao would seem to be a good candidate for approximating our term for "tradition." An etymological analysis of dao would further lend credence to such an understanding. The character is formed out of two elements, *pi* 疋 "foot," or "to lead through," and *shou* 首, "head," also in the sense of "leader," or, as Ames and Hall point out, "foremost,"[33] which surely can be extended further to the idea of "the most important" or "the essential." Thus, it would seem entirely in order to understand dao as the "leading forth of what is essential."

To what extent, then, was tradition considered an authority? Confucius famously stated that he was simply a transmitter of past wisdom and not an innovator.[34] This statement is often taken as evidence of the conservative spirit of his teachings, but it should probably rather be seen as merely exemplifying Confucius's own modesty as well as his respect for cultural tradition. For the aim is not mere preservation. In the first part of the apothegm quoted above, Confucius states that learning without reflection leads to confusion. This is a clear disapproval, and disavowal, of mere preservationism. The word *wang* 罔, which I have translated as "confusion," can also mean "disorientation," and, in fact, Zhang Weizhong explains it as "disorientation that leads to nothing."[35] Evidently, those who simply stick to old methods and norms without reflecting on how to adapt them to new situations are unlikely to be successful in their efforts. They will effect nothing at all. In the *Zhongyong* 中庸, Confucius is reported to have said that those who are "born into the present age and yet return to the ways [dao] of the past will cause themselves misfortunes."[36] In the *Lunyu*, moreover, Confucius says that "one who realizes the new by reviewing the old can be called a proper teacher."[37]

Confucius thus emphasizes the importance of reevaluating what is traditional. Tradition is surely of vital importance as a foundation for proper behavior, but it should not dictate in a dogmatic manner how one should behave. Instead, proper behavior should be formulated with regard to a critical reexamination of tradition itself.[38] The most concrete form of such an examination entails personalizing the values and practices that constitute the given tradition, for new situations continuously call for new responses within the framework of its paradigms. Such responses, when thoughtful and creative, take into consideration the relevant values and past practices belonging to the tradition. However, it is up to the agents as concrete persons to reinterpret the significance and meaning of these values and practices by constantly adapting and re-adapting them to the current circumstances. "Proper behavior" is therefore not only proper in the sense of conforming to traditional values and practices; it is also "proper" in the sense of being the manifestation of a personal "appropriation" of the tradition as such. By responsibly continuing the tradition, persons make it their own—that is, they make it "proper" to them.[39] And, obviously, this can be done in a multiplicity of ways. Confucius would therefore surely agree with

MacIntyre's argument that "[t]raditions, when vital, embody continuities of conflict."[40] The point is not to *return* to the ancient ways, or the ancient tradition. The frequently discussed *junzi zhi dao* 君子之道, the way of "refined," "cultivated," or "edified" persons,[41] the way within the way, refers precisely to the endeavor to continue forging the path that constitutes the tradition, to continue *making* the tradition—for without such an endeavor, the tradition runs the risk of becoming a thing of the past, a dead tradition.

The Temporal Sequence of Practice and the Chinese Notion of Time

In the introduction, I pointed out some reasons for the generally antagonistic attitude to ritual in modernity. As an archetype of traditionalism par excellence, ritual action is by and large regarded as consisting in a fixed sequence of mechanistic and repetitive gestures both devoid of and inhibiting individual and creative thought. According to this view, which has been fostered by historical, political, and social factors, ritual is appropriately associated "with the primitive, tribal, and nonrational."[42] This view was duly reflected in anthropological and sociological treatments of ritual until after the midtwentieth century, in particular those influenced by Durkheimian and Marxist approaches that make a strict demarcation between the religious and the profane or secular.

The social sciences, ever since their rise in the late nineteenth century, have been marked by a struggle to establish themselves as a proper discipline of science. This has resulted in a methodological ambivalence as to how to approach their subject matter and what kind of results to seek. Thus, whereas most social scientists have appreciated and emphasized the particularity of their human objects of study, they have at the same time been constrained to yield to the scientific demand for objectivity, explainability, and, therefore, generalization. The consequence of such an imperative has been a certain conflation of disparate, yet conceptually related, social practices. For the demand for an objectifiable, generalizable explanation has led to an imposition of a mechanistic model upon these practices or to their categorization and reification in some form. It has led to the tendency to view culturally established practices as following a fixed and an ostensibly "logical" sequence in which the components all have a direct and decipherable symbolic reference to the cultural tradition as a whole. Pierre Bourdieu has launched a criticism of this view that has particularly instructive implications for our discussion.

In his seminal study, *The Logic of Practice*, Bourdieu is concerned with the epistemological status of the social sciences. The objectivist approach that I sketched above was later met with a phenomenological or a subjectivist reaction that had the potential of resulting in some kind of productive synthesis. Bourdieu deplores, however, that the social sciences have been left with an artificial and unfortunate dichotomy between these approaches, both of which suffer from serious shortcomings for the aim of understanding the dynamism of the human habitat. He therefore attempts to go beyond both objectivist and phenomenological approaches in pursuing "a reflexive return to the subjective experience of the world and also the objectification of the objective conditions of that experience."[43] The former of these two aims shall, so to speak, stalk my discussion in this section on time and temporality.

According to Bourdieu, one of the chief problems with the scientific approach to practice consists in the discrepancy between the presupposed notion of time in the scientific outlook and the way in which time unfolds in actual practice. Scientific analysis is inherently detemporalized in the sense that it arrives after the fact, and, having at its disposal sufficient time to overcome the effects of time, it then reconstructs the events according to a synchronized or static scheme or synopsis. Hence, a gap arises between the supposedly "objective" spectator and the "subjective" agent of the practice. The former, when reconstructing the process, tends to see a fixed or mechanized sequence of actions, each of which has a determinate symbolic reference to the culture to which the agent belongs, while not necessarily being transparent to the agent. The latter, however, being immersed in and living the process, obviously sees it in a very different manner. He experiences all the uncertainties and cognitive challenges that accompany practically any temporal succession of action. If social scientists had considered closely the rituals that they themselves perform every day, Bourdieu writes, such as a polite conversation, "the seemingly most mechanical and ritualized of exchanges,"

> they would have discovered the unceasing vigilance that is needed to manage this interlocking of prepared gestures and words; the attention to every sign that is indispensable, in the use of the most ritual pleasantries, in order to be carried along by the game without getting carried away by the game beyond the game . . . the art of playing on the equivocations,

innuendoes and unspoken implications of gestural or verbal symbolism that is required, whenever the right objective distance is in question, in order to produce ambiguous conduct that can be disowned at the slightest sign of withdrawal or refusal, and to maintain uncertainty about intentions that always hesitate between recklessness and distance, eagerness and indifference.[44]

A well-performed ritualized action, then, while certainly following a preestablished pattern to a certain degree, is performed well precisely by *not* being a simple automatic repetition. Bourdieu makes a compelling comparison with the performance of music:

> Practice unfolds in time and it has all the correlative properties, such as irreversibility, that synchronization destroys. Its temporal structure, that is, its rhythm, its tempo, and above all its directionality, is constitutive of its meaning. As with music, any manipulation of this structure, even a simple change in tempo, either acceleration or slowing down, subjects it to a destructuration that is irreducible to a simple change in an axis of reference. In short, because it is entirely immersed in the current of time, practice is inseparable from temporality, not only because it is played out in time, but also because it plays strategically with time and especially with tempo.[45]

Bourdieu's insight into the discrepancy between the temporality of science and that of practice serves us well in this respect. Apart from reminding us of the inevitable gap that arises between "external reconstructors" and "internal agents," his observation also prompts us to observe that one's way of relating to practices and events will be largely influenced or even conditioned by one's presupposed, and, for the most part, implicit notion of temporality. This takes us to the very particular Chinese conception of time, which, in fact, suggests that the notion of ritual necessarily involves individuality, creativity, and a keen sense for the situation at hand.

Tang Junyi 唐君毅, in his study of the special characteristics of classical Chinese cosmology, has pointed out that the Chinese notion of time is inseparable from the notion of space and is thus an inherent quality of all things. Classical Chinese contained no independent concepts for time and space until they were imported into the language by Buddhist thought.[46] This indicates that Chinese temporality is characterized by a high level of concreteness and cannot easily be abstracted or objectified into a one-dimensional, linear, sequential movement of divisible units, as has been the dominant understanding of time in the West, at least since the seventeenth century.[47] Tang takes the example of the modern Chinese word for "cosmos," *yuzhou* 宇宙. In classical Chinese, *yu* 宇 means "up, down, and in all four directions," indicating extension or space in its totality, and *zhou* 宙 means "going back to the past and arriving in the present," indicating duration or time in its totality.[48] The cosmos is thus understood as the combined totality of time and space, neither of which can be clearly separated.[49] This also explains the dynamic concept of constantly changing reality in Chinese thought, for if time and space, and hence matter, are ultimately inseparable, there can be no room for an understanding of reality as static.[50]

The idea of the totality of time and space is, moreover, not an idea of an absolute totality, but of one relative to human experience. This can be derived from the way in which the notions of time and space are originally formulated. Tang says that "[t]o say 'going back to the past and arriving in the present' and 'up, down and in all four directions' is to place ourselves at the centre. Thus, 'tracing back from the present to the past' means 'past and present,' 'left, right, in front of and behind' means 'the four directions,' and 'above our head and under our heels' means 'up and down.'"[51] Ancient Chinese thought is consistent in its tendency to explicitly consider things from the point of view of the human being. The emphasis is on "function," not on "essence"—on the way in which things "work" or what they "do," not on what they "are." The role of philosophy and knowledge, therefore, consists in enhancing the ability of human beings to realize a harmonious relationship with their environment. This particular epistemological, or perspectival, anthropocosmic orientation is a partial explanation for the lack of conceptual oppositions so important in Western thought such as appearance/reality or subjectivity/objectivity. Provided that we can detect some kind of *telos* in the Chinese approach to reality, it is certainly not the attainment of an "objective truth" to be conceptualized, but rather a "practical skill" to be mastered, demanding openness, perspicacity, and engagement with regard to an ever-changing reality. Such a *telos*-as-skill can thus never be attained once and for all. On the ancient Chinese outlook on reality, François Jullien says that "reality—every kind of reality—may be perceived as a particular deployment or arrangement of things to be relied on and worked to one's advantage. Art, or wisdom, as conceived by the Chinese, consequently lies in strategically exploiting the propensity emanating from that particular configuration of reality, to the maximum effect possible. This is the notion of 'efficacy.'"[52] Given the fundamental role of time in the Chinese worldview, one might pose the provocative question whether Confucius and his followers were even capable of regarding ritual observance as a mere mechanistic repetition of a fixed sequence of actions. It seems at least clear that persons who aim at such repetition rather prove themselves as decidedly unskilled, concentrating as they do on "copying" a past deed instead of maintaining vigilance and responding appropriately to the particular circumstances in which they find themselves.[53] This view can be reinforced through an analysis of the particular role of time in the Confucian tradition.

Despite the comparative lack of reference to cosmological issues in the *Lunyu*, it contains a memorable passage where Confucius offers us his view of the flow of time: "While standing on a riverbank, the Master said with a deep sigh: 'Doesn't time pass by just like this, never ceasing day or night!'"[54] By comparing the ongoing succession of days and nights with the flow of water in a river, Confucius is entirely in accordance with other more cosmologically oriented thinkers of classical China who describe reality as a process of constant change. In fact, although Confucius and his immediate followers generally focused on social and ethical issues and, unlike the Daoists, tended to refrain from cosmological elaborations, few if any would hold that their worldview did not rest upon some conception of cosmology.

Much has been written on the difference between the Confucian and the Daoist philosophical outlooks. The Chinese scholar Fang Dongmei 方東美 once summarized the main difference between Confucians and Daoists by characterizing them respectively as "persons of time" (*shijian ren* 時間人) and "persons of space" (*taikong ren* 太空人).[55] Praising Zhuangzi's indifference to the affairs of the mundane world in his soaring through space by riding the clouds, Fang (following, in fact, Bertrand Russell) maintained that the ostensible Daoist view that "understanding time is of little importance" was "the gate to wisdom."[56]

Tang Yinan 唐亦男 argues that Fang's (and Russell's) interpretation of the Daoist attitude to time is mistaken, and demonstrates that Zhuangzi's view of time and space was in fact much in line with Tang Junyi's account of the general Chinese view of time and space as inseparable modes of reality. However, he acknowledges that Fang's characterization of the Confucians as "persons of time" may be befitting, for the notion of time plays an enormously important role in the Confucian philosophy.

A seminal source for the largely implicit early Confucian conception of cosmology is the ancient *Classic of Changes* (*Yijing* 易經). Although incorporated into the list of Confucian "classics" during the Han dynasty, this work expresses a worldview predating all the schools of thought in China of the Warring States period and can thus be regarded as representing something like a pan-Chinese cosmological vision.[57] Most contemporary scholars would now agree that both Daoists and Confucians alike shared the philosophy of the *Yijing* as a kind of cosmological foundation.[58]

The *Yijing* presents an art of divination dating back to the Shang dynasty, although the book itself was probably composed in the Zhou dynasty—hence its alternative and original title, *Zhouyi* 周易, or *The Changes of Zhou*. The *Yizhuan* 易傳, or the *Appended Remarks* (also called *Shiyi* 十翼, or *The Ten Wings*), which interprets the *Yijing*'s prognostications and elaborates on its relation to cosmology, is a much later composition. The *Yizhuan* was long believed to be the work of Confucius himself and is in fact ascribed to him by Sima Qian 司馬遷, the great Han dynasty historian, in his *Historical Records* (*Shiji* 史記). This attribution was later questioned and has now been disconfirmed by textual analyses of *Yizhuan* bamboo scrolls excavated among the Mawangdui archeological finds in 1973. These scrolls strongly indicate that it was written no earlier than the end of the Warring States period, or around 200 BCE, and certainly by more than one author.[59] The *Yizhuan*, however, is undoubtedly a Confucian work, written in response to Daoist challenges in order to give expression to Confucian views of cosmology.[60]

The *Yijing* is an elaborate expression of the Chinese cosmological view that reality is in a constant flux of generative change. In the classic, these changes are symbolized by means of broken and unbroken horizontal lines, later to be identified with the cosmic interactive tendencies attributed to yin 陰 and yang 陽. Three lines arranged in vertical order compose a so-called "trigram" (*sanhua gua* 三畫卦). By exhausting the different combination of lines, there are a total number of eight different trigrams. Two trigrams placed on top of each other make up a "hexagram" (*liuhua gua* 六畫卦). The hexagrams, sixty-four altogether, form the substance of the divinatory symbolism. It is important to remember that by embodying the processes of reality, the hexagrams themselves are conceived of as being in a constant process of transformation. The lines are displaced from the bottom to the top and thus a displayed hexagram is always about to yield to a new one. Thus, the constant process of generative (and degenerative) change through time can never be left out of consideration.

The system of the *Yijing* has been regarded as one of the more obscure products of the Chinese tradition. The main reason for this obscurity is beyond doubt its fluidity. The hexagrams are meant to provide an indication as to whether taking certain measures in a particular situation is auspicious or not on the basis of the symbolic combination of its broken or unbroken lines. The interpretation proceeds by mutually correlating either the lines or the trigrams of which the hexagrams are composed, whereby each interpretive element represents a complex set of propensities based on the rich symbolic polarity of yin and yang. However, there is no one fixed method for such an interpretation. The interpreter can choose from virtually unlimited possibilities of correlation and hence reach practically any desired conclusion. A. C. Graham has suggested that this extreme fluidity of the system is not without significance: resting upon the Chinese worldview of the unpredictability of events, it has the heuristic function of unblocking the mind to possibilities that would otherwise not have been envisaged: "An openness to chance influences loosing thought from preconceptions is indispensable to creative thinking. In responding to new and complex situations it is a practical necessity to shake up habitual schemes and wake up to new correlations of similarities and connexions. . . . The Yi . . . is designed for responding to unique and complex situations in which correlative thinking must be fluid."[61] Graham's observation underscores the importance of personal vigilance and perspicacity in the ancient Chinese view of reality as ever changing and indeterminate. A similar point has been made by Tu Weiming 杜維明. Rejecting notions of the Chinese worldview as being either cyclic or spiral, he argues that it is "transformational": "The specific curve around which it [reality] transforms at a given period of time is indeterminate, however, for numerous human and nonhuman factors are involved in shaping its form and direction."[62]

The processual and transformational nature of reality necessitates a conscious awareness that excludes the possibility of a fixed or given order and, in a sense, is prepared for anything. Such awareness necessitates in turn a high evaluation of the skill required to respond to one's environment in the most appropriate or expedient way. It moreover sheds light on the generally cautious approach to things found in Chinese thought and culture. One always observes carefully before acting. Summarizing his brief analysis of the role of time in Chinese thought, Zhang Dainian

張岱年 emphasizes both of these points: "Persons of initiative should advance only after having followed the advances of the moment. Moreover, they should be capable of initializing an action that is proper to every aspect of the situation."[63]

Hitting the Mark: Zhong 中, Shizhong 時中, and Zhongyong 中庸

There is more to gain from the ancient *Classic of Changes* on the notion of time. In the *Yizhuan*, which, we might recall, was composed by Confucian thinkers in the Warring States period, there is much to suggest that the important but disputed Confucian idea of zhong 中 is closely associated with time and timeliness. The character zhong occurs frequently and in various contexts in the ancient Chinese corpus. Zhong's most common meaning is prepositional, functionally equivalent to the English "in," "inside," or "between," which, in fact, corresponds to the *Shuowen* lexicon's explanation of the term through the character nei 內. The *Shuowen* also associates it with the character zheng 正, "upright," "straight," or, as Ge Rongjin comments, "not biased and not partial, properly placed."[64] Despite the apparent differences between these meanings, we can detect their semantic relationship.[65] To be inside or between, that is to say, to be central, has also the implication of being "properly placed." There is at least one unambiguous case in which Confucius uses zhong in this prescriptive sense, where he says, in explicating his idea of "correcting the application of names" (zhengming), that "if government decrees and penal law are not on the mark [zhong], the common people will not know where to place their hands and feet."[66] To be "not on the mark" thus carries the meaning of inappropriateness.

In the *Yizhuan*, the character zhong is used to signify the lines occupying the central places of the hexagrams. As the name indicates, a hexagram is composed of six lines. The central places of a hexagram correspond to the second and the fifth lines, which again are the most important in determining whether or not an intended action will be auspicious.[67] Since a hexagram represents a given situation or "time," the trick consists in making opportunities out of the propensities of the moment as indicated by its central lines.[68] Another way of expressing this in the *Yizhuan* is shizhong 時中, which we may translate provisionally as "time centering," where time (shi 時) signifies the hexagram as such. Since, however, shi refers to the particular point of time in question, it is perhaps more appropriately translated as "moment." Further, by associating the meanings of zhong as depicted above, we may construe shizhong as hitting the mark of the moment, which would then make sense of the reference both to the specific prognostications of the hexagrams as well as to one's approach to things in actual reality.

The shizhong reference in the *Yizhuan*, commenting on the hexagram *meng* 蒙, or ignorance, would thus read like this: "As for ignorance [meng] and discernment [*heng* 亨], it is with discernment that one proceeds to hit the mark of the moment."[69] In the *Yijing*, meng is explained through its contrast, heng. In a modern edition of the classic, this passage is explained as follows: "Why the contrasts of ignorance and discernment? Because things change by following circumstances. Ignorance is a lack of knowledge, but having learned, a lack of knowledge is able to turn into knowledge, meng is able to change into non-meng."[70]

It is on the basis of the dynamic interaction of its central lines, the second being unbroken *yang* and the fifth a broken yin, that the hexagram indicates good conditions for ignorance to change into discernment. Tang Yinan argues that the idea of shizhong in the *Yizhuan* suggests an approach to reality that is particularly Confucian—namely, to identify things in their particular location of temporality, observe their transformational development, and then choose the most opportune moment to realize an appropriate or effective action.[71] He quotes the Qing dynasty Confucian scholar Hui Dong 惠棟, who not only identified the notion of shizhong as the core of the wisdom of the *Changes* but also as a supreme illustration of the entire Confucian tradition. Marveling at the *Changes*, he has the following to say: "The way of the *Changes* is indeed profound! To sum up in a word, it hits the mark of the moment." He then continues: "Pointing out the excellence of Confucius, Zisi wrote in the *Zhongyong*: 'A *junzi* hits the mark of the moment.' Mencius also said: 'Confucius was the sage whose actions were timely.' The implementation of the zhong standard began with the *Zhongyong*, in which the standard of shizhong was illustrated by Confucius, even as it was handed down from Yao and Shun as their model of thinking."[72]

The vital role of time in the Confucian philosophy is also emphasized by Ge Rongjin. He notes that the specific formulation of shizhong first appears in the *Yizhuan*, in which, he adds, the notion of time is generally found in the prescriptive context that people's actions ought to try to "hit the mark" (zhong) by following the process of time.[73] He argues, moreover, that the idea is also prominent in the thought of Confucius himself. In one passage of the *Lunyu*, Confucius discusses the steadfastness of some of the more excellent personalities of the ancient era, but then says: "I, however, differ from all these, for I have no 'must not' or 'must.'"[74] Ge Rongjin comments on this passage as follows: "That is to say, not to limit oneself to conventional rules, not to imitate that which is conventionally considered permissible, but to be flexible at all times, and thereby adapt to the variations specific to any situation—this is to 'have no "must not" or "must".'"[75]

The concept of zhong in its philosophical use, then, frequent in the Confucian literature in combinations such as zhongdao 中道, zhongxing 中行, not to forget zhongyong 中庸, seems to be closely associated with the notion of shizhong and thus with the idea of conduct involving flexibility, adaptability, and appropriateness to the particular situation at hand.

A particularly elusive zhong concept is zhongyong. The work bearing this title, attributed to Confucius's grandson, Zisi, and, following its first canonization during the Han dynasty, incorporated into the *Liji*, is not easily decipherable. The Western exegetical tradition of Chinese philosophy has tended to follow James Legge in translating and thereby explaining *Zhongyong* as the *Doctrine of the Mean*.[76] To a student of philosophy, this title immediately calls to mind Aristotle's ethics of the mean (*mesotes*) between two extremes, and in fact, his particular ethical approach has frequently been compared with the spirit of the *Zhongyong*, and even the Confucian notion of zhong altogether. Such a comparison, if sufficiently sophisticated, can certainly be of value. But it can also lead to distortions if either party or both are underrepresented or too simplified in the analysis or if one goes too far in identifying Aristotle's mesotes and the Confucian zhongyong.

I shall, in this discussion, not venture to delve deeply into the philosophy of Aristotle. Suffice it to say that his notion of mesotes implies a criterion for virtuous action in the form of a rationally chosen mean between extremes.[77] Although the mean emerges as a functional category through the mediation between *theōria* and *praxis*, which involves an abstraction that certainly upsets the comparison, let alone identification, with the Chinese notion, it nevertheless retains a strong sense of concreteness by being relative to the circumstances in which it finds its application. The procedure for arriving at the "mean" consists neither in an exact calculation nor in a simple derivation of the particular from the universal, as is sometimes held, but indeed relies on a complex interactive scheme of emotional and cognitive elements. The moral excellence of the Aristotelian exemplars consists largely in having developed a profound sense or "feel" for the situation in which they find themselves and is therefore far from being some kind of "fixed middle."[78]

The inevitable question is whether we can find a comparable idea in the Confucian philosophy. We can certainly find passages in the *Lunyu* and other Confucian writings that may at first glance indicate something of the sort. For example: "Zigong asked: 'Which is of superior character, Zizhang or Zixia?' Confucius replied: 'Zizhang oversteps while Zixia falls short.' Zigong asked: 'So is Zizhang better?' Confucius replied: 'To overstep is just as bad as falling short.'"[79]

Confucius also says that if one is not able to find people of zhongxing 中行 to associate with, then one had better turn to the hasty or the timid: "The hasty rush into things, the timid are left with things undone."[80]

How should we understand zhongxing in this context? To pursue "the due mean" (Legge), to "steer a middle course" (Waley), or "temperate" (Ames and Rosemont)? Is Confucius proposing a "mean"? Though an element of such a thought may be present in his philosophy, it certainly does not involve any kind of theory of a general mean. The "mean," zhongxing, means something much more specific.

Let us first consider the meaning of being either too hasty or too timid. Too hasty or timid for *what*? The clue to an answer is contained in the concept of learning (*xue* 學). The hasty fail to reach the standard of the junzi by speaking of things before accomplishing them, and, more importantly, by engaging in reflection without having the patience to learn. This is supported by a passage where Confucius specifically advises Zizhang to speak and act cautiously.[81] The timid, on the other hand, also fail by not investing enough individuality in their affairs. They concentrate too much on learning at the expense of creative reflection and active engagement. This corresponds to the character of Zixia, who emphasizes learning above anything else but appears extremely cautious with regard to active engagement in the world. Confucius certainly recommends cautious engagement, but without any or with too little engagement, human beings would simply subjugate themselves to the largely unpredictable forces of the environment.

The "theory of moderation" consists specifically in this. Mencius, in the following passage, virtually seems to be providing a direct corrective to the understanding, or misunderstanding, of zhong as referring to a general theory of moderation:

> Mencius said: "Master Yang held on to egoism. Even if he could benefit the world by pulling out a single hair, he still would not do it. Master Mo advocated concern for each and everyone. If he could benefit the world by sacrificing himself,

he would do it. Zimo held on to the middle [zhong 中]. Holding on to the middle is not as far off. However, holding on to the middle without assessing the situation [quan 權] is like holding on to one extreme. Those who detest holding on to one extreme detest it because it impairs the way [dao 道]. One thing is singled out at the expense of a hundred others."[82]

The notion of quan, which I have translated as "assessing the situation," originally refers to a steelyard, and has the verbal meaning "to weigh." Zhang Dainian explains quan in this usage as "the assessment of relative weight that enables one to adapt to changes in the situation."[83] In the passage above, Mencius is arguing that clinging to a norm or a principle without regard for the particular situation, whether that norm is some kind of "middle way" or "moderation," is no better than advocating some kind of extremism. Thus, an understanding of zhong in this philosophical context merely as a centre or middle is too circumscribed. It requires the additional and more important meaning of "being on the mark" in every circumstance of the constantly changing reality in time.[84]

Let us try to get closer to the meaning of "being on the mark" and look at another passage from Mencius in which he compares the adherence to dao to the skill of craftsmanship. Gongsun Chou, one of his disciples, complains that it is too difficult to reach dao and requests a more realistic ideal. Mencius answers in the following manner: "A great craftsman will not change or give up his guideline for the sake of a clumsy worker. Yi [a master archer] did not alter his standards of drawing the bow for the sake of a clumsy archer. Those who are junzi have their bow stretched, and although eager to shoot, do not let the arrow fly at once. They take their stance by being precisely on path [zhongdao 中道], and those who are able to follow them do so."[85] Zhongdao, then, implies to maintain an established standard, in this case, the high standard of archery, and not to compromise it for the sake of less adept individuals. Mencius's comparison of "reaching the dao" with the mastering of a craft or skill is not unparalleled. In the Lunyu, Zixia says that "[j]ust as the numerous craftsmen stay in their shops in order to master their business, so do junzi learn in order to gain access to their way [dao 道]."[86] The process toward becoming a junzi is comparable to the acquisition of a practical skill in the sense that it requires the appropriation of a knowledge refined and cultivated throughout a long tradition.[87]

Thus, there is every indication that the notions of zhongdao or zhongxing imply adherence to the path, the standards, the tradition initiated by the Zhou kings. In the *Zhongyong*, there is an extremely suggestive passage containing the same formulation of overstepping (*guo* 過) and falling short (*bu ji* 不及), as in the *Lunyu* passage on Zizhang and Zixia cited above: "Confucius said: 'I know why the dao is not traveled. The wise overstep it, while the simple-minded fall short of it. I know why the dao is not evident. Those of superior character overstep it, while the unworthy fall short of it. There is no one who does not eat and drink, but the ability to savor [*neng zhi wei* 能知味] what one eats and drinks is rare indeed.'"[88] Two elements in this passage deserve special attention. The first is Confucius's unusual admonition of the wise (*zhi zhe* 知者) and those of superior character (*xian zhe* 賢者) for missing the dao by overstepping it. The second element is the remark on eating and drinking, which apparently is meant to clarify his intended meaning. If we compare the first with the passage on Zizhang and Zixia where Confucius ends by saying that "to overstep is just as bad as falling short," can we then infer that he means, in this passage, that to be wise or of superior character is just as bad as being simple-minded or unworthy? Hardly. There is certainly an irony at play here. In the *Zhongyong*, Confucius is also purported to say, "People all say about themselves: 'I am wise,' but when driven forward they end up in all kinds of nets, traps, and pitfalls without any of them knowing how to avoid them. People all say about themselves: 'I am wise,' but when they decide to conform to zhongyong, they cannot adhere to it for even a month."[89] Wisdom or knowledge (*zhi* 知) in early Confucian tradition is always primarily of a practical nature. It involves perspicacity for the circumstances at hand and the ability to act upon them in the most fruitful or appropriate manner. Hence it is also said in the *Zhongyong* that wisdom consists in bringing things to completion.[90] There is also a particularly illuminating passage in the *Lunyu* where Confucius says that wisdom consists in devoting oneself to what is appropriate for the people and to show respect for ghosts and spirits while at the same time distancing oneself from them.[91]

Those who claim to be wise but then reveal themselves to be incapable of fulfilling the tasks of the world are probably precisely the ones who do not take distance from ghosts and spirits: they devote themselves to all kinds of esoteric and otherworldly theories and practices and forget how to deal with events in ordinary life. They reflect too much and learn too little.[92] Confucius criticizes such tendencies on various occasions. The best known and the most eloquent is probably the following: "Zilu asked about how to serve the spirits and the gods.

Confucius said: 'Not yet being able to serve people, how do you expect to be able to serve the spirits?' Zilu said: 'May I venture to ask about death?' Confucius replied: 'Not yet understanding [zhi 知] life, how do you expect to understand death?'"[93]

The initially obscure comment on eating and drinking now becomes a little clearer. Those who claim to be wise pay too little attention to the things belonging to ordinary life and strive to understand things of which they have no immediate experience. They eat and drink, like everyone else, but, because their mind is elsewhere, they do not even know how to distinguish good food from bad; they do not *savor* it.[94] Due to the routine nature of daily life, they disregard its importance and look for the unusual and the strange, claiming to be aspiring to a higher level of wisdom. As we have seen, however, wisdom in the classical Chinese tradition consists precisely in realizing the deeper meaning and function of everyday life and the ability to discern all its nuances, particularities, and interconnections in order to enhance one's skill in dealing with it. The path, the dao, the *tradition*, that which we have learned from previous generations, is precisely that which enables us to obtain the knowledge to contribute to a more integrated and harmonious society, a contribution which is also an essential precondition for our own personal development. "Overstepping" the dao is thus something comparable to locking oneself in an ivory tower. Conversely, "falling short of" the dao is simply mindlessly and uncritically going about one's business without even the slightest attempt to comprehend the reasons and implications for one's own and other people's actions. Zhongdao, on the other hand, is to stay firmly on the path demanding continuous creative application on the basis of a careful assessment of the dominant propensities in the current circumstances. This is the tradition initiated by the sage kings of antiquity, the tradition which Confucius wants the people to return to and cultivate further.

If my analysis is correct, then it is evident that the rather problematic notion of zhongyong is a further and a more specific elaboration on this theme. Zhong, as already mentioned, is explained in the *Shuowen* lexicon with *nei*, "inside," and with zheng, "straight" or "upright," the latter of which I have emphasized in my interpretation. The term *yong* 庸 is explained with its homophone *yong* 用, "to employ," "to use," "to exercise." In the *Erya* 爾雅, the oldest Chinese treatise on characters, it is also interpreted as *chang* 常, "constant," "regular," or "ordinary." Ge Rongjin suggests that by combining these interpretations, we can have a reasonably good idea of what yong entails. He says that zhongyong could thus be understood as "exercising the ordinary way of zhong, the ordinary actions that people practice."[95] The rich semantic character of the classical Chinese language makes it indeed hard to come up with one succinct formulation in English of this polysemous notion. I suggest, though, that it refers to the endeavor of maintaining appropriate conduct according to the standard of the wisdom handed down by tradition and embodied and expressed in ordinary practices and habits.[96] Thus, as indicating what is "appropriate," the notion of zhong receives its reference from the cultural tradition—in other words, actions are appropriate insofar as they are perceived as embodying the values of the tradition.[97] But we must be careful of not confusing it with a simple conformity to tradition. While there is certainly *deference* to tradition, there is also a need for *difference* when novel circumstances are encountered and traditional values need to be interpreted or translated into action. Owing to the consistent Chinese sense of reality as a continuous process of change in time, the details of one's circumstances are never the same, and thus the circumstances themselves are always novel. In this way, the emphasis is on actions as "appropriate," both in the sense of being a realization of values suitable to the tradition *and* as a personal "appropriation" of the tradition. To zhong, or to "hit the mark," then, is an intelligent combination of the (strictly speaking) inseparable social and personal investments in every single moment.

Nothing in this is foreign to the Confucian philosophy or, as a matter of fact, to the broader Chinese tradition of thought. On the contrary, the idea of maintaining a focus on the here and now is one of the more consistent and specific features of Chinese thought. A poetic and metaphorical passage in the *Daodejing* 道德經 says:

Do not go out your door in order to know the world.
Do not peer outside your window in order to know the
   way of heaven [*tiandao* 天道].
The further one goes, the less one knows.
Thus, the sage knows while not traveling far,
Understands clearly while not gazing into the distance,
Succeeds while not doing things in this way.[98]

An old Chinese idiom (*chengyu* 成語), common in literature and refined speech, describes the folly of overlooking the obvious, or that which belongs to one's immediate environment, and concentrating all one's efforts on the distant: *shejin qiuyuan* 捨近求遠, literally "to seek far and wide for what lies close at hand." This expression is most germane to the criticism of the purportedly wise persons in the *Zhongyong*. In the *Lunyu*, Confucius also states that the way to become a person of "communal humanity" (*ren* 仁), a person who combines all the ideal Confucian characteristics, is to "correlate one's conduct with those near at hand."[99] To excel as a human being means, for Confucians, to excel as a social being and therefore requires a concentration on and engagement in one's own social reality. The source of wisdom is right here, or as Confucius laconically says, "How could communal humanity [ren] be at all distant? As soon as I want communal humanity, it has arrived."[100]

It should now be clearer how the notion of zhong relates to ritual propriety. Ritual propriety is the most powerful medium through which one appropriates and expresses one's tradition. If zhong implies a deep sense in which one can "hit the mark in one's actions" or "to act appropriately" in every situation with regard to the social values of the tradition, then it would be expected that Confucians recommend a particular concentration on ritual propriety as a heuristic device for learning this sense.[101]

It should be acknowledged that Confucians, as well as most if not all ancient Chinese thinkers, never aspired to some kind of transcendent version of truth according to which moral universal values could be realized: the criterion for what is "right" to do is located within culture. It is then a matter of contemplating and deciding what cultural norms, what tradition, what dao are in some way superior to the others. I would hold that the different choices made by the different thinkers constitute the main difference between the Chinese philosophical schools. What unites the Confucian thinkers is the belief that the tradition, the dao, initiated by the Zhou rulers, is the most promising one for realizing a society characterized by the harmonious coexistence of its members. It is worth reiterating the point that this does not imply a simple nostalgic return to Zhou culture and society. This point seems to be emphasized by Confucius himself: "Human beings are able to broaden the tradition (dao); the tradition does not broaden human beings."[102]

I shall conclude this section by turning to Xunzi, who, of all the ancient Chinese thinkers, provides the most explicit account of the relationship between li 禮 and zhong 中. In his section on the "Teachings of the Confucians," he says that "[t]he way [dao 道] of the ancient kings consisted in exalting communal humanity [ren 仁] whereby they followed zhong in enacting it. What is meant with zhong? I say that it consists in ritual propriety [li 禮] and appropriateness [yi 義]. The way that I am speaking of is not the way of heaven [*tian zhi dao* 天之道], nor the way of earth, but the way followed by the human being and embodied in the conduct of the junzi."[103] This remarkable passage virtually sums up the seminal points in my previous discussion. First, zhong, the focus that enables us to be on the mark, to get it right, consists in the practice of li, the customs that have been transmitted through cultural tradition and are thus the strongest manifestation of its continuity and existence. Li is complemented by yi, "appropriateness." Second, Xunzi seeks to clarify what he means by dao through an exclusion of possible (mis)understandings: It is *not* the way of heaven or earth, *not* a process of nature, but precisely the "way followed by the human being"—it is the cultural tradition.

CHAPTER TWO

Second Assemblage

From Reason to Intelligence

In the previous chapter, I touched upon the dichotomy of reason and tradition as it has emerged in modern Western discourse. Here I shall provide a more focused and critical discussion of the notion of reason or rationality. Through engagement with the Enlightenment notion of reason, the ultimate aim is to formulate a complex Chinese equivalent of reason and show how it, in fact, harmonizes itself with traditional modes of behavior. The li customs, then, are far from being conceived as irrational or obscurist. On the contrary, they strengthen and maintain reasonable conduct within society.

Since the discussion proceeds from the perspective of education, I shall approach the topic of reason by considering the difference between education and indoctrination, beginning with modern views of Confucius's status as an educator. The wide-ranging ambivalence, both in the West and in China, as to whether he should be regarded as an educator or an indoctrinator of feudal values will be brought into association with modern and predominantly Western attempts to distinguish between education proper and indoctrination. While most would hold, prima facie, that these two are quite distinct, a further exploration of their differences and overview of seminal attempts to clarify such differences reveal that there is arguably no clear line by which their separation can be articulated.

I shall argue that the modern Enlightenment notion of reason has significantly exacerbated this analytic problem and that the ambivalent attitude to Confucius's worth is ultimately founded upon a discourse that is ostensibly rational in its rejection of appeals to traditional or emotional modes of human life. Education, then, is ultimately taken to be founded upon this narrow pillar of reason.

A brief exposition of Max Weber's critique of reason, value, and power shows that a certain paradox has emerged in the above-described way of thinking, such that an exclusivist notion of reason is insufficient for the task of accounting for human freedom and thus for an education devoid of indoctrination. Because of the near dogmatic faith in its supreme value, the glorification of reason in our times may in fact have produced a particularly vicious kind of indoctrination that presents a mere fabrication of "the rational" by hidden and self-serving powers in modern society, by and large successfully implanted in the modern mind.

I shall then turn to the criticisms of John Dewey and Pierre Bourdieu of the traditional notion and understanding of "reason" as an independent entity and their suggestions for alternative ways of accounting for human social behavior. Both thinkers claim that reason must be understood as emanating from and operating within social practices and therefore that it cannot be a viable concept unless it is tied to tradition, or, in their preferred terms, "habits" and "habitus," at work there. This may at first seem to relativize reason, but in fact, it rather localizes it more intimately in the particular cultural and social environment to which it is supposed to apply. In this sense, it enables us to come to a better understanding of what may be called the "organic mechanisms" of these social interactions and processes.

Last, by drawing implicitly on the ideas of Dewey and Bourdieu, I shall attempt to outline a model of what constitutes the functional equivalent of "reason" or "the reasonable" according to the early Confucians, especially Mencius and Xunzi. Both of these thinkers strive to reformulate and enrich the Confucian vision to make it meet the intellectual needs of their time. Consequently, I will argue, their well-known disagreement about the quality of the human being's "natural dispositions" (*renxing*) is largely of a practical kind, resting upon their differing appraisals of what are the most urgent issues to the Confucian philosophy. The renxing issue, and its treatment by Mencius and Xunzi, provides an opening to the complex notion of "the reasonable" or "the intelligible" in Confucianism and its relation with tradition and cosmological forces.

Education and/or Indoctrination: A Borderless Distinction

We have seen that the attainment of a particular kind of practical wisdom is the primary aim of the Confucian teaching. This wisdom is at the same time a social kind of wisdom. By enabling each individual to enrich society, it facilitates the harmonious integration of its members. Moral education, then, lies at the heart of the Confucian philosophy.

While Confucius has frequently been described as an educator, there has, generally speaking, been more skepticism about whether he was "really" a philosopher.[1] But even the epithet of educator is not without its challengers. For at least in the People's Republic, there has been considerable ambivalence as to whether Confucius should be regarded as an educator or as a mere propagandist or indoctrinator of feudal values.

I have already allowed that Confucius certainly meant to return to the tradition initiated by the ancient sage-kings and continued by the first Zhou dynasty emperors. Since this return included a revival, however modified, of the ceremonies and rituals enacted within that culture, and since ritual tends to be perceived as an instrument of mystification and obscurantism, it is perhaps not surprising that his philosophy would be regarded as "partisan teaching" or indoctrination for the old order rather than as education proper.

A recent example of such a perception can be seen in Gou Chengyi's 勾承益 study of li 禮 in the pre-Qin period. Gou claims that the Lunyu introduces a tendency to formalism and consequently to dogmatism (jiaotiaohua 教條化) in its portrayal of the li customs. He concedes that its particular kind of dogmatization is based on a thorough understanding of the original nature of the customs. It therefore possesses, he says, a certain "abstract nature," whose function is to influence people's inner sense of values, whereas the "dogmatism" found in the Yili 儀禮 and the Liji 禮記 is much more concrete and exhibits an effort to control people's external behavior.[2] However, he argues, the distinct style of the Lunyu of easily recited and thus easily memorized aphorisms or maxims (geyan 格言) functions as an ideal linguistic carrier to fulfill the spirit of the li teachings by spreading and popularizing them: "The results of this kind of language-art was to make the Lunyu in its totality betray its character as a collection of choice specimens of aphorisms."[3] Gou's argument is marked by the familiar confusion of consequences and intentions that we have encountered in the works of other Chinese critics of early Confucianism. While he attributes the problem of dogmatism in the Lunyu to later interpretations, scholarly, political, and popular, rather than to Confucius himself, he simply assumes that there must be something inherently dogmatic about the work itself.

It is a common view among contemporary Chinese commentators, in particular those influenced by Marxist-based points of view, that Confucius was a conservative or even a reactionary. He is portrayed as striving to maintain the status quo, and thus as sacrificing individual aspirations for the sake of the whole.[4]

The tension resulting from the general modern uneasiness with tradition is closely related to the problem of indoctrination in Western and Western-influenced discourse. For in the wake of the Enlightenment, Marxism, critical theory, and various other movements of thought that designate themselves as "progressive," indoctrination has been associated in particular with traditionalism and tendencies to conserve and reinforce the predominant relations of power and economic distribution in society. There is much to be said about such an association, not least today in our increasingly complex societies of mass media, societies that sponsor the continuous outpouring of information and where we repeatedly witness consistent and often successful attempts at monopolizing the media market in order to control the flow and content of information for both political and economic or commercial purposes. Ironically, however, these very "progressive" movements have tended to install arguably even more grotesque mechanisms of indoctrination and propaganda in the societies where they have gained actual power. The point is that it is simplistic and shortsighted to blame tradition as such for being the source of distortion and false consciousness. Both traditionalism and antitraditionalism can easily fall prey to dogmatism or a kind of conservatism aiming at the protection of certain narrow interests.

It seems evident that the defamation of Confucius as a mere indoctrinator of feudal values is yet another aspect of the apotheosis of reason in modernity and the subsequent uneasiness with tradition per se. The modern demand for a persistent forward-looking orientation has simultaneously established the tradition of rejecting any tradition, and this is clearly incommensurable with the outspoken veneration by Confucius and his followers for the tradition initiated by the former sage-kings. The real issue, then, is not that Confucius was an indoctrinator, but that he was indoctrinating ideas that arose in the past.

In order to establish this point, however, a closer look at the concept of "indoctrination" is first needed. With a relatively clear idea of what constitutes indoctrination, one ought to be able to ascertain the extent to which, if any, it characterizes the Confucian teachings. Normally, indoctrination is associated with certain "teaching" methods and the expectation of an uncritical acceptance of the content "taught." Most people, and especially educators, would argue that indoctrination ought to be clearly distinguished from education and kept out of its range. Such a distinction, however, has proven to be problematic.

We may note, first, that the English word "indoctrination" is itself highly ambiguous. Its predominant connotation is the pejorative one of a systematic and uncritical inculcation of ideas that serves narrow interests. But it *can* also be synonymous with "instruction," though it is rarely used in this way. An etymological analysis is not particularly helpful either. The Latin *doctrina* means "teaching" or that which is taught, so "indoctrination" could be adequately described as "the imparting of teachings" or simply "to teach." Although the word "doctrine" was later restricted to the teachings of the Christian Church, from where it has acquired its modern and more general pejorative meaning as a synonym of "dogma," it is nonetheless no less ambiguous than "indoctrination."[5]

In modern Chinese, the distinction between "education" and "indoctrination" is even more obscure. The words *guanshu* 灌輸 and *jiaodao* 教導, both of which can mean indoctrination in the pejorative sense of the word, can also mean "to imbue with" (knowledge, thoughts, etc.), "to teach," or "to give guidance to" and are frequently used in both senses.[6]

In a Western-informed argument, a successful separation of education and indoctrination would ultimately base itself upon the concepts of truth and reason, whereby these concepts would be considered an essential component of the first and not of the latter. According to such an analysis, truth and reason are taken to be "objective," "value neutral," and, ultimately, to serve everyone's interests. Being devoid of truth and reason, indoctrination, on the other hand, has the deliberate subjective, value-laden objective of serving the interests of only a few at the expense of the many.

Most attempts to analyze these concepts philosophically follow this line of thought. A classic formulation is, for instance, that of sociologist Michio Nagai, who uses the categories of content and method to distinguish between education, or teaching, and indoctrination:

1. In regard to content, teaching is primarily concerned with objective valid knowledge, such as the sciences, mathematics and logic. Indoctrination is concerned, on the other hand, primarily with subjective unverifiable knowledge, such as national ideals, class ideologies, family norms, mores, moral conviction, religious creeds and the like.

2. In regard to method, indoctrination utilizes non-rational means; teaching, on the other hand, utilizes open

examination, disinterested exchange of ideas and unrestricted analysis.[7]

Nagai concedes that this is merely a hypothetical distinction, and, to be sure, when closer examined, it turns out to be highly questionable. Let us first take a look at the content part. Nagai makes the distinction in terms of supposedly "objective," value-neutral disciplines, on the one hand, and, on the other hand, "subjective," value-laden ones. One immediate objection to this distinction is that the claim of science to objectivity is certainly not beyond dispute. It is a characteristic feature of scientific theories that they continue to be refuted and replaced by more accurate, or more applicable, ones. Further, the notion of "science" is unclear. Is psychology a science, or anthropology, or economics? They certainly strive to be such, but most theories in these fields are highly disputed and controversial. Moreover, these domains of knowledge are anything but value-neutral, for a particular conception of the function of society usually reflects political tendencies. A Marxist conception of society is vastly different from a neoliberal one. A third objection is of a more practical nature. Given that indoctrination ought to be eliminated, this distinction suggests an almost unthinkable reduction of the educational curriculum to the disciplines of logic, mathematics, and perhaps some of the supposedly more reliable sciences.[8] If it is a sufficient condition for instruction to include values in any form in order to be classified as indoctrination (in its pejorative sense), then there is not much of our present day so-called education that is not indoctrination.

In fact, this was the conclusion of some thinkers during a heated and intriguing discussion about the difference between education and indoctrination that took place in the United States in the wake of the Depression. Owing to the variety of often conflicting social and political plans that teachers who were eager to restore order in American society introduced to classrooms, the question arose whether they ought to present various views impartially or rally for the plans that they endorsed themselves. Many argued that schools ought to take a positive stand with regard to social reform. One of these was George Counts. When asked whether schools ought to practice indoctrination, he responded in the following manner: "I am prepared to defend the thesis that all education contains a large element of imposition, that in the very nature of the case this is inevitable, that the existence and evolution of society depend on it, that it is consequently eminently desirable, and that the frank acceptance of this fact by the educators is a major professional obligation."[9] In other words, since education is always already indoctrination to a significant degree, it is futile to try to purge education of indoctrination. Instead, the responsibility of educators should consist in appraising the divergent positions on the basis of which they select the "best one" for presentation. Although Counts's position was not without support, most believed that it represented a total surrender to the vagueness of an important distinction on the mere account of its philosophical unsettledness. Among these were John Dewey and John L. Childs. In response to Counts, they write that "[i]nstead of recommending an imposed indoctrination, we are striving to challenge all the indoctrinations of conscious dogma and of the unconscious bias of tradition and vested interest which already exist."[10]

These words clearly display a modernist tone. However, Dewey and Childs did not maintain that education, as distinct from indoctrination, was a wholly rational practice in the sense of being entirely value-neutral and objective. They argued, on the contrary, that because education is an affair of action, and because human action always implies preference, "the scheme of education itself cannot be impartial in the sense of not involving a preference for some values over others."[11] Education, no less than any other human endeavor, is always involved with value.

Reason I: Max Weber's Paradox

Before exploring further Dewey's position, I would like to turn to Max Weber once again. For with their association of education with action and value, Dewey and Childs recall Weber's views of the nature of values and their decisive role in determining human action. In fact, following the founding of the Weimar Republic in Germany after World War I, a fierce controversy took place in Germany about the acceptability of having academic instructors explicitly espousing their personal political views in the classroom. This discussion was prompted by several cases of socialist intellectuals being discharged from their academic positions on grounds of their political beliefs. The multitude of social and historical factors involved in this controversy makes it an immensely complicated one, and I shall therefore disregard its particularities here. I believe, however, that Weber's views on this issue, which are closely bound up with his skepticism of the Enlightenment ideals and the Enlightenment notion of reason, contain interesting implications for the discipline of education, and, in particular, its method, as it has been formulated in the modern West.

Weber held that the notion of reason preached by the Enlightenment thinkers as containing the key to true values amounted to nothing more than a myth. In fact, he ironically referred to the Enlightenment (*Aufklärung*) as a "transfiguration" (*Verklärung*) of reason.[12] Weber argued that it is not reason that determines values, but the other way around: reason is dependent on and relative to values. When things or actions are appraised as reasonable, they are appraised according to the values, usually socially constituted but ultimately individual, of the appraiser. If I consider something as a good, then I will consider it reasonable to pursue this good, provided, of course, that I take reasonableness as a justification of my actions.

Now reason can certainly help me to obtain that which I conceive as a good. However, it merely enables me to find the best and the most efficient way to do so, not to assess the worth of my pursued end. It is what Weber identifies as "instrumental" or "means-end rationality" (*Zweckrationalität*), which he sharply distinguishes from "value-rationality" (*Wertrationalität*). The former, therefore, accepts a given end as a justification of the measures taken to reach it, while the latter is oriented toward values, and according to which actions are justified for their own sake. These two kinds of rationality are derived from the way in which people assign meaning to their actions. According to Weber, however, values are beliefs, not facts, and therefore it cannot be assessed or determined by a discipline of science what values should be considered "correct" or "true." At the end of the day, this assessment or determination is up to the person in question. It is a personal, and not a professional, choice.[13]

Our modern idea of freedom and democracy is closely tied up with the Enlightenment notion of reason. We see this already in Kant, who considers the "autonomy" of reason as a path toward liberation from the bondage of tradition—the human being's "self-incurred immaturity." Weber, however, by pessimistically denying the possibility of the autonomy or independent use of reason, simultaneously casts strong doubts on the possibility of freedom in this sense.

This conclusion is evident from Weber's discussion of power (*Gewalt*). For Weber, power does not necessarily imply physical force, nor is it restricted to the formal power to rule. Thus, the agent exercising the supreme authority in a state is not necessarily the sovereign government. Power is the ability to make others act according to one's own wishes and interests. Hence, for example, in a reign of terror, cruel dictatorships rule by virtue of their superior physical force and people's fear of that force. It is, however, inevitable that the latter, while openly conforming to the government's wishes, will clandestinely seek to undermine it and its interests through their actions. Successful indoctrination, however, is a much more effective kind of enforcement. For in such a case, people willingly act according to a value-orientation that promotes the interests of the indoctrinator. They will act so whether publicly or privately, since they are acting in the belief that they are promoting their own good. In this context, Weber makes use of and twists Kant's famous dictum of the practical imperative for a free moral action: the supreme ruler of society is one who is able to influence the actions of the ruled in such a way that they behave *as if* they were following a maxim of conduct for its own sake.[14]

Indoctrination has been and probably still is a tool used in most, if not all, parts of the world. Weber's point, however, is more specific, relating to our particular modern Western belief in the supremacy of reason. Reason, famously depicted by Plato as the sunlight meeting our eyes when we finally succeed in escaping from the gloomy cave, and revealing to us our previous blindness by illuminating the "real" appearance (and nature) of things, is, for Weber, yet another illusion. In fact, we have simply gone from a cave in which we were blinded by the lack of light to another in which we are blinded by excessive (artificial) light. However, believing that we have left all caves, we have sunk even deeper into the abyss of illusion, for we have come to convince ourselves that we have overcome all previous illusions. This is the essence of value-rationality, a nonrational adoption of values now taken to constitute rational approaches to the world in the specific form of the Enlightenment notion of rationality. Weber, who was strongly influenced by Nietzsche, refers, in this respect, to the latter's notion of the "last human beings."[15] Nietzsche describes them partly in the following satirical manner:

> No herdsman and one herd! All want the same, all are the same: those whose opinions are different voluntarily commit themselves to a lunatic asylum.
> "Previously, the whole world was mad"—say the subtlest ones, and blink.
> One is intelligent and knows everything that has happened: in this way, there is no end to one's scoffing.[16]

Weber's ideas may admittedly be considered unnecessarily extreme and even pessimistic. What remains, however, is that the notion of reason, at least as understood by the Enlightenment and immediate post-Enlightenment thinkers, is insufficient to determine either acceptable methods or the content of education. What counts as rational in a given society is determined by the dominant (*non*rational) beliefs of that society. Moreover, if education proper requires freedom, freedom, in turn, requires the independent use of reason, and yet, if reason is defined according to our deepest values, then it seems impossible to exert a meaningful critique of those values. Thus, from a Weberian point of view, education will necessarily be a kind of enforcement or coercion.[17] C. J. B. MacMillan comes to a similar conclusion through an analysis of Ludwig Wittgenstein's ideas of language games and world pictures:

> [I]n a modern democratic society, the desired goal of education is that each student develop a set of beliefs that are rationally grounded and open to change when challenged by better-grounded beliefs. In order to develop such students, however, it would seem that they must acquire a belief in rational methods of knowing which must itself be beyond challenge, i.e., held in a manner inconsistent with its own content. Thus, students must be indoctrinated in order not to be indoctrinated.[18]

According to these compelling views, rationality turns out to be a particular (cultural) method of discourse following certain (cultural) rules. It is founded upon certain assumptions about the nature of knowledge and truth. Thus, Nagai's typical definition of indoctrination through its utilization of "nonrational means" is largely vacuous. It would perhaps enable us to exclude extreme measures such as coercive brainwashing or authoritarian drills from the category of education. However, the dividing line is far from being clear. I. A. Snook, who proposes a distinction between education and indoctrination in terms of the instructor's intentions, argues that the notion of nonrational method, as a criterion of indoctrination, is unacceptable, not only because of its vagueness, but also because "it makes no allowance for the efficient, cunning, or well-trained indoctrinator."[19]

According to Snook's implications, such an indoctrinator must be someone who is capable of lending his or her instruction an appearance of rational authority while, in fact, he or she is indoctrinating the audience, that is to say, making them internalize values that are in the perceived interests of the indoctrinator.

To this Weber would surely add that an indoctrinator could very well be using a rational method, namely, a means-end rational one—the most efficient method for making students believe what the indoctrinator takes to be in his or her interest that they believe. The problem still remains how to understand the notion of the "rational": rational from what perspective and for whom?

Reason II: The Quest for Reason in China

One of the greatest problems with the notion of reason in post-Enlightenment discourse is precisely that it purports to be the final authority, often without elaboration, resting on a fixed unchanging base that supposedly unites all the variations belonging to individual cases. That base, if not taken to be metaphysically grounded, is frequently identified with Western logic and its rules. However, as Weber points out, such a foundation is insufficient as a guide for human action—unless, of course, we *all* subscribe to a *single* system of values, prescribing a universal framework of social stratification and justice. Such a possibility is now generally considered to be not only unthinkable but also to rest upon an obsolete, arrogant, and chauvinistic monomania. It is, however, certainly still present as an unannounced presupposition in the most important dimensions of human experience.

In classic Western discourse, the scope of reason is not limited to human conduct. In much of Western metaphysics, human reason is portrayed in some form or another as a microcosm of the macrocosm of the inherent order in the totality of being. Thus, the "reason in nature" is ultimately the "same" reason as the one that human beings are expected to follow in their actions.[20] This unquestioned assumption of a single-ordered world was also the underlying factor in the recurrent attempt by early Western interpreters of Chinese thought to identify *the* single element in Chinese philosophy that would more or less correspond to a Western notion of reason. The most popular candidates have been dao 道 and li 理.[21]

The former has been tempting for two reasons: first, because of its seemingly metaphysical or even divine nature in Daoist literature, most notably in the *Daodejing*, and second, because of its alternative meaning as "discourse" or "speech," both of which taken together recall the Greek *logos*.[22] In the present work, dao's association with reason is particularly ironic, considering that I have argued for its affinity to the Western notion of tradition.[23] Two things, however, should be noted in this respect: first, there is a discrepancy between the Confucian and the Daoist uses of the notion; second, and more important, the irony only arises because of the unfortunate antagonism between reason and tradition in Western discourse, as already discussed.

Given the absence of such an antagonism and the will to be flexible in one's interpretation, one can possibly see reason as being, to some extent, embedded in dao—that is, of course, depending upon our understanding of "reason." For if we still insist upon a notion of reason that is supposed to be a universal authority at all places and at all times, we will find either nothing of value in the Chinese classics or a pleasant but deceptive reconfirmation of our already held convictions. If, however, we open up the vista and grant the possibility of a plurality of reasons, then dao would seem to potentially encompass such a notion.

In the latter half of this section, I will first revisit the discussion of dao and reason, and, after a treatment of Dewey's and Bourdieu's views of human behavior as socially embedded, turn to li 理 and reason in conjunction with other seminal Confucian notions.[24] It should be made quite clear at the outset, however, that I do not accept any view identifying a single Chinese concept as either corresponding to the Western kind of reason as such, or even as its functional equivalent. The Western notion of reason itself is a complex cultural thought-model,[25] and it is even questionable whether one can identify a *single* such notion at all. At the same time, however, this does not mean that the Western and Chinese notions are wholly incommensurable. There is certainly a Chinese functional equivalent, but it is composed of a cluster of interacting ideas operating on different levels.

I want to take the discussion to a more elementary level and first consider some basic understandings of reason. The English "rationality" and "reason" both derive from the same Latin root, *ratio*, meaning "reckoning," which again derives from *reri*, "to think." Thus, at its most basic level, it merely signifies the ability to think. However, it has an obvious relation to mathematics as "ratio" and "reckoning," the latter of which, according to the *Collins English Dictionary*, means "to calculate or ascertain by calculating." This concept carries a long philosophical history, which is traceable to the Greek *logos*. I will not discuss this complex history in any detail. This has already been done by others, for instance by Hall and Ames, who convincingly argue that the Western notion of reason is derived from cosmogonical reflections, according to which the ordered world (cosmos), as we supposedly know it, came into existence from a disordered world (chaos). This effected order has then become something of a model for the ideal order in the human realm as well.[26] Suffice it to say, for the present purposes, that the heritage of the Pythagoreans, Plato, and Aristotle has provided the notion of reason with a significance combining cosmological, mathematical, and ethical principles in such a way that it tends to point to a single ordering principle governing all.[27]

Let me turn to another word more or less corresponding to "reason," the German *Vernunft*. Being of Germanic origin, Vernunft carries a lighter philosophical baggage than "reason," although it of course shares its meaning, especially when used in the wake of the German idealist tradition initiated by Immanuel Kant.[28] The word derives from the Old High German verb *firneman*, meaning "to hear" or "to ascertain." The modern meaning of Vernunft, according to the *Duden Deutsches Universal Wörterbuch*, is "[t]he human being's intellectual ability to acquire understanding, recognize connections, gain an overview of things, form judgments, and act in accordance with these."

Note that there is considerable openness to this definition. For instance, it does not presuppose that this intellectual ability is based on any particular rules, such as (Western) logic, which, in turn, the English "reason" and "rationality" both do. The first two definitions of the word "rational," according to *Collins*, are formulated thus: "1. using reason or logic in thinking out a problem. 2. in accordance with the principles of logic or reason; reasonable."

Now the Chinese kind of reason is certainly closer to the open-ended German definition than to the English one. As we shall see, however, the Chinese kind is much more concrete and emerges as the ability to negotiate effectively between the established tradition and the unforeseen changes in one's environment. There is further ambivalence as to its relation with the cosmological forces, depending on the author in question.

The dao of the *Daodejing* certainly does imply some kind of ordering in the continuous process of the myriad things, and, in this sense, some kind of reason in the way of things. But it is not a transcendental "principle." As Xu Fuguan 徐復觀 has pointed out, if we construe it as a principle (*yuanli* 原理), it will be static, which seems to go against its spontaneously active nature as described in the *Daodejing*. We must, Xu continues, think of it instead as a force or dynamism (*dongli* 動力).[29]

Dongli, however, is an unfortunate term, for it implies a mere moving power without any kind of ordering. For the sake of retaining that sense, I propose a pun on Xu's suggestion, whereby we accept the term of dongli, but use a different li, namely, the other potential candidate for reason. We could translate this dongli 動理 as "dynamic patternings."

By understanding dao as "dynamic patternings," the many recommendations of Daoists to "follow the dao" or "act according to dao" make more sense. Following the dao would then mean that the best way to proceed in the world is to harmonize one's actions with the operations of the cosmos, in this case, by engaging in "dynamic patterning" oneself. For although there is little to suggest that cosmogony played any significant role in the development of Chinese thought, there is still a tendency to identify and pursue a certain correspondence or harmony (he 和) between cosmological and human arrangements. In fact, Tang Junyi has asserted that one of the fundamental characteristics of Chinese philosophy is the view that there is a consistent continuity or harmony (heyi 合一) between the human being and the cosmos.[30] Tu Weiming almost echoes Tang Junyi in the following statement: "[T]he notion of humanity as forming one body with the universe has been so widely accepted by the Chinese, in popular as well as elite culture, that it can very well be characterized as a general Chinese worldview."[31] Accordingly, "rational behavior," from a Daoist point of view, is to align oneself with cosmic operations. The difference here is that "rational" is neither single-ordered nor absolute, but continuously unfolding in an endless process of change as creative responses to new circumstances.

In this regard, there is nothing of fundamental difference in the Confucian philosophy. Admittedly, and as I have noted, most of the pre-Qin Confucians do not concentrate in particular on cosmic operations. In the Lunyu, the notion of "dynamic patternings" would rather seem to operate within the scheme of the dao of tradition, whereby the junzi zhi dao 君子之道 describes an excellent and exemplary instance of the personalization of a traditional mode of engaging with the world. To the extent that we can speak of rationality in this context, it is derived from tradition, much in the same way as Gadamer describes it. The Zhongyong, however, quite explicitly establishes a connection between the cosmic or the natural and the human in its opening sentences: "What tian commands is called natural dispositions (xing 性). Drawing out the natural dispositions is called the proper way (dao 道). Cultivating this way is called education (jiao 教)."[32] These three sentences are as pregnant with meaning as they are short. Tracing the chain backwards, education is seen as the cultivation of the proper way, or of the cultural tradition. The cultural tradition, on the other hand, refers essentially to certain manners of developing our faculties, which again are received from nature. Thus, the rational has rather the sense of the reasonable: It means making use of our natural faculties for the sake of personal and cultural growth, for the sake of "broadening the way," or, as we may formulate it, "broadening the tradition."[33]

Reason III: Reasonable Alternatives

The dominant notion of reason in the modern world has its source in Plato, from where it describes an ascending trajectory through Christian scholasticism and the Enlightenment, reaching its highest glory in certain modernist movements such as positivism and futurism. But then its star begins to fade, almost certainly to a large degree due to the "irrational" inhumanity of the two world wars, perpetrated by ostensibly the most rational of peoples. The perception, following Nietzsche, Weber, and other critical and anthropologically and sociologically oriented thinkers, that the concepts of reason and the rational were utilized to justify domination of one culture over another, or one segment of society over another, has also led to a consistent challenging of reason's authority by, among others, postmodern, left-wing, and feminist thinkers, as well as numerous writers and artists.

Hence, today, one has several different alternative notions of reason to choose from, all of which attempt to get away from its narrow chauvinistic heritage. This state of affairs, however, does not mean that any of the available notions have filtered into the general Western way of thinking to any significant degree, at least not yet. I believe, in fact, that the general understanding of reason is still that of being logical (proceeding according to fixed rules), universal (transcendent), and ultimately infallible (leading to truth).

In this section, I will indicate a different, and, in my opinion, a more useful and realistic formulation of reason by drawing from the ideas of John Dewey and Pierre Bourdieu. It seems to me that the relational and praxis-oriented notion of "the reasonable" that can be derived from the accounts of human behavior provided by these authors lends itself well to a positive comparison with the complex Chinese, especially Confucian, functional equivalent.

John Dewey, in his *Human Nature and Conduct*, rejects the traditional perception of reason as being opposed to impulse and habit: "Rationality . . . is the attainment of a working harmony among diverse desires. 'Reason' as a noun signifies the happy cooperation of a multitude of dispositions, such as sympathy, curiosity, exploration, experimentation, frankness, pursuit—to follow things through—circumspection, to look about at the context, etc., etc."[34] This view resonates with the reference I made to Nietzsche in the introduction concerning objectivity and perspectives. In fact, there are quite a few passages in Nietzsche's works that, leaving aside his unmistakable rhetorical style, express practically the same view. In the *Gay Science*, for instance, he mocks those who hold "reason [*intelligere*] to be something conciliatory, just, good, something that is essentially opposed to the impulses; when it is simply a *particular relation of the impulses with one another.*"[35]

Both Dewey and Nietzsche, then, reject the notion of reason as a particular faculty set aside from the other human faculties. Such a notion is posed as isolated from, and more often as, ideally, the reigning counterweight to most other human propensities. Pierre Bourdieu, in criticizing "rational actor" anthropologists, who purport to explain rational conduct solely through the notion of "reason," makes an illuminating point in this respect. He says that "by refusing to recognize any other way of founding it in reason than by giving reason as its foundation, they simply introduce a being of reason, an ought-to-be, as a *vis dormativa*, in the form of an agent all of whose practices have reason as their principle."[36]

Bourdieu refers here to the ironic circular explanation in Molière's play from 1673, *The Imaginary Invalid* (*Le Malade Imaginaire*), that opium puts people to sleep because it possesses the *vis dormativa* (a somnolent potency). Bourdieu sees the "liberal subjectivist" approach to human practice as no less circular. A cause, the "faculty of reason," is fabricated and reified to assess and explain practice on the basis of its conformity to the cause. It is, moreover, attributed universally to individuals without taking into consideration the particular qualities of the society to which the model is being applied. This rational model, however, is of no explanatory value if the agents, whose conduct it is meant to explain, do not explicitly share this particular notion as a valuable or in some ways superior model for action. Instead, Bourdieu suggests, one must realize "that decision, if decision there is, and the 'system of preferences' which underlies it, depend not only on all the previous choices of the decider but also on the conditions in which his "choices" have been made, which include all the choices of those who have chosen for him, in his place, pre-judging his judgments and so shaping his judgment."[37] Reason, in other words, is but an empty word if it is not considered as a construction arising out of the interaction between a particular person and that person's particular environment in all its physical, cultural, and historical dimensions. For, as Bourdieu continues,

> if one fails to recognize any form of action other than rational action or mechanical reaction, it is impossible to understand the logic of all the actions that are reasonable without being the product of a reasoned design, still less of rational calculation; informed by a kind of objective finality without being consciously organized in relation to an explicitly constituted end; intelligible and coherent without springing from an intention of coherence and a deliberate decision; adjusted to the future without being the product of a project or plan.[38]

Bourdieu consequently suggests that "rational" is too narrow a concept, too constrained by the rules of formal logic, and, in the context of economics, for example, too closely associated with the specific Euro-American capitalistic (Weber would say means-end rational) notion of maximum gain for minimum costs. With the plethora of other kinds of value operating in every society, there will be different designations of what sort of social, economic, or other conditions are deemed "reasonable."[39]

Let us now go back to John Dewey for a moment. In his *Democracy and Education*, first published in 1916, he writes that "'[r]eason' is just the ability to bring the subject matter of prior experience to bear to perceive the significance of the subject matter of a new experience. A person is reasonable in the degree in which he is habitually open to seeing an event which immediately strikes his senses not as an isolated thing but in its connection with the common experience of mankind."[40] On grounds similar to Bourdieu's, Dewey prefers speaking of being "reasonable" to being "rational." Reason is nothing outside of or apart from one's experience of the environment. To be reasonable, in Dewey's sense, is to be habitually open to perceive novel events in the maximally broad range of their interconnections with other phenomena already experienced. One must be *habitually* open, because it has to be a lasting disposition and not merely an isolated whim.

Dewey gradually came to abandon the word "reason," surely because its unfortunate historical baggage had constrained his readers to understand his use of it in an all too narrow sense and opted instead for the word "intelligence."[41] This preference is already latent in his earlier works where "intelligence," notably "social intelligence," receives a much more elaborate discussion than does "reason." Intelligence, moreover, cannot be adequately comprehended apart from understanding the functionality of "habits."[42]

In its mundane use, the word "habit" has a rather negative connotation. It tends to call to mind a "bad habit," a thoughtless routine, or an idiosyncratic or eccentric act that serves no further purpose. "Habit" is thus sometimes used as an explanation or a reason for a certain action or behavior, but, if accepted as such, it accounts for an action that is either meaningless or in some ways reprehensible (and even neurotic)—otherwise the reason or explanation is normally regarded as insufficient: "Why do you drink so quickly?" or "Why do you utter the word 'like' several times in every sentence?" could both be answered with "It's just a habit." It would, however, be an apologetic explanation, admitting that the actions in question are undesirable.

Dewey and Bourdieu argue, however, that habits play a much more fundamental and vital role in human existence and living. Tasks and actions that are practically, if not literally, necessary for us to execute in order to get through our day, that may appear to be spontaneous, and, to an alien wholly unfamiliar with human life, arbitrary, are to a significant degree the effects of habit. In most cases we do not deliberate on the purpose or the exact execution of these actions, but if we were asked why we perform them, we would hardly respond in the apologetic manner as stated above: "It's just a habit." For these actions are far from being devoid of purpose, even though we may not always bring that purpose to consciousness when about to perform or while performing them. In other words, we can justify these actions, at least to someone who is adequately familiar with our environment and shares or understands, at least in part, our valuations.

Dewey introduces the notion of habits into moral discourse with the aim of offering a practical and nonreductionist explanation of the complexity of human behavior. He sees the practicality of the notion in its dynamism as referring to social functions, arts, or skills that we have acquired through our interaction with the environment.[43] Thus, instead of attributing tendencies or dispositions to an isolated or abstract self, Dewey argues that virtues no less than vices are habits that have taken form through "interactions of elements contributed by the make-up of an individual with elements supplied by the out-door world."[44] Habits are therefore in continuous formation, as the already formed habits will condition our approach to other tasks, which, in turn, may or may not modify the habits themselves. It depends on the intensity and the quality of our experience whether a refinement of our habits will take place or not.

Now habits, Dewey reminds us, are not only physical actions, such as picking one's nose or approaching people one knows by slapping their backs, but also certain manners of thinking and perceiving. Without the restrictions involved in these habits, we would probably need to figure out the most mundane of our operations over and again every single day. If I cannot find my toothbrush in the morning, I will not look for it in my wife's handbag (unless, perhaps, I have excluded all other possibilities), as it would contradict the reality to which I am accustomed. Habits help us focus and find our way through our familiar surroundings, or, as Dewey says, they "prevent thought from straying away from its imminent occupation to a landscape more varied and picturesque but irrelevant to practice. Outside the scope of habits, thought works gropingly, fumbling in confused uncertainty."[45]

To be sure, many of us have found ourselves in a cultural setting in which we did not know how to comport ourselves, in an environment to which we did not know how to respond appropriately. In such cases, we are not in possession of adequately relevant habits that can inform our behavior in these very situations. In our own cultural setting, however, we may be able to function appropriately and elegantly without giving it a single thought. It is through habits that we "know how" to act. Dewey criticizes the liberal individualist doctrine of "a single, simple and indissoluble soul" for having been "the cause and the effect of failure to recognize that concrete habits are the means of knowledge and thought."[46]

These examples further point to the social formation of habits. It is through the social and cultural conditions of human impulses that the generation of the abundance of active and reactive patterns takes place, not to mention the variable modes of behavior between cultures. In fact, our performance may even be seriously interrupted if we concentrate too hard on the microsequences that make up our habits. On the other hand, of course, habits can also totally exclude reflection. Generally speaking, habits are conservative powers that restrict thought, which is instructive in the sense that they can lend thought direction but obstructive in the sense that they can take complete control over thought processes, transforming them and themselves into routine. This is the reason why the liberation of one's impulses is of importance. Impulses or instincts are, Dewey argues, the primary, unformed raw material and basic resource of habits. They are, in their most simple form, devoid of meaning and only acquire meaning as soon as they become habitual. The "*meaning of native activities is not native; it is acquired.*"[47]

What matters, however, is not to block new impulses, because they are triggered by exposure to new experiences, and it is through these that one forms habits and learns how to engage effectively with one's environment. In fact, a healthy balance between acquired habits and native impulses contributes to the construction of reason or intelligence. Intelligence, Dewey says, "is the sum-total of impulses, habits, emotions, records, and discoveries which forecast what is desirable and undesirable in future possibilities."[48] The aim, therefore, is to form a multitude of habits by being open to new experiences to be mastered. This requires not only that previously formed habits are brought to bear on and adapted to the situation at hand, but also that one's impulses and instincts are given sufficiently free reign to forge new and different approaches and perspectives. Let us not forget that habits, in a Deweyan sense, are not only physical actions, but also ways of thinking about and viewing the objects of our attention. There is, then, in this particular respect, an intriguing similarity between the Deweyan notion of habits and Nietzschean perspectivism: both are calls for a multiplicity of approaches to what we experience.

After all, reason turns out to be itself a sort of habit, an acquired "instinct" as it were.[49] Reasonable or intelligent action is to be "habitually open to seeing an event . . . in its connection with the common experience of mankind."[50] Dewey's idea of reason or intelligence, then, is always "social intelligence": hence the reference to the common experience of humankind, and not merely to the experiencing individual's own prior experience. Reason or intelligence is thus the habit of regarding events in their entire interrelationships with other events and things, but it is a communicable and hence, at least to a significant extent, common way of regarding events.

Bourdieu's discussion differs from Dewey's in that its aim is not to offer a practical moral account of human action. At the same time, however, Bourdieu's more focused social scientific approach resonates with Dewey's ideas and, in my opinion, complements them.

The protagonist in Bourdieu's discussion is not "habit" but *habitus*, referring to a "system of structured, structuring dispositions" which is "constituted in practice and is always oriented towards practical functions."[51] Habitus is historically and thus culturally established, generated by the previous experience of certain conditions to which it refers back in such an "objectivist" manner that it forms the basis of all subsequent perception and experience of this class of conditions. In this sense, it "is the active present of the whole past of which it is product."[52] However, it neither mechanically determines responses to conditions, nor is it unchangeable between persons or in the unfolding of time. The habitus is no less structured as it is structuring and is therefore in continuous modification by the culture's particular individuals whose experiences are always in some sense unique. But by disposing actors to behave in a certain way depending on the overall conditions of the social field, it forms the generative basis for norms of action and thus enables continuity, regularity, and consistency in social practices: "In short, being the product of a particular class of objective regularities, the habitus tends to generate all the 'reasonable,' 'common-sense,' behaviours (and only these) which are possible within the limits of these regularities, and which are likely to be positively sanctioned because they are objectively adjusted to the logic characteristic of a particular field, whose objective future they anticipate."[53] Every field, then, generates and sanctions a certain "logic of practice"[54] determined by the wider historical and cultural framework in which it has been directed. Therefore, while there is a certain level of consistency between cultures in that human beings all over the world have similar physical needs, the patterns of behavior generated by these needs are modified by the conditions in which these cultures live, and, last, by the habitus structured by and simultaneously structuring these conditions.

There is a definite advantage to Dewey's and Bourdieu's suggestions of how to formulate the basis for meaningful human action. For one thing, they both abandon the essentialist models of innate faculties, such as a reified kind of reason, and propose instead models of relationality between the acting individuals and their environment. Second, the idea of "the reasonable" emerges as a product of social processes and as an agent that then produces other social processes: "the reasonable" itself becomes habit or habitus. One would then expect that reason presides over a certain flexibility in that it is constantly being shaped by the changing circumstances in our social and natural environment.[55]

This is, in fact, how I see the Confucian equivalent of "the reasonable" as arising primarily from the dialectic relationship between ritual and the sense of the appropriate, or li 禮 and yi 義, most clearly accounted for by Xunzi, who adds to this pair the notion of li 理, which is often understood as constituting "reason" in ancient China. For this discussion, to which I shall now turn, Dewey's and Bourdieu's accounts of human conduct and the reasonable serve as quite suggestive models for coming to an understanding of the Confucian idea of reason embedded in tradition.

Reason IV: The Interplay of Li 禮, Yi 義, and Li 理

In one's approach to Chinese philosophical terms, definitions or questions as to what this or that *is* can be seriously misleading. It is not without significance that a Chinese discussion of philosophical notions tends to be conducted in a pluralistic, relational mode; that is to say, two or more notions are normally discussed together, and only very rarely do we encounter attempts to produce a definition of the notions in isolation from each other. In the context of a world in a constant process of change, the notion of fixed definitions would in any case be inappropriate. Everything evolves and changes, and thus the best one can do is to look for configurations between things in the present moment.[56]

While in most classical Chinese writings, we may find explanations that appear to be definitions, we may, in the same writings, also find other and quite different explanations of the same notions. In such cases, the factor of time is again of vital importance, for the Confucian writings are no theoretical "treatises," but circumstantial discussions that base themselves on the perceived dominant or most meaningful propensities of the situation at hand. Thus, an effort is made to make the discussion relevant to the opportunities involved in the situation, and, when the topic is a meaning of a term, the strands of the term most germane to the situation and to those involved are extrapolated.

Hence, a different kind of question is more appropriate, namely, what is the functional relationship between the various moral and social skills and characteristics in the Confucian world? Perhaps a step toward answering this question consists in considering the underlying target of Confucian social and moral philosophy. And this will bring us straight to one core topic of this work: education.

It is surely no coincidence that the first passage of the *Lunyu* brings up both the pleasure of learning and of socializing: "The Master said: 'To learn and then to apply at the proper time what one has learned—is this not a source of pleasure? To have friends arriving from distant places—is this not a source of joy?'"[57]

Learning, as we have seen before, always implies the practical learning of improving one's functional ability in the social sphere. Education is thus not restricted to a particular "sector of education." Education is, to speak with Dewey, who puts this most aptly for our purposes, a "social function," and further, "a process of renewal of the meanings of experience through a process of transmission."[58] Society and communal living, for Dewey as for the Confucians, are the primary seats of learning. The notion of personal cultivation or self-improvement (xiushen 修身) is always concealed, so to speak, in the background of the Confucian discourse.

In the next section, I will provide a more focused discussion of education in the Confucian context and of the Confucian notion of personal cultivation. What matters, for the moment, is to keep in mind that this perspective of learning is seldom if ever absent in the Confucian discourse.

The Confucian philosophy generates and makes use of a large number of specific terms, all of which enjoy a certain level of importance. Most would agree, however, that among the more important ones are communal humanity (ren 仁), the sense of appropriateness (yi 義), ritual propriety (li 禮), and wisdom (zhi 知 or 智). These are all frequently brought up in the *Lunyu*, but it is especially in the *Mencius* that these are identified, combined, and presented as constituting the key terms. In fact, they are so important that Mencius appears to convey them as belonging to the natural make-up of the human being, or at least of the junzi:

> While a vast territory and a large population are what junzi desire, their joy [*le* 樂] consists not merely in this. While taking a stand in the center of the world and bringing peace to the people between the four seas is what junzi take joy in, their natural dispositions [*xing* 性] do not consist merely in this. As for these natural dispositions, great deeds do not add to them, nor do straitened circumstances detract from them. This is because they have already been allotted these tendencies. To their natural dispositions belong communal humanity [ren 仁], appropriateness [yi 義], the observance of ritual propriety [li 禮] and wisdom [zhi 智], which are rooted in their thoughts and feelings [xin 心]. These manifest themselves in the mildness of their faces, amplify themselves in their backs, and extend to their limbs, rendering their instruction clear without a single word being uttered.[59]

It is often held that *xing*, as it occurs in the *Mencius*, and in the slightly earlier *Zhongyong*, refers to a general and given human nature.[60] This belief has been reinforced by Mencius's apparent claim, prefiguring Jean-Jacques Rousseau, that the human being is "good" by nature. On clarifying what Mencius means by this, he says, in a most difficult passage involving a number of complex notions:

> Considering their spontaneous (re)actions [*qing* 情], [human beings] are capable of becoming good [*shan* 善]. That is what I mean by good. As for their becoming not good [*bu shan* 不善], it is not the fault of their (natural) endowments [*cai* 才]. People all have a sense [*xin* 心] for compassion; people all have a sense for shame; people all have a sense for respect; people all have a sense for distinguishing between right and wrong. The sense for compassion constitutes communal humanity [*ren* 仁]; the sense for shame constitutes appropriateness [*yi* 義]; the sense for respect constitutes the observance of ritual propriety [*li* 禮]; the sense for distinguishing between right and wrong constitutes wisdom [*zhi* 智]. Communal humanity, appropriateness, the observance of ritual propriety, and wisdom are not fused onto us from the outside—we already have them.[61]

In this passage, I translate qing 情, which is otherwise often translated as "emotions" or "fact," as "spontaneous (re)actions." Qing is here applied or, rather, observed, as a test for the quality of xing.[62] For something to be observed, however, it has to be observable, and thus it is unlikely that Mencius is referring to emotions per se or to something internal. The term rather seems to indicate how people act or react to events without deliberation, such as in Mencius's well-known example of how people spontaneously react when seeing a child falling into a well.[63]

Without joining the ongoing discussion on the status of the Mencian notion of renxing, it seems clear that Mencius is establishing a connection, in line with the ideas expressed in the *Zhongyong*, between the human being's moral capacities and the natural realm. Qing, indicating the quality of xing, emanates from xin, the heart-mind complex, which I chose to translate above in a functional manner as (incipient) "sense." In his discussion of renxing, Mencius is responding to other thinkers who claim, like Gongduzi, that renxing is neutral, neither good or bad, or, like others, that it can become both good and bad, or, like others yet, that some people's xing is good and others' bad.⁶⁴

In order to appreciate Mencius's claim of the shan-ness of renxing, I believe that it is important to consider the philosophical and social context in which he makes the claim. It was surely important to Mencius, in his continuing Confucius's philosophical and educational mission, to establish the genuine possibility of realizing the "goodness" or harmonious socialization of human beings. As we have seen from our discussion of wisdom (zhi 知), the Confucian philosophy is a philosophy of "realization" in the dynamic sense of the word. It seeks to motivate rather than to ascertain or discover. In fact, discovery is never an objectified act dislocated from its consequences.

Confucius lived in a time in which the Zhou dynasty had already undergone a significant disintegration, and violence escalated between the remaining states. Mencius, moreover, found himself in a society where wars were even more frequent, resulting in, as the late D. C. Lau put it, "a growing cynicism toward morality which is implicit in Legalist doctrines based on a view of man as purely egoistic and motivated solely by the thought of reward and punishment. With the prevalent atmosphere Mencius was in profound disagreement. In his view man is basically a moral creature."⁶⁵ I would tend to agree with Lau that Mencius held the human being to be "basically a moral creature." Of importance, however, is the manner in which he held this view. It is certainly not a factual or teleological claim parallel to the Aristotelian one of human beings being social animals by nature. Confucius himself says in the *Lunyu* that human beings "are similar in their natural dispositions (xing 性), but differ in their habits (xi 習)."⁶⁶ This claim invites the policies characteristic of Confucius and his immediate followers: first, that the emphasis is on practice, learning, and personal cultivation rather than on discovery; and second, no less important in this context, that what is crucial is an optimistic attitude. This latter point requires some further explanation.

During Confucius's time, cynical or pessimist views were not restricted to Legalist thoughts. Chen Jingpan refers to the "pessimists" during the time of Confucius as "those who grew weary of the deplorable conditions of the time, and felt no hope of salvation for the corrupt social order."⁶⁷ Some of these are brought up in book 18 of the *Lunyu*, for instance Jie Ni 桀溺, whose name can be translated as "Boldly Sunk"⁶⁸ and who says, cynically, to Zilu upon hearing that he is Confucius's disciple: "The whole world is flooded in disorder, and who is going to change it? You follow one who avoids some people, but would it not be better to follow those who avoid the world altogether?"[69] When Zilu reports this conversation to Confucius, the Master responds, as it says, interestingly, with frustration or disappointment (*wu* 憮): "It is impossible to associate with birds and beasts [like the hermits purport to do]. If not with the people, who are of my kind, with whom shall I then associate? If the proper way [dao 道] reigned in the world, I would not go about changing it."[70]

It is notable that Confucius does not challenge Jie Ni's lamentation that the "world is flooded in disorder." He is disappointed in Jie Ni's defeatism and in his conviction that nothing can be done and that it is best to withdraw from the world altogether. Elsewhere in book 18, which, in fact, appears to be dedicated to the defeatists of the time, he lists names of seven outstanding individuals whose talents were "lost to the people" as they all retired into privacy from the world.[71] Moreover, when Confucius, riding his carriage, hears "the madman of Chu" 楚狂, another recluse, singing a cynical poem about the futility of doing anything at all in this doomed world, Confucius gets off his carriage with the intention of speaking with him, but in vain as the "madman" disappears. The frequent reference to the recluses and Confucius's remarks about them indicates that he admired their talents and abilities and therefore deplored their decision to retire from the world instead of participating in his quest for stability and harmony.

In this apparently wide-ranging atmosphere of despair and cynicism, Confucius describes himself as "a person who is so eager [*fen* 憤] that he forgets to eat, who is so optimistic [le 樂] that he forgets to worry, and who does not even realize that old age is impending."[72] Above all, Confucius emphasized the importance of motivation for the ability to learn and to work on the improvement of society. As long as one can inspire this motivation in oneself, there is nothing preventing that person from becoming a junzi 君子. Confucius makes clear that his admired abilities and wisdom are far from being inborn but have come about through his fondness of the ancient culture and thus from his untiring efforts in extracting wisdom from it.[73] In a well-known passage from the same book, he says that he never refuses instruction to those who are only able to afford a piece of dried meat, the most humble of gifts in ancient Chinese society, implying that it is the willingness to learn that is the most important factor.[74]

It is this optimistic ethos or spirit of Confucius that Mencius inherits and carries further. In my view, it constitutes the primary motive of Mencius's particular formulation of renxing as shan. He makes it quite clear that anyone has the opportunity to become even a sage (shengren 聖人). In one place he says that all one has to do in order to become a sage is to model oneself after the ancient sage-kings Yao and Shun; in other words, all one has to do is appropriate the cultural tradition initiated by them and carried further by Confucius.[75] Elsewhere he says that "the sages and I are of the same kind" and that what constitutes our difference is that "the sages were simply the first to grasp our common sensibilities [xin 心]," likening the sages to the famous cook Yi Ya whose culinary excellence consisted in his grasping the general preferences of the human palate.[76]

To consider renxing as either evil or variable between individual human beings would, for Mencius, be a kind of defeatism. But by regarding the xing as containing sprouts that may enable human beings, and *all* human beings, to become good, the Confucian motivational factor is in place. Despite the turmoil, horrors, and misery caused by the constant wars in Mencius's days, he maintains the Confucian hope for the realization of a better society. This, however, is not to say that his idea of renxing is a pure pragmatic construct. It entails the firm conviction that if given the right conditions and environment, in a manner similar to agricultural products, human beings will develop their best abilities as they grow up. What are the best abilities of agricultural products? That they nourish people. What are the best abilities of people? That they nourish society. An ideal person, indeed, a junzi, let alone a sage or shengren, is one who grows up having affection for the people who enabled him to grow up and then extends this affection to the larger society, such that he or she will contribute to the maintenance, growth, and development of that society. It is here that Mencius introduces the interplay between xing 性, the original natural endowments or tendencies, and *ming* 命 or *tianming* 天命, often translated as "destiny," but probably more appropriately understood as the "forces of circumstances."[77] These are two interacting sides of the same process:

> Mencius said: "The disposition of the mouth toward good taste, of the eyes toward beauty, of the ears toward pleasant sounds, of the nose toward fragrances, and of the four limbs towards ease and rest are cases of xing 性; yet, because these

depend on ming 命, junzi do not refer to them as their xing. The tendency of communal humanity [ren 仁] to characterize the relationship between father and son, of the sense of appropriateness [yi 義] to characterize the relationship between prince and minister, of ritual propriety [li 禮] to characterize the relationship between guest and host, of wisdom [zhi 知] to characterize persons of excellence [xianren 賢人], of sages [shengren 聖人] to follow the way of tian 天 are cases of ming; yet, because these depend on xing, junzi do not refer to them as their ming."[78]

Xu Fuguan[79] has pointed out that this passage should be understood in combination with the following: "Mencius said: 'Seek and you shall obtain it; let go and you shall lose it. If this is the case, then seeking is useful for obtaining and that which is sought is within yourself. But provided that there is a proper way of seeking, while obtaining still depends on the forces of circumstance [you ming 有命], then seeking is of no use for obtaining, and the sought for lies outside of yourself.'"[80]

In this passage, Mencius is referring to the heart-mind or what he takes to form the core of human thoughts and feelings, which we may understand as sensibility (xin 心). The problem here is that if we do not locate in some sense the excellent qualities of human beings within ourselves, then whether they develop or not will not depend on us, but somewhat arbitrarily on external circumstances. Ming does not imply destiny in a strong, deterministic way, but it nevertheless points to forces that are ultimately beyond our control. Thus, although it belongs to the natural disposition of human beings to desire good food, beauty, rest, ease, and so on, our success in satisfying such desires depends significantly on the force of circumstances. Despite all our hard work and determination, it takes no philosopher to tell us that our goals can easily be frustrated by some unforeseen occurrences in our immediate environment and that we may not reap what we sowed. However, the development of our moral capacities depends largely on our own efforts. Naturally, environment and the force of circumstances play an important role, and it is unrealistic to expect, as Mencius himself points out, that people will dedicate themselves to self-cultivation if they do not have proper means of support.[81] Nevertheless, as he also notes, "great persons are those who do not lose their child-like sentiments" or heart-minds (xin 心), despite all the hardships in their circumstances.[82] This is a matter of effort and determination. Moreover, if one's moral development were left wholly to the force of circumstance, then one would not be compelled to take responsibility for one's mode of action and could always find excuses in the environment—the sought for would lie outside oneself. Human life can thus be seen as an ongoing negotiation or dynamic interaction between xing and ming, both of which exert strong influences on the human being, without, as is typical in Chinese thought, either of them dominating the other.[83]

Mencius can thus be credited with having provided an important and apparently needed link between the moral philosophy of Confucius and the cosmological forces without thereby having forced them into some kind of categories of necessity or determinism. It is tian 天 that provides the human being with xing, but the development of xing, although clearly affected by external circumstances, ming, ultimately depends on the exertion of the human being. In comparing people's xing with the human senses, Mencius then asks in what way the human sentiments, heart-mind, or thoughts and feelings (xin 心) are similar and then answers his own question: "It is what is called li 理 and yi 義 . . . li and yi please my heart-mind in the same way as good meat pleases my palate."[84] This answer provides a gateway to Xunzi's formulations, which, in my opinion, most clearly express the Confucian kind of reason or intelligence.

In light of the foregoing discussion of the optimistic attitudes of Confucius and Mencius, turning to Xunzi may not seem too promising, and even paradoxical, since he is best known for his claim, contradicting Mencius, that renxing is not "good" (shan 善) but "evil" (e 惡). This would appear to reveal Xunzi as a "defeatist" or a "pessimist."[85] However, as many commentators have noted, the asymmetry is not perfect here. Kurtis Hagen, for instance, has recently argued that Xunzi's slogan, *xing e* 性惡, usually rendered "human nature is evil," does not adequately reflect his position and that a more appropriate English translation would be "[o]riginal human nature is problematic."[86] Further, according to the Japanese Sinologist Ōmuro Mikio, "[w]hile [Xunzi] concludes that human nature is *e* [crude], he agrees with Mencius' doctrine of the goodness of human nature at its root. At least, one piece of evidence is the optimistic ethical doctrine that if one accumulates virtue by means of ritual propriety, even the ordinary person on the street may be cultivated into a sage."[87] According to this view, Xunzi held renxing to be good in the sense of being transformable, which, in my opinion, is to stretch his position somewhat. Xunzi is quite explicit in his rejection of Mencius's conception of renxing. The most plausible reason for his rejection, however, is that he disliked its passive implication of personal cultivation as a mere drawing out of the natural, because it seemed to imply a position similar to the Daoist, especially Zhuangzian, one of following nature or tian 天, a view with which Xunzi was familiar and criticized explicitly.[88] In any case, Xunzi clearly wants to emphasize that moral cultivation requires enormous effort and does not come about "just like water flows downwards." At least in this respect, Mencius appears to Xunzi as something of an armchair philosopher, or, more appropriately, a "mat philosopher": Mencius "expounded this while sitting on his mat, but would his error not be obvious if he rose up, proving unable to establish it or showing its general application in practice?"[89]

Hence, Xunzi's disagreement with Mencius rests on the former's accentuated focus on practice and discipline rather than on original constitution and the plasticity of natural things, humans included. He sets this tone right at the beginning of the work bearing his name: "Learning must never be halted. Blue dye is taken from the indigo plant, but it is bluer than the indigo. Ice is made from water, but it is colder than water."[90] The same applies to human beings' moral qualities: they derive from renxing but are an improvement of it through conscious exertion.[91] "Hence, [the human being] requires the enculturation according to a teacher's standard and the guidance of li and yi."[92]

In summarizing the main differences between the positions of Mencius and Xunzi as to the cultivation of humankind, A. C. Graham makes an intriguing observation:

> Mencius puts more stress on the benevolence [ren 仁] which flows spontaneously from the goodness of man's nature [renxing 人性]. Xunzi on the other hand sees ceremony [li 禮] as the alternative to punishment in imposing order on man's anarchic desires. As for yi 義, "the right, morality," its importance remains constant, although less obtrusive than the other two. For Xunzi yi (not, as for the West, reason) is the defining characteristic of the human; he says so explicitly in laying out a chain of being from the mineral through the vegetable and animal to man.[93]

Graham then quotes at length from Xunzi who says that what distinguishes human beings from other beings in the world is that they "possess vital energy [qi 氣], life [sheng 生], knowledge [zhi 智] and also a sense of appropriateness [yi 義], making them the most noble (beings) in the world."⁹⁴ We have already seen that Xunzi takes yi (appropriateness) together with li (ritual propriety) to form the method for "hitting the mark" (zhong 中) in enacting communal humanity (ren 仁) and thereby continuing the cultural tradition (dao 道).⁹⁵

Xunzi certainly takes a step away from the tighter relationship between the cosmological forces and the human dimension established in the Zhongyong and the Mencius, and in this sense he reinforces the stance of Confucius, who was generally wary of making such connections and, moreover, emphasized the importance of the effort of persistent learning. In his discourse on nature or heaven (tian lun 天論), Xunzi makes it quite clear that the way of tian and the way of human beings are two processes and that we should predominantly focus our attention on the affairs of society. However, these are not entirely disconnected; after all, tian affects the circumstances (ming 命) of human beings.⁹⁶ Xunzi formulates the connection more carefully with the notion of li 理, "patterns" or, more actively, "patterning," which reflects the norm-making functions of its homonym li 禮 and of the sense of appropriateness, or yi 義. Robert Eno has observed that Xunzi establishes a close analogy between the two kinds of li: "Ritual li are, in essence, the extension of natural principles [li 理] into the human sphere."⁹⁷ Hall and Ames make a similar point but with regard to the general Confucian attitude to tradition and reason: "Li 理 understood here as 'pattern' or 'coherence' is inclusive of the more narrowly defined li 禮 as ritual. It entails being aware of those constitutive relationships that condition each thing and which, through patterns of correlation, make the world meaningful and intelligible."⁹⁸

For Xunzi, it is the development of the triad of li 理, li 禮, and yi 義 that produces a junzi. Why yi? Because it is through the ability of making appropriate distinctions between things that meaning is constructed.⁹⁹ Xunzi says quite explicitly that "yi is 'to pattern' [li 理], hence (proper) action follows."¹⁰⁰ Yi is in fact the mediator between the greater patterns of things, li 理, and the traditional patterns of conduct, li 禮. Yi could thus be understood as the "sensibility" necessary for cultural adaptation and development—that is, for effecting the appropriate changes in social patterns responding to the constant process of change taking place in the greater patterns of nature. Without such changes, the tradition stagnates and fails to fulfill its role of effecting human flourishing. Xunzi says: "That which has remained unchanged through the hundred kings suffices to be considered the connecting thread of the cultural tradition [dao 道]. Approach all rises and falls by applying this thread. If one patterns [li

理] this thread, there will be no chaos. Not to know this thread is not to know how to respond to changing circumstances."[101] Knoblock argues that with "connecting thread," or *guan* 貫, Xunzi means the rituals.[102] It seems to me, however, that Xunzi is rather speaking of the spirit of the tradition, that to which I have already referred as the particular *mode of thinking* characterizing the Western Zhou dynasty according to Confucius and his followers. While particularities of the tradition change, including rituals,[103] the spirit, the mode of thinking, remains constant. The "connecting thread" is therefore more correctly identified with the sense of appropriateness or yi.

The Confucian qualitative intelligence thus emerges in its clearest form in Xunzi's philosophy. It is embedded in the Zhou tradition and formulated by Xunzi as a combination of li 禮 and yi 義.[104] Hence we could speak of li as the habits that form and inform the sensibility of yi, which in turn prevent li from stagnating by modifying it and adapting to the ever-changing circumstances or patternings of the li 理 of tian 天. The triad of li 禮, yi 義, and li 理, then, ensures cultural continuity, personal signification, and flexible adaptation to changes in the natural forces of circumstance.

To use the language of Dewey, this kind of intelligence bases itself on the habits of tradition but is necessarily open to individual impulses as long as these have something positive and useful to offer. Bourdieu could add to this that the habits, being both structured and structuring, ensure both continuity and constant readaptation of the cultural tradition. Dewey's and Bourdieu's novel approaches to reason enable us to see, from a Western point of view, how models of reasonable behavior are constantly being formed within the field of a culture in its historical evolution and on the basis of its particular circumstances. Accordingly, the difference between the positions of Mencius and Xunzi turns out to consist in their efforts to interpret and adapt the Confucian philosophy to the particular historical circumstances in which they lived: Mencius emphasizes an optimistic attitude, a firm belief in the possibility of improving the human condition; Xunzi stresses the importance of hard work and conscious exertion. Both of these—we could call them optimism and activism—are integral features of the Confucian spirit.[105]

The next task consists in explicating how the Confucian thinkers conceive of the individual's appropriation of this kind of intelligence in the process of learning.

CHAPTER THREE

Third Assemblage

Education as Humanization

Thus far, the approach to the underlying theme of this work, education and ritual propriety, has been largely oblique. This chapter will take a more direct approach to the roles these play in the classical Confucian philosophy.

In the first section, I begin by providing a general philosophical and etymological discussion of the notion of education, upon which I return to the hermeneutic philosophy of Hans-Georg Gadamer and provide an overview of his development of Georg Wilhelm Friedrich Hegel's notions of "edification" (*Bildung*) and "experience" (*Erfahrung*). Gadamer's emphasis on the cultivated "sense" (*Sinn*), informed by a balanced interaction with tradition, constitutes, I argue, the core of his vision of the educated individual. This could be seen as a suggestive prelude to a discussion of John Dewey's philosophy of education and experience, which, incidentally, is also significantly influenced by Hegel's philosophy. As before, Dewey turns out to provide an illuminating perspective from which to approach the Confucian philosophy of education.

Confucian education, and its relationship with ritual propriety, is in fact the topic of the last three sections, though not without rather elaborate theoretical foregrounding. In the second, I turn to the "aesthetic" as an explanatory notion to understand the peculiarities of the Chinese tradition. This takes me to a discussion of recent sophisticated analyses of ritual and its pedagogical and noetic functions that have a bearing on a productive understanding of li.

The third section takes the idea of aesthetic noesis to more concrete dimensions and focuses especially on the relationship between ritual propriety and music in order to seek out the Confucian view of personalization and creativity in human action. This requires a discussion of the Confucian view of the difference and mutual bearing of the internal and external modes of human behavior, a topic that is best represented by the *Wuxing* 五行 essay, an ancient philosophical document only recently unearthed in China.

In the fourth and last part, I begin with a discussion of the proposed Confucian methods and aims of education in the sense of teaching. With reference to the indoctrination *Problematik*, I show that Confucius develops and uses teaching methods that are in fact particularly well suited for the circumvention of indoctrination without having to resort to a blurry notion of rationality. His didactic modes clearly show that the aim of teaching is not to produce a person who simply conforms to social norms, but one who has the ability and desire to "hit the mark of the moment" in every situation of life.

But teaching is only one half of the story, and the last pages are dedicated to arguably the most fundamental aspect of the Confucian vision—namely, personal cultivation (xiushen 修身 or *xiuji* 修己) or the individual's efforts in constructing and refining his or her own character. Personal cultivation as the prime process of humanization is inseparable from the role of li. To become human, I argue, always more and more human, is the overall but never finally attainable aim of Confucianism. In the absence of li, this aim would be meaningless, and Confucianism would "not know where to place its hands and feet."

Education through Experience: Reconciling Tradition and Reason

The once supreme status of knowledge and reason that resulted from the apprehension of the Enlightenment as an antidote to and liberator from the oppressing yoke of tradition has, through groundbreaking post-Enlightenment thinkers, been humbled and degraded. This has also resulted in a certain circumspection among contemporary philosophers, who by and large have turned away from the aim of "founding" truth-claims to the one of revealing presuppositions, or, to use Gadamer's term once again, pre*judgments*, that constitute hidden agendas in practically every kind of discourse.[1] Among contemporary philosophers, whether labeled "continental" or "analytical," this tendency has been gaining the upper hand.

It is inevitable that this reevaluation of reason should have a palpable impact on the philosophy of education. For if the reevaluation proceeds along the lines of a reconciliation of tradition and reason, which it always does to at least some extent, it also effects a change in the normative outlook on education.

The first gestures of such a reevaluation can be found as early as in the philosophy of Hegel. As is well known, the richness of Hegel's philosophy has influenced or generated many diverse and even contrasting tendencies of thought. The separation and disputes between the so-called "right-wing" and "left-wing" Hegelians may be said to have laid down the basis for political discourse in the twentieth century and beyond. However, in his philosophy of history, Hegel also attempted to find a way to reconcile the Enlightenment antagonism between tradition and reason. After having liberated themselves from the authority of tradition, Hegel argues, it is necessary for human beings to revisit their relationship with that which has been transmitted from the past. The key to this reevaluation is found in Hegel's notion of *Bildung*.

In its contemporary everyday use, the German word *Bildung* means education or cultivation. Originally, it was used to describe when something "takes shape." It then came to refer to the external manifestation of things, such as the shape of the limbs, and generally to the formation of natural phenomena. With Johann Gottfried Herder, the term began to receive its contemporary sense of a process toward cultural sophistication or cultivation and was then further developed by Hegel in this direction.[2] It should, however, be distinguished from the word *Ausbildung*, literally "outwards formation," which specifically denotes formal (vocational) education. *Bildung* is a more general notion of human cultivation.

The two notions of *Ausbildung* and *Bildung* correspond more or less to the two Latin roots of the English "education," *educere* and *educare*, as depicted by Hall and Ames:

> The first means "to evoke, lead forth, draw out"; the second "to cultivate, rear, bring up." *Educare* resonates with the sense of education as rationally ordered guidance; it is the logical and rationally ordered mode of education. On the other hand, *educere* suggests the creative side of education that is complicit with aesthetic understanding. Education construed primarily as *educere* suggests that one "extends" one's inner tendencies through a mode of *self*-cultivation that is, in fact, self-*creation*.[3]

In most Indo-European languages, in fact, the term for education in the broader sense implies a process of becoming, as suggested by the etymological root of *educere*. In French, education is *formation*. In Icelandic, the most archaic Germanic language still spoken, the word for education is *menntun*, derived from the noun *manneskja*, meaning "human being." Thus, the fuller meaning of the word *menntun* is "the becoming of a human being" or, alternatively, "humanization." It has a close semantic association with the word for culture, *menning*, from which it can be inferred that an important connotation of *menntun* is "acculturation" or "cultural sophistication." To be educated means to be cultured, to have reached farther on the human path, to be, as it were, "more human," and this is also the main sense evoked by the German *Bildung*.

With the concept of *Bildung*, Hegel attempted to reconcile the dichotomy that the Enlightenment had prized open between reason and tradition. It was evident to him that the normative dimension of thought and action emanates directly from the authority of tradition, expressed through his notion of *Sittlichkeit*—that is, concrete morality as embodied by real people, or "mores." However, with the Enlightenment insistence upon liberation from the yoke of tradition through the individual use of reason, the ostensibly "free" subject was left alone to rely only upon itself as a rational creature. As a consequence of a move from one extreme to another, it is this "alienation" from historical reality that calls for the notion of *Bildung*. The sense of alienation brings about the abstract, rationally oriented self's need to reconcile itself with its concrete, historically constituted environment. *Bildung* is precisely this process of reconciliation or mediation. The past is "superseded" (*aufgehoben*) by the present, which means that it is simultaneously preserved, and not simply annulled, as the more radical proponents of the Enlightenment would have it.

As might be expected from Hegel, he understands not only the objectification or concretization of the individual as *Bildung*, but the entire "objective" course of history as a universal process of *Bildung*, in which the objective, universal spirit returns to itself in a superseded form. Thus, progress, for Hegel, is constituted by a dialectic interplay between past, present, and projected future.

Bildung is a core topic in the hermeneutical philosophy of Hans-Georg Gadamer. While developing further Hegel's insights, Gadamer stresses the understanding of *Bildung* as a process in which the individual acquires an "aesthetic" kind of wisdom. That is to say, to be *gebildet*, "edified," means to have a profound "sense" (*Sinn*) for one's social and ethical environment, a sense which cannot be derived from theoretical knowledge. Such a sense rests, at least partly, upon having thoroughly appropriated one's cultural environment and the tradition and history to which it belongs. It therefore involves the nurturing of such qualities as taste, judgment, and tact that are more often than not ignored in Western discourse on the grounds of their ostensible lack of "objectivity." Gadamer, however, argues that persons who are *gebildet* in this way are persons that have not only moved beyond the narrow scope of their private interests and concerns, but even beyond the limits of the interests of their community or group to adopt a genuine interest also in other cultures, their history, and the future development of our communal living in the world.[4] He says that the essence of edification consists in "a general and communal sense" (*ein allgemeiner und gemeinschaftlicher Sinn*), for it involves

> a general sense for scope and distance with regard to oneself, and, as far as this goes, an elevation of oneself to generality [*Allgemeinheit*]. To view oneself and one's private aims from a distance means to view them as others do. This kind of generality is certainly not a conceptual or intellectual generality. No particularity can be derived from the general; it leads to no conclusive proofs. The general viewpoints to which the edified person remains open are to him no fixed criteria that are always valid, but merely points of view that possible others may have at present. In fact, as far as this goes, the edified consciousness is rather characterized by sense. For every kind of sense—for example, a sense for faces—is surely general to the extent of the sphere that it comprises and of the field to which it opens itself, by which it then grasps the differences within that opening. The edified consciousness exceeds any natural sense in that the latter is limited to a particular sphere. The former operates in all directions. It is a *general sense*.[5]

This general sense borders on or is formed through a combination of a common sense and a sense for one's community. The latter is derived from the humanist tradition as *sensus communis*, or, as Gadamer puts it, drawing on Shaftesbury, "a sense for the common good, but also *love of the community or society, natural affection, humanity, obligingness*."[6] Referring to Giambattista Vico, he further says: "What gives the human will its direction, Vico says, is not the abstract generality of reason but the concrete generality which is exemplified by the commonality of a group, a people, a nation or the whole of mankind. The formation of this communal sense is therefore of decisive significance."[7]

With his emphasis on the importance of "sense," Gadamer takes a clear distance from the Hegelian formulation, which rests for the most part upon abstract and universal conceptualization. While Hegel conceived of history as the continuous progress of freedom, his notion of freedom was ultimately subjected to the concept and its ostensible universality. This universal truth inherent in language, Hegel believed, contained also a certain kind of moral vocation. Thus, *Bildung*, as one commentator has pointed out, consisted for Hegel in such a promotion of universality: "Those who tie themselves to the particular and lack the ability to abstraction and generality are '*ungebildet*,' and such a failure can only be understood as moral failure."[8]

Since Gadamer's edified sense is one that has been cultivated out of natural sense, Gadamer prefers speaking of aesthetic or historical consciousness instead of sense.[9] It is tempting to see a parallel here between Gadamer's idea of edification and the Confucian "way," as expressed in the *Zhongyong*, of "drawing out the natural dispositions and then cultivating that way"—in effect, education, or *jiao* 教. Gadamer's notion of sense, or aesthetic or historical consciousness, is clearly practical in that it does not derive from a theoretical, universal concept, but must base itself on concrete experience.

It is the notion of experience, especially what Gadamer calls "hermeneutic experience" (*hermeneutische Erfahrung*), that enables the aesthetic or historical consciousness to come to fruition and develop its profound sense for its surrounding life-world. "Experience" has long been an important topic in German philosophy, but Gadamer makes especially use of Hegel's and Wilhelm Dilthey's elaborations. The latter developed the notion of *Erlebnis*, or "lived experience," as an antidote to the scientific notion of experience as *Erfahrung*. In Dilthey's use, *Erlebnis* is distinguished from *Erfahrung* in that it refers to unique and unrepeatable experiences. As Georgia Warnke puts it, "*Erlebnis* is supposed to signify the wholeness and intensity of human experiences against scientific abstraction; what is experienced in this sense contains the entire wealth of feelings and emotions that make an experience peculiarly one's own."[10]

Warnke further points out that *Erlebnis*, in its application, "is compatible with the Hegelian sense of *Erfahrung* as a learning experience."[11] In his celebrated *Phenomenology of the Spirit*, Hegel describes experience as a dialectical movement of consciousness in relation to its object: "This *dialectical* movement that consciousness directs not only at itself, but also at its knowledge and its object, *insofar as the new true object springs to it therefrom*, is really that which is called *experience*."[12] Experience follows a dialectical scheme in the sense that its structure constitutes a "reversal of consciousness" (*Umkehrung des Bewußtseins*), a transformation in the way of thinking.[13] Hegel's emphasis on experience as a "learning experience," according to which consciousness directs itself to the objects of its attention and is changed by them, is what attracts Gadamer to his version of the concept.[14] Thus, while certainly adopting elements of the Diltheyan *Erlebnis*, he opts for the Hegelian *Erfahrung*, though without supposing, as Hegel did, that in the history of mankind, experience comes to a "completion" at which "the dialectic of experience ends with the overcoming of all experience by reaching absolute knowledge, that is to say, in the perfect identity of consciousness and object."[15] Experience is for Gadamer on the contrary a never-ending process whose truth is contained in itself:

> The truth of experience always contains a reference to new experience. Hence someone who is held to be experienced has not merely become such *through* experience but by being open *to* experience. The perfection of one's experience, the perfect being of what we call "experienced," does not consist in having knowledge of everything and a better understanding of everything. On the contrary, the experienced one reveals himself rather to be one who is radically undogmatic, who, because he has had so many experiences and learned from experiences, has a particular ability to have new experiences and to learn from experiences. The dialectic of experience has its proper completion not in epistemological closure, but in that openness for experience that is freely enacted in the experience itself.[16]

It is this openness of experience that is able to elevate itself to a "general sense," to an aesthetic consciousness that must at the same time be historical. The cultivated general sense is simultaneously historical consciousness because, in contrast to Hegel's demand for conceptual abstraction and universality, they both identify the uniqueness of the "other." The difference is that in its dimension as historical consciousness, the cultivated general sense "looks in the other of the past not for a case of general lawfulness, but for one of historic singularity."[17] Thus, just as the general sense calls for openness to the other, it requires, because of its historical dimension, a compatible openness to tradition. Gadamer says that tradition is not an object to be studied, but a language to be spoken.[18] That is to say, tradition, if it is not to be a dead relic of the past and if we want to learn, or rather, gain experience from it, is analogous to a communication partner. It must be approached in much the same way as we approach, with intentionality, other people from whom we expect meaningful communication. "Here lies," Gadamer points out, "the equivalence to the hermeneutic experience. I must acknowledge tradition [Überlieferung] in its claims. Not in the sense of a mere recognition of the otherness of the past, but in such a way that it has something to tell me."[19]

Edification, then, as cultivation of the human sensibility, requires the experience of one's unique historicity and therefore the willingness to learn from tradition. It is worth reiterating that Gadamer is not proposing a blind submissiveness to tradition. Tradition ought not to be mistaken for a general law to be followed but is rather to be seen as a collection of often inciting experiences handed down to us from the never repeatable past. In the constant flow of time and change, the historical consciousness with all its experience does not hold on to the past, but tries to apply what it has gained from it to the unpredictable future. "To be experienced," Gadamer says, "really means to be aware, to know, that one is not master of time and of the future."[20]

We shall now move to the educational philosophy of John Dewey, for it also concerns a demand for a move toward transcending the classical dichotomy of tradition and reason by means of education. Dewey was, in fact, like Gadamer, influenced by Hegel, and his particular ability to synthesize apparent contradictions may be traceable to Hegel's influence on his thinking. One synthesis typical of Dewey, however, and less conspicuous in Hegel, is the pragmatic one between philosophy and concrete issues.[21] Hence, while Dewey's philosophy may certainly be understood more broadly and generally, he developed his philosophy of education without ever taking his eyes off its applicability in real educational situations, that is to say, in schools. The part of Dewey's philosophy of education on which I will focus here developed within the context, to which I have already alluded, of the social reform debates in the United States, where this dichotomy was formulated as between "traditional" and "progressive" education. Dewey critically characterized the tendencies dominating this debate as "Either-Ors," that is to say, a kind of philosophy that recognizes only two and "no intermediary possibilities."[22] For Dewey, the contrast drawn between "traditional" and "progressive" education was a case of a false dilemma. Proponents of the latter, wanting it to replace the former, tended to reject all of its methods and approaches in toto and to propose others that were their exact opposites. Dewey argued that this was a case in which old problems were simply replaced with new ones and emphasized therefore the importance of analyzing and appraising the methods and approaches of traditional education in order to discern the extent to which they were of value.

Dewey's philosophy of education is rich and complex and involves a number of notions. Here I shall take into consideration the interrelation between only three of these, namely, "experience," "growth," and the already discussed "habit." I restrict my discussion to these because I believe that they are the most helpful for gaining an insightful perspective on the Confucian approach to education.

"Experience," in Dewey's sense, does not merely refer to the state of perceiving or being aware of phenomena; it is a notion implying value and achievement and appears to be influenced by the Hegelian *Erfahrung*. While "primary experience" is obviously of fundamental importance as the raw material for a more reflective and impressive kind of experience, it is the quality of the experience that is produced through reflection on and interaction with these primary experiences that is to be assessed. In a manner close to Gadamer, Dewey suggests that if the experience generates the disposition, indeed, the habit, to open up to other experiences—if, in other words, the experience produces growth in terms of further experiences—then the experience can be said to have been of value. For Dewey, education, real education, is virtually synonymous with such experiential "growth."

This is also what Dewey means with his principle of "the experiential continuum."[23] This principle is a criterion for qualitatively distinguishing between experiences. Those that enhance this continuum are valuable; those that arrest it are not. Dewey's approach rests upon his view that the continuous change of human beings results from their interaction with their environment. All my experiences change me in my attitudes, in my dispositions, and in my openness toward experiencing more of the world. In short, they change my habits:

> The basic characteristic of habit is that every experience enacted and undergone modifies the one who acts and undergoes, while this modification affects, whether we wish it or not, the quality of subsequent experiences. For it is a somewhat different person who enters them. The principle of habit so understood obviously goes deeper than the ordinary conception of a habit as a more or less fixed way of doing

things, although it includes the latter as one of its special cases. It covers the formation of attitudes, attitudes that are emotional and intellectual; it covers our basic sensitivities and ways of meeting and responding to all the conditions which we meet in living.[24]

It serves us well, in this respect, to recall Dewey's words, already quoted in the last section, that a "person is reasonable in the degree in which he is habitually open to seeing an event which immediately strikes his senses not as an isolated thing but in its connection with the common experience of mankind." Education enhances reason insofar as it stimulates the formation of the habit to regard events and phenomena in their interconnectedness with other events and phenomena as experienced by human beings in general.

By referring to the common experience of mankind, Dewey is highlighting the importance of communication and meaning. Communication enables the continuous existence of human co-living; it, so to speak, "defragments" human beings and effects their cultural relatedness. As he says in *Art as Experience*, "[c]ommunication is the process of creating participation, of making common what had been isolated and singular; and part of the miracle it achieves is that, in being communicated, the conveyance of meaning gives body and definiteness to the experience of the one who utters as well as to that of those who listen."[25]

Meaning, a major condition for the existence of the experiential continuum, is created through the perceived relationship of action and its consequence, or, in Dewey's preferred terms, "doing and undergoing."[26] But in communal living, a consequence of an action manifests itself most dramatically in the responses from others: "Experience is the result, the sign, and the reward of that interaction of organism and environment which, when it is carried to the full, is a transformation of interaction into participation and communication."[27]

Communication, then, is the field in which meaning is most intensively created. This also exemplifies the extent to which our activities—if they are to be meaningful, not only to others but also to ourselves—are dependent upon others' responses. In the case of anger, for example, with "a human being, it is as meaningless as a gust of wind on a mudpuddle apart from a direction given it by the presence of other persons, apart from the responses they make to it."[28] Without meaning, there is no stimulus to project the action of the present to future actions; in short, there is no continuity, only isolated, disconnected actions. This is why, as Dewey says, "continuity and interaction . . . intercept and unite. They are, so to speak, the longitudinal and lateral aspects of experience."[29] Continuity proceeds from the past, through the present, and is projected toward the future. Through interaction with one's environment and society, the latter of which builds on meaning acquired from the past, new meaning is produced: "The past is carried into the present so as to expand and deepen the content of the latter."[30] This carrying-into, expansion, and deepening together describe an instance of growth, for the newly created meaning does not cancel the older acquired meaning; it rather supersedes and enriches it by constructing upon it.[31]

The aim of education, then, to the extent that we can speak of an educational aim, is to induce in the student the habit of proceeding toward such experiential growth of meaning. In a sense, this calls for a certain preservation of the experiences of the past, but a preservation that is readapted to the objective conditions of the present with which we find ourselves in interaction at every moment. That the aim of growth is simply more growth, and the aim of education more education, statements for which many commentators have criticized Dewey as being too vague,[32] means precisely that the learning individual is both carrier and cultivator of the tradition to which he or she belongs, including the practical and scientific means to deal effectively and fruitfully with the environment. This is what constitutes "reason" in Dewey's sense. It is, as we have seen, "the ability to bring the subject matter of prior experience to bear to perceive the significance of the subject matter of a new experience." Reason, according to Dewey, does not relate to timeless truths, but designates the ability to maintain and develop the "experiential continuum" in the ever-changing circumstances within the endless process of time.

It is notable that Gadamer and Dewey share a similar sense of what constitutes "experience," probably due to their shared source in the Hegelian philosophy. They both maintain that without experience, there can be no education in the proper sense of the term. Experience, moreover, is only worthy of the name if it contains emotive and sensitive elements. A wholly unemotional experience would hardly be an experience at all, for it would make no impression on the individual and therefore have no impact on his thought and habits.

Aesthetic Consciousness and Ritual Knowledge

Nowhere does the feature of a world in constant motion and change, a world of "*dongli* 動理," where nothing is permanent and eternal, manifest itself more clearly than in the human habitat. Generations perish and new ones come into existence, human dwellings and other constructions are built and destroyed, and different cultures come and go, usually leaving some impact on the culture and people left behind. Moreover, it is not only in this broader historical context but also in the narrower context of the mundane that the human society is an arena of constant transformation. Language, arguably the human being's most profound and complex system of communication, enabling cohabitants to gain virtually an infinity of different views of the same affairs and events, is, in itself, a source of endless perceptual and perspectival transformations. Through the projection of meaning and personalization of our world, we in fact create innumerable worlds—by no means incommensurable worlds, but still ones that differ from one another and that are themselves in constant transformation. An otherwise dreary bus stop where I wait every day undergoes transformation as soon as I learn, say, that this was where my parents met for the very first time. Our knowledge of things, as Hegel wrote, really changes the things themselves: the internal effects a change in the external no less than the external in the internal.[33] Through the interaction of these dimensions, our ordinary environment, as the Chinese philosophers also remind us, becomes an endless source of wonder and curiosity. Marcel Proust once wrote, most aptly for this context, that the only true voyage would be not to travel through a hundred different lands with the same pair of eyes, but to see the same land through a hundred different pairs of eyes.[34]

Our ordinary reality is therefore an endless source of learning. The content of this learning, however, is ultimately practical and has a bearing on our way of living in our familiar environment. Due to our ordinary reality's rich and constantly regenerated manifoldness resulting from the process of change and all the different perspectives simultaneously at play, learning how to handle it and comport oneself within it is indeed a difficult and a never-ending task.

If this continuous process of the world comes to full realization, there can hardly be a perception of any constants to be learned. All one can speak of are tendencies, likelihoods, possibilities that are apprehended by drawing analogies from previous experience. Such experience obviously does not provide laws but merely approximations to what might be expected in the future. In other words, what one needs to learn is not a law but the ability to appraise situations in light of one's overall understanding and appropriation of previous experience—both one's own, but also of others, that is to say, of one's tradition, and, to the extent that these are accessible and relevant, of other traditions.

It is, in other words, a kind of sense or sensibility, much the same as Gadamer's *Sinn* or aesthetic consciousness. As it happens, the notion of aesthetic consciousness is most germane to the context of Chinese philosophy, for in recent years, the attribution of the "aesthetic" to the ancient Chinese worldview and cosmology has been receiving increasing recognition among comparative East-West scholars.

How should "aesthetic" be understood in this context? For Gadamer, the notion of the aesthetic consciousness figures as a key to the title of his seminal work, *Truth and Method*, for it constitutes an expansion of the basis on which truth—in the sense of a continuously evolving and ever-renewed meaningfulness—unfolds itself in the human world. That is to say, the human endeavor of understanding, Gadamer argues, does not proceed along fixed rule-governed procedures or methods, but is a skill that manifests itself in virtually all human activities. Gadamer's aesthetic consciousness is probably most clearly exemplified in the way in which we experience works of art. As before, experience is here taken in the Hegelian sense as a learning experience. Art can teach us to see things from new points of view and therefore enhance our skill of interacting with our environment and create new meaning. With some qualification, one might say that this learning experience consists in discovering and assimilating new perspectives that open up to novel ways of world orientation.[35]

Art and aesthetic consciousness, then, represent a mode of understanding that since Kant's subjectivization of aesthetic taste in his *Critique of Judgment* has tended to be disregarded as inferior to the ostensible exactitude of the mathematical sciences and of logic.[36] Gadamer's project could therefore be seen as an attempt to expand the horizon within which modern thought can satisfactorily justify its own operations. The attribution of "aesthetic" to Chinese worldviews is closely related to this understanding in that it is contrasted with rational "methodo-logical" approaches. The emphasis on uniqueness and particularity that Gadamer sees in aesthetic consciousness, as opposed to the aspiration to universality and lawfulness of rational thought, is precisely that which comparative East-West scholars have discerned as indicating ancient Chinese and even East Asian approaches. Expressing the difference between what they call, on the one hand, "logical" or "rational" order, and, on the other hand, "aesthetic" order, in terms of perspectives of experience,

Hall and Ames write that "[o]ne attends to the manner in which the experienced items instance a given pattern or set of formal relations, the second notes the manner in which just those experienced items constitute themselves and their relations to one another in such a way as to permit of no substitutions."[37]

That is to say, the elements comprising the aesthetic order are celebrated as sui generis. The implications that this has for the performance of ritual propriety as order-establishing acts are impressive. First of all, the performance is always a particular personal performance in particular circumstances that are constitutive of that person's momentary situation. The narrow view of ritual propriety as a set of formal, preestablished, and repetitive gestures is precisely traceable to an outlook that proceeds from and assumes a "rational" ordering in which the elements are perfectly substitutable, an ordering, in other words, which is purely formal.

Second, and consequently, the emphasis is on the personalization of these performances, not only because the order established through a performance is personal, but also because it is through the performance itself that the person learns about his or her role in society and therefore how to respond as well as contribute to it. Ritual, then, can function as a tool for learning, and we may be justified in speaking of "ritual knowledge."

It is worth reiterating, at this stage, that li is not confined to formal rituals or ceremonies, it but constitutes a wide range of interhuman or ethical behavior, gestures, and responses informed and partially prescribed by the cultural tradition. However, considering merely the category of ritual *qua* ritual, there is much to indicate that it enables the individual to better internalize and personalize a sense of the values of that tradition. Insofar as ritual promotes invariance, of course, a certain disciplining takes place that may contain educational value. Hardly anyone would deny that learning requires some formal repetitive elements in order both to memorize certain things and to inculcate some level of discipline. Drills or rote learning can be seen as types of such formal elements, and while they are by and large condemned by educationalists today, some degree of rote learning is surely necessary. But formal measures are also useful, indeed inescapable, for cultivating discipline. Without an adequate level of discipline, the whimsical randomness of our incessant quest for immediate satisfaction will condemn us to perennial frustration. This is what Alfred North Whitehead has called "the rhythmic claims of freedom and discipline."[38] Discipline paves the way to freedom, both at early stages of our education and whenever training new skills, though, as Whitehead further qualifies this combination, "the subordinate stiffening of discipline must be directed to secure some long-term good."[39] Catherine Bell points out that the "ritual-like qualities of disciplined routines for molding individual dispositions" are often compared with the educational process.[40] To the extent that educational institutions are concerned not only with the transmitting of information through instruction, but also "with fundamental forms of socialization that involve the internalization of cultural values," they will certainly emphasize the imitation of a considerable level of formal actions and appearances. As Bell notes,

> [f]rom the basic requirements of punctual attendance and alert responsiveness to bells, to the subordination of ego through uniformity of dress or submission to authority, it is clear that the most important things learned in school are not in textbooks. These ritual-like practices socialize young people to accept certain forms of authority (seniors, experts, and texts, for example), to interpret hard work in the classroom or the playing field as the source of rewards and prestige, and to associate personal well-being with the cooperative social order of the group.[41]

This aspect of ritual as an instrument for the enforcement of discipline and relative uniformity is far from being a revolutionary discovery and is presumably the most obvious reason for its use in virtually all cultures in human history. Rituals are everywhere expected to be performed according to preestablished patterns, no less by Confucians than by others. Without such patterns, rituals could be performed any way one likes, and thus they would both lose the structure that preserves their identity as rituals and fail to inculcate the desired discipline in the performers. The *Liji* 禮記 contains numerous detailed descriptions of how exactly to perform certain rituals, ceremonies, and sacrifices depending on the occasion. Thus, there is a significant degree to which invariance is an element of li.

However, there is a different side to the potential educational value of ritual actions, one that is hidden behind our usual understanding of ritual as purely formal and invariant. Suggesting, in fact, that ritual is normally quite open to novelty and functions as a venue of learning how to deal with the world, Theodore W. Jennings warns against overemphasizing the formalist element in ritual: "Ritual action is a means by which its participants discover who they are in the world and 'how it is' with the world. If we concentrate attention on ritual as an entirely fixed and unvarying sequence of actions, we are likely to overlook this aspect of ritual knowledge altogether."[42]

Jennings acknowledges the pedagogical function of ritual in its repetitive performance as a "transmission and illustration of knowledge gained elsewhere and otherwise,"[43] that is to say, as a tool supporting the continuity of tradition. However, by emphasizing the *noetic* function of ritual, he takes issue with the dismissal of variation in the performance of ritual as incidental. He argues that it is precisely the variation that makes possible "the view that ritual may be understood as a search for an understanding of the world, as a mode of inquiry and of discovery."[44] Jennings further draws on the work of Victor Turner, who has argued that the process of gaining knowledge is intrinsic to the ritual itself.[45] The variation in the enactment of ritual, then, is explained through the participants' exploration for the "right" or "appropriate" movements or actions depending on the situation in which the performance takes place. The repertoire of ritual performance, Jennings suggests, "provides the necessary framework for exploration in much the same way that a mastery of relevant data and theoretical construction is indispensable for 'scientific' exploration and discovery."[46] According to this intriguing simile, ritual may function as a classroom or, indeed, a "cultural laboratory" in which the values and norms of the culture are not only transmitted but also developed further. Ritual certainly encourages that it be imitated within relatively fixed boundaries, but this is not where the story ends. As Jennings further argues, leaning on interpretations of ritual action in cultures in which a relatively clear line is drawn between fields of ritual action and nonritual action, that is, where ritual is explicitly assigned a strong formal role, "[r]itual serves as a paradigm for all significant action. While the ritual itself may be specifically 'religious,' it serves as a paradigm for all important action whether or not that action is, in some restricted sense, religious. The performance of ritual, then, teaches one not only how to conduct the ritual itself, but how to conduct oneself outside the ritual space—in the world epitomized by or founded or renewed through the ritual itself."[47] Through the practice of ritual one acquires a certain sensibility for the most fitting actions even external to the ritual itself. It is, for instance, no coincidence that the Chinese characters for *ti* 體 ("body") and li 禮 are cognates, as "they reference 'a living body' and 'embodied living' respectively."[48] Being enacted through bodily action, ritual is capable of providing one with a sense for appropriate movements as well as for appropriate responses to others' responses to one's movements, such as in a dance or while practicing martial arts. As Linda Ekstrom and Richard D. Hecht have observed,

> in ritual, meaning flows into the individual and is experienced in the body. Ritual constructs the body and also embodies the epistemic dimension of the ritual experience. Ritual is as much epistemological as it is sensual. It is through the senses as well as the intellect that the body is formed and reformed, and only the body makes ritual experience possible. This is not a tautology, but a necessary recognition of how the body is believed to mediate ritual and to be transformed by it. In ritual, humans are all experiential learners.[49]

Ritual, then, trains certain skills that demand agility and quickness, preventing lengthy contemplation, and that are informed by the most "sacrosanct"—in the broadest meaning of that word—field of culture. Gerardus van der Leeuw has written about ritual dance: "In the dance man discovers the rhythm that surrounds him . . . He discovers the rhythm and invents a response. . . . He places his own movements and those of the creatures which surround him in an ordered whole."[50]

In the Chinese world, as Poul Andersen has pointed out, dance serves in fact as a metaphor for the ideal action of the junzi and is at the same time "conceived as a kind of prototype of ritual action."[51] One may infer from Andersen's discussion that dance—and thus ritual—mediates a skill or sensitivity for correlating one's movements with those of the ever-changing external circumstances. The following passage from the Xunzi, illustrating great Confucians' (daru 大儒) skill in handling affairs with a "dance-like description," as Robert Eno has observed,[52] makes this point: "They move along with time, bowing or rising with the times; a thousand moves, ten thousand changes, but the tradition [dao 道] they follow is one and the same."[53]

However, an illuminating corrective to Jennings's thesis has been offered by Ron G. Williams and James W. Boyd in a sophisticated study based on Zoroastrian ritual that also has implications for the present topic. By comparing the ritual to an artwork, Williams and Boyd propose that the noetic function of ritual is not exclusively traceable to its variations, but it can also consist precisely in the invariance *intended* by its practitioner: ritual is, in this sense, "an unchanging instrument of transformation."[54] Williams and Boyd summarize their thesis as follows:

> Whatever else it may be, a ritual is akin to an artistic masterpiece. An artistic masterpiece is that which rewards attention over time. Those who bring the ritual repeatedly into existence, by their careful performances, may count themselves fortunate to stand regularly in the presence of its virtual power and to be engaged thereby in processes of learning and discovery for which it acts as guide. They may be certain as well that it is a guide like no other—one that rightly takes precedence over the vacillations of theological doctrine. The real coherence is in ritual.[55]

Williams and Boyd thus inquire into the nature of ritual from the point of view of the practitioners, or, to use Bourdieu's term, "internal agents." The difference between Bourdieu, on the one hand, and Williams and Boyd, on the other, is that the latter are interested in the view of the ritual as a performance to be repeated over time. They readily acknowledge that the ritual will not be perfectly invariant every time and, strictly speaking, perhaps never, but emphasize that it is characteristically the *intention* of the practitioner to preserve the ritual by maintaining its formal structures when performed.[56] What one learns thereby is parallel to what one learns when repeatedly engaged with a masterpiece artwork: one discovers new perspectives that enable one to acquire a skill to deal more effectively with one's environment. In fact, Williams and Boyd argue, "if there is any mismatch between the necessary structures of an artwork/ritual and the performer/practitioner, it is the practitioner who is called upon to change, not the artwork."[57]

A successfully performed ritual, then, effects a change, indeed, growth, in the one who practices it. Its pedagogical function is comparable to that of an artistic masterpiece. For in both cases, the ritual and the artwork, it lures us into further interaction with itself, causes us to focus on certain realms of our experience, and conveys some kind of message, which, however, we ourselves must interpret or even create.[58] Through a repeated engagement with the ritual we will, over time, acquire a deeper and broader understanding of the communal sphere to which it applies. Considering dance as a prototype of ritual, note the following description of the meaning of dance by Xunzi:

> How do we come to realize the meaning of dance? I say: we cannot see ourselves (move) with the eyes, we cannot hear

ourselves (sing) with the ears. Thus, it can only happen when the order of every episode of gazing down and lifting up the face, of bending and straightening, of advancing and retreating, and retardation and acceleration is executed with proper restrained control; when the strength of bone and flesh has been so thoroughly trained that every movement is in such agreement with the rhythm of the drums, bells and ensemble that there is never an awkward or wayward motion; and when these, through constant practice, are combined into a meaning that is realized again and again.[59]

It is tempting to suggest that this repeated involvement also provides one with the skill or sensitivity to respond appropriately to extraritual circumstances. For these two are surely interrelated: a deeper understanding of the meaningfulness of the ritual (or the dance), "realized again and again," involves a deepening of one's sense for the norms of the community; it generates, so to speak, a *general* sense in much the same way as Gadamer speaks of the active engagement with artworks. As emphasized by Dastur Kotwal, the Zoroastrian priest who serves as Williams and Boyd's primary source, the priest whose life is dedicated to the performance of the rituals must also embody the values of the rituals and strive to enhance his own righteousness.[60]

These considerations of the noetic character of ritual provide illuminating perspectives on the social application of the Confucian li 禮. There are, of course, important differences that need be taken into account. However, due to its particular character, li, if anything, seems even more capable of encompassing a dual pedagogical/noetic function than other kinds of ritual. The main reason is, of course, that li does not exclusively belong to a separate sphere of ritual that takes place outside of mundane life. Thus, the validity of the suggestions made by Jennings and Turner that learning how to perform a ritual also entails learning how to conduct oneself in situations external to the ritual as such is far from being a necessary condition for the noetic function of li. As a "performance," li is not confined to solemn or formal occasions, but its application extends to every occasion involving interaction between people, and, for those "advanced" enough, acts undertaken even in solitude. As long as a ritualized life does not only take place externally, then, it can be a way of gaining profounder awareness and understanding of one's relationship with one's environment and society.

It therefore remains to be seen to what extent internalization, that is to say, conscious reflection leading to creative personalization, is meant to play a role in the performance of li.

Internalization and Efficacy: Li 禮, Yue 樂, De 德, and Ren 仁

Crucially, the process of learning does not begin in formal institutions, but in the family. It is through family relations that an individual gradually acquires a sense and understanding of her place, roles, obligations, and reasonable expectations as to what she may expect from others. While certainly entailing cultivation of one's person, such learning is not aim-directed in a simple sense as the relations and all that they engender are changing with time along with all those involved. Thus, the configuration of these relations as informed by li is in a continuous process of reevaluation. Roger T. Ames speaks of li as "achieved propriety in one's roles and relations,"[61] thus emphasizing that li are first and foremost enacted in the dynamic context of family relations. Learning to become a social human being is what Confucian self-cultivation is all about, for one's identity is also to a considerable extent constituted by the roles, relations, and obligations one has as a member of a given group or, indeed, groups, for one is bound to have several overlapping identities depending on the context. My identity as a stepfather differs from my identity as a grandson or a teacher, and yet all these identities make up what I am. How these identities differ is most clearly exemplified through the ways in which li is enacted in the relational profile particular to each of them. However, while there is certainly a blurry frame within which my enactment of li is expected to take place in each of my roles, I nevertheless have considerable scope to creatively personalize that enactment in each case.[62]

Book 10 of the *Lunyu* is a collection of detailed descriptions of Confucius's behavior in various formal and nonformal situations, the latter of which include his comportment while eating and sleeping and even the way in which he mounts his carriage. These descriptions betray the extensive scope of li according to Confucius's own embodiment of it in real life. As Ames and Rosemont have noted, li applies to "a way of life carefully choreographed down to appropriate facial expressions and physical gestures, a world in which a life is a performance requiring enormous attention to detail. Importantly, this li-constituted performance begins from the insight that personal refinement is only possible through the discipline provided by formalized roles and behaviors."[63]

Li, then, is something of an artwork of life to be accomplished through discipline and training and is, as the *Lunyu* records, best exemplified by the life of Confucius himself. Note, however, that Confucius's comportment is not presented as constituting universal rules to be imitated. It is, on the contrary, highly personalized as manifesting the particular character traits of Confucius himself, and therefore a mode of action inimitable by others. Due to the perceived continuity between the inner and the outer, every action enjoys its particularity as an action performed by that particular person in that particular circumstance and her particular phase of life. Consider, for instance, the following description of Baron von Landwagen from Ivan Goncharov's nineteenth century novel *Oblomov*, which might well be a description of a li-oriented manner of comportment:

> He was exquisitely polite, never smoked in the presence of ladies, never crossed his legs, and severely criticized the young men when during a visit they allowed themselves to lean back in an arm-chair or raise their knees and boots on a level with their noses. He kept his gloves on even indoors, removing them only when he sat down to dinner. He dressed in the latest fashion and wore several ribbons in his buttonhole. He always drove in a carriage and pair and took great care of his horses: before stepping into the carriage, he first walked around it, examined the harness and even the horses' hoofs, and sometimes took out a white handkerchief and rubbed their flanks and backs to see whether they had been well groomed. He greeted acquaintances with a polite and affable smile, and strangers coldly at first, but his coldness was replaced by a smile as soon as they had been introduced to him, and his new acquaintance could always count on it in future. He discussed everything: virtue, high cost of living, science and society—and with equal precision; he expressed his views in clear-cut and well-balanced sentences, as though speaking in ready-made maxims written down in some textbook and circulated among society people for general guidance.[64]

The descriptions of Confucius in the *Lunyu* and elsewhere and, for that matter, the description of Baron von Landwagen here may indicate that the issue of li revolves merely around "correct" external behavior. Indeed, in the classical Chinese corpus, li is sometimes described as belonging to the external, that is to say, as conveying interhuman respect (*gong* 恭) in the social sphere in order to reach a state of harmony (*he* 和) between people. Peng Lirong 彭立榮, for example, quotes the following two passages from the *Lunyu* to point to the primary functions of li:

> Master You said: "Achieving harmony [he 和] is the most valuable function of li. In the tradition [dao 道] initiated by the former kings, this produced elegance and both small and great affairs proceeded from there. But when things are not functioning, to harmonize things on the basis of [supposed] knowledge [zhi 知] of harmony without regulating them through li is bound to fail."
>
> The Master said: "What can I see in someone who, when holding an influential office, is not tolerant, when observing li, is not respectful, and, when overseeing the mourning rites, does not grieve."[65]

Both passages imply that the main function of li is to harmonize external interaction within society. But this implication is deceptive, and, in fact, a more complete reading of the former passage makes it evident that an exclusive concentration on the external—in other words, a kind of imposition of "harmony"—will not suffice. It must be done through li, precisely because li, in its best spirit, demands that the harmonizing action comes from within and is, therefore, authentic.

As is paradigmatic for apparent dichotomies in Chinese thought, the relationship between the "inner" (*nei* 內) and the "outer" (*wai* 外) is portrayed as one characterized by mutual influences and as strictly inseparable. It is probably Zhuangzi who provides the most succinct formulation of their inseparability in the ancient Chinese philosophical tradition with his notion of "inner sage and outer king" (*neisheng waiwang* 內聖外王).[66] However, the *Zhongyong* also says that "[c]onsummating oneself is an instance of communal humanity [ren 仁] and consummating other things is an instance of wisdom [zhi 知]. This is bringing one's natural tendencies [xing 性] to a state of virtue [de 德] and is the way of integrating the inner [nei 內] and the outer [wai 外]."[67]

The apparent schism between the inner and the outer is further brought to expression in the *Liji*'s discussion of music (yue 樂) and ritual (li 禮), where music is presented as belonging to the "inner" and ritual to the "outer" aspects of human life.[68] But even here the distinction is only provisional or, I am tempted to say, "pragmatically analytical." For yue and li belong together as complementary practices acquired by the people so that social order will be produced and maintained *by* the people: "Li, music, penal law [xing 刑,] and government decrees [zheng 政] all aim at the same thing, namely, to assimilate the minds [xin 心] of the common people and produce order in the way."[69] Note that the former two relate to the practices of the people themselves, whereas the latter two, penal law and government decrees, are external administrative modes for effecting social order. Confucius, for his part, is quite clear on his own preference: "The Master said: 'If led with government decrees [zheng] and controlled with penal law [xing], the common people will refrain [from committing crimes] but will be without a sense of shame. If led with moral virtue [de] and controlled through the observance of li, they will not only develop a sense of shame but will also order themselves.'"[70]

One of the most frequently cited passages from the *Lunyu*, one in which Confucius explains to the outraged Zilu why he would begin by correcting the application of names (zhengming 正名) if he were to rule the state, is clearer yet on the priority and the complementariness of li and yue:

> When names are not applied correctly, language will not accord with things; when language does not accord with things, affairs will not be taken care of; when affairs are not taken care of, the observance of ritual propriety and the playing of music will not flourish; when the observance of ritual propriety and the playing of music do not flourish, government decrees [zheng] and penal law [xing] will not be on the mark; if government decrees and penal law are not on the mark, the common people will not know where to place their hands and feet.[71]

We have already seen that "not knowing where to place one's hands and feet" implies a situation of *anomie*, that is to say, one in which at least relatively established norms are unavailable. The point is that negligence of the social or cultural foundations of emotions and practices will result in a state of alienation between the people and those in power, which, in turn, results in a state of social *anomie*. In order to be a responsible and active citizen, one needs to have faith in one's society, enjoy the feeling of security, and, last, have certain emotional dispositions such as the belief in one's ability and possibility to take care of affairs, in short, some level of optimism.

The crux of a well-ordered, harmonious, and dynamic society, then, consists in starting at the right end. And it is precisely one of the distinguishing particularities of the Confucian philosophy that it emphasizes the development of certain personal sensibilities as the foundation of society. This is why li and yue are considered prior to zheng and xing.

Now yue as music and le as joy or optimism are in fact expressed by the same character, 樂. Their original identification can be traced back to the joy expressed in the music and dance during harvest celebrations in China's antiquity. Music is moreover indispensable to the sacrificial ceremonies for the ancestors and, in fact, constitutes certain parts of these ceremonies.[72] Li and yue, therefore, representing the moral and the artistic tradition, cannot be fully separated. As Confucius stresses, these are not mere external performances, but must be properly internalized in order to be truly functional: "When speaking time and again of ritual propriety, how could I just be talking about jade and silk? When speaking time and again of music, how could I just be talking about bells and drums?"[73]

The importance of the internalization of certain dispositions is alluded to throughout the Confucian corpus of the pre-Qin period. Nowhere, however, does it receive as detailed a discussion as in the recently discovered *Wuxing* 五行 document, or *The Five Kinds of Conduct*, a pre-Qin text possibly written by Confucius's grandson, Zisizi, or his students and excavated in Mawandgui for the first time in 1973 and again at Guodian in 1994. The *Wuxing* emphasizes the distinction between conduct that is merely externally appropriate and conduct proceeding from within. In its first paragraph it says that "[w]here communal humanity [ren 仁] takes shape from within, it is called virtuous conduct [de 德]; where it does not take shape within, it is called mere (proper) conduct."[74] The same argumentative pattern is then repeated in the passage about yi 義 (appropriate conduct), li 禮, zhi 智 (wisdom), and sheng 聖 (sagacity), all of which are core Confucian notions. An important implication here is that actions executed with skill and authenticity, on the one hand, or by sheer imitation, on the other, are bound to be vastly and noticeably different. The latter will, quite literally, be hollow, as they are based on mere imitation of external form. Mencius, for instance, is in no doubt that one's physical deportment reveals most clearly what lies behind one's actions: "To the natural dispositions of exemplary persons [junzi 君子] belong communal humanity [ren 仁], appropriate conduct [yi 義], li 禮, and wisdom [zhi 智], which are rooted in their thoughts and feelings [xin 心]. These manifest themselves in the mildness of their faces, amplify themselves in their backs and extend to their limbs, which, in turn, instruct them without uttering a single word."[75]

With regard to the *Wuxing* argument, Pang Pu has pointed out that the difference between the two kinds of conduct also indicates different stages of learning, whereby "if one has neither grasped it nor effected its formation in one's heart, all that remains is the embodiment of the action, which is then called simply 'action' (xing 行)."[76] In other words, imitation is merely second rate and perhaps only useful as a kind of drill for those in whom the Confucian moral skills have not yet taken shape.

The qualitative difference described in the opening lines of the *Wuxing, The Five Kinds of Conduct*, between "virtuous conduct," proceeding from within, and "mere (proper) conduct," being only external, consists in *de* 德, which may be translated provisionally as "virtue."[77] The five kinds of conduct are the familiar ones of ren 仁, yi 義, li 禮, zhi 知, and sheng 聖, of which the last, sagacity, is presented as the final stage of personal cultivation.[78] It is de 德, however, that enjoys a particular privilege as signifying the harmony between the five actions together: "If (all) five of the virtuous conducts are in harmony [he 和], one speaks of virtue [de]; if (only) four of the virtuous conducts are in harmony, one speaks of goodness [shan 善]. Goodness is the way of human beings; virtue is the way of tian 天."[79]

De obviously proceeds through some stages here, from describing the characteristics of a single action as such to the harmony that obtains among all of them. But it is even more complicated than that. As Ames and Hall explain, de connotes in the early philosophical literature "the insistent particularity of things." The conventional translations of de, "virtue" or "power," they continue, define "the particular as a focus of potency within its own field of experience . . . The earliest Confucian literature tended to limit its concerns to human experience, where this qualitative dimension of de more nearly suggests both "excellence' and 'efficacy' as what we can truly be and do if we 'realize (zhi [知])' the most from our personal careers as members of a specific community."[80] Elsewhere, they add to this: "Given the intrinsic relatedness of particulars in this conception of existence as process, de is both process and product—both the potency and the achieved character of any particular disposition within the unsummed totality of experience."[81] These two semantic or connotative pairs of "excellence" and "efficacy," on one hand, and "process" and "product," on the other, are particularly germane to the complex meaning of de in the *Wuxing* passage. As excellence, it points to an achieved state of personal character, a product reaped from the process of learning. As efficacy, it signifies the external "potency" in that character's actions.

"Potency" has a twofold meaning here. First, it points to the ability to be able to make the most of one's circumstances, and obviously, a sage, who has appropriated all five kinds of conduct, is here the supreme virtuoso. The *Wuxing* expresses this by invoking the notion of timeliness: "A sage realizes [zhi 知] the way of *tian* 天. To realize it, and thereby put it into practice [xing 行], is appropriateness [yi 義]. To put it into practice in a timely manner [shi 時] is de."[82]

The second meaning of potency points to the transformative effects one is capable of having through one's comportment. The *Wuxing* uses an artistic, indeed, musical image to convey this idea: "[Opening with] the sound of bells and [concluding with] jade tubes is to possess de 德. The sound of bells is goodness [shan 善]. The timbre of jade is sagacity. Only those who possess de are able to [open with] the sound of bells and [conclude with] jade tubes."[83] A similar passage occurs in the *Mencius*. In fact, it seems probable that Mencius is referring directly to the ideas presented in the *Wuxing*.[84] It is illuminating to look at the *Mencius* passage as well:

> Bo Yi was the sage who was pure. Yi Yin was the sage who was responsible. Liu Xiahui was the sage who was easygoing. Confucius was the sage whose actions were timely. Confucius may be said to have "assembled the great symphony."[85] "Assembling the great symphony" means to [open with] the sound of bells and [conclude with] jade tubes. The "sound of bells" means to begin with a rhythmic order [*tiao li* 脩理]; the "jade tubes" means to (carry through and) bring the rhythmic order to a conclusion. Beginning the rhythmic order is the affair of knowledge [zhi 智]; (carrying through and) bringing the rhythmic order to a conclusion is the affair of sagacity [sheng 聖]. Knowledge is comparable to skill and sagacity is comparable to strength. It is like when shooting an arrow from a distance of hundred paces: its getting there is a matter of your strength; its hitting the mark is not a matter of your strength.[86]

Having reached sagacity means possessing the virtuosity or potency to see things through to the end. Remember that, according to the *Wuxing*, one needs to have harmonized all the five conducts, among which sagacity is the ultimate stage, in order to rise above a "mere" shan-ness 善 and become a de-inspired sage. Now de 德 is often presented as an almost mysterious power to govern and control without having to force things or, in government, resort to violence. In the *Lunyu*, Confucius describes the effects of de thus: "The de of the junzi 君子 is the wind, while the de of the petty person [*xiao ren* 小人] is the grass. When the wind blows, the grass necessarily bends."[87] De is often associated with musical impressions. Knoblock has noted that *de yin* (德音), literally "virtuous sound," is a common expression in the *Book of Odes* (*Shijing* 詩經). He explains this idea such "that the 'sounding' of the true 'inner power' produces change in all that hear it, [the junzi's] charisma transforms all who know of him, just as a sound struck on one instrument produces sympathetic vibrations wherever it extends."[88] This musical metaphor catches the image of the junzi, who, wherever he goes, effects transformations by "touching" people's sentiments through his way of living and interacting.[89] A true junzi can thus be recognized through his demeanor. The *Wuxing*, then, underscores the importance of internalizing the de-excellence, and of building in oneself a charismatic de-character for the sake of acquiring genuine efficacy.

However, the *Wuxing* repeatedly stresses the necessity of a joyful or optimistic disposition in order to be efficacious. In fact, the entire process of developing de requires certain inner sentiments that are therefore authentic. Consider, for instance, the second strip of the *Wuxing*: "If junzi have no heart-felt worries [*you* 憂], they will lack heart-felt wisdom [*zhi* 智]; if they lack heart-felt wisdom, they will not have heart-felt enjoyment [*yue* 說]; if they do not have heart-felt enjoyment, they will not have heart-felt feeling of security [*an* 安]; if they do not find security, they will not be optimistic [*le* 樂]; if they are not optimistic, they will not have the potency to be efficacious [*de* 德]."[90]

One should be wary of reading this as a linear causal development in which each successive stage signifies the completion of the previous one. The de-inspired junzi still has heart-felt worries, but he worries about the state of his community and, of course, about his own deeds and dispositions. Now the entire passage can be read as a sociopsychological account of the necessary conditions for a vibrant and effective society. Without the sensitivity necessary for enjoying things in one's immediate surroundings, for instance, without being able to savor the culinary specialties of one's home place, one cannot be at ease. One does not feel at home and lacks a feeling of security. And if there is no inner feeling of security, one is incapable of believing in one's own ability to improve the less perfect aspects of one's culture and society: in short, without optimism, one cannot be efficacious.

The "efficacy" contained in de, however, is not a mere ability to carry through actions to the end without considering the quality of the action as such. An excessive concentration on the power of the de-inspired junzi can be misleading.[91] One of our important gains from the *Wuxing* consists precisely in an unusually clear presentation of what de really consists in. De turns out to be the internalization of the supreme Confucian qualities of ren 仁, yi 義, li 禮, zhi 智, and sheng 聖. Consequently, there can be no presentation of a meaningful notion of "efficacy" in isolation from these qualities.

Of these, ren, which I have referred to as "communal humanity," is undoubtedly one of the most important. If de is the potency to initiate things and bring them to completion, ren makes sure that these things are worth initiating at all. The character for ren is composed of the characters for the human being (ren 人) and the numeral 2 (er 二). Hence, and as many have pointed out, ren 仁 stresses the unavoidably social aspect of human existence. A human being is never alone, is born of other human beings, and is not able to develop him- or herself without other human beings—in short, without some sort of society the human being would not be human. Ren reminds us that our mode of living and our actions always involve other persons, thus implying a social or communal sense. As such a sense, it lends a vital qualitative direction to our behavior. Skill or efficacy in the sense of de is certainly of profound importance in the Confucian tradition, but if disengaged from the social sense of ren, it runs the danger of degenerating into a kind of means-end rational mode of action typical of the greedy, vain, and egocentric "petty person" (xiao ren 小人) who seeks to manipulate situations exclusively for his or her own benefit. While, as Confucius points out, "there are occasions on which the junzi fails to act in accordance with ren, there are no occasions on which the petty person acts according to ren."[92] This complete lack of the sense of ren is precisely what makes such persons petty and distinguishes them from those who are junzi.

In the process of education and refinement, therefore, the sense expressed through ren must be present and evolving. Otherwise, the process will not lead to the formation of a junzi. This is also why Confucius asks, rhetorically: "What does someone who is not ren have to do with the observance of ritual propriety? What does someone who is not ren have to do with the playing of music?"[93] If the aesthetic experience of li and yue are to have any effects on the character development of the person, this can only be meaningful if it enhances and refines that person's sense of ren. Conversely, a person who is not ren is bound to perform both li and yue in a superficial and meaningless manner.

The process *qua* process of learning is described in the *Wuxing* both as analogous to and mediated through the experience of art, producing a particular kind of consciousness or sensibility that informs sagacious and exemplary behavior, which, again, has the effect of stimulating others to strive for their own cultivation. The aesthetic sense and aesthetic experience acquired through li and yue are therefore far removed from, say, the Western modernist notion of *l'art pour l'art* that was meant to liberate art from social commitments. On the contrary, a Confucian would maintain that art can never be disengaged from moral considerations, though this does not mean that the artist or performer must necessarily present some moral claims. It is rather, as Eliot Deutsch has pointed out, explaining the Chinese attitude to artistic creation, that "one [will] inevitably be disclosed in one's work as the kind of person one is."[94] One might further argue that considering the absence of body-soul dualism in the Chinese worldview, as well as the close interplay between the inner and outer, it is but to be expected that the (inner) character traits of a person are considered to be observable in that person's (outer) works and actions. Such a view clearly goes hand in hand with a development of a refined kind of discernment to evaluate persons' "authenticity" by observing their every move in the smallest detail.

There are clearly affinities between the ways in which both Gadamer and Dewey understand experience and the roles that li and yue play in the Confucian philosophy. Li and yue are meant to enhance one's engagement in the dynamic configuration of the social environment and foster an elevated sense of community by revealing the impossibility of personal development, according to the value of humanness within the framework of tradition, outside of society. This aspect will become clearer in the next section.

Further, the insights of Jennings, and Williams and Boyd's correctives to these insights, offer illuminating perspectives from which to approach Confucian ritual propriety. From one point of view, a performance of li is always personalized and particular, depending on the person performing and the situation at hand. Therefore, it demands of the performer an endeavor to assess the situation and present a personal interpretation of the meaningful variables of the situation through a personalized performance. From another point of view, Confucians, no less than others, also expect those who perform rituals to do so according to preestablished patterns. Without such patterns, obviously, the rituals would be arbitrary and eventually lose the structure that preserves their identity as rituals. Invariance as an element of li has the educational function of continuously revealing, partially but significantly through the performer's hermeneutic creativity, new latitudes of the social meaning and message of the ritual. While performances of li are described in minute detail in various ancient writings, the descriptions do not include the exact meanings for the parties involved. These need be interpreted by each. And it is here that personalization and internalization come in. As pointed out by Wu Zongjie and Hu Meixin, "[l]inguistic meaning arises when the participants reflect on [their] own identity and relationship with [their] circumstances through a dialogue with the situation. Therefore, meaning arises as situated understanding which is, and has to be, based on reflection on the dialogic relationship between [. . .] individual and the community."[95] The generation of meaning, as Wu and Hu continue, "is always relative to local, historical and social, and personal context, and one may make different meaning at a different stage of one's life with one's evolving cultural identity."[96] Thus, there is necessarily a hermeneutic openness to the practice of li customs, an openness that demands individual creation of meaning on behalf of the practitioner. Otherwise, the customs are merely empty relics devoid of meaning.

As has been shown in these pages, li encompass both formal and informal kinds of conduct. From a pedagogical point of view, one might say with some simplification that the more formal aspects are to be applied at one's early stages of learning, while more spontaneous, personalized, and informal patterns will emerge at advanced stages. The former has to do with appropriating one's cultural legacy; the latter, with its expression, interpretation, and thus development. Tradition and culture must be continuously revised and reinterpreted in light of the novel circumstances arising in the constant transformation to which we refer as "reality." And this revision and interpretation can only be done by us, as indicated in Confucius's saying that "[h]uman beings are able to broaden the tradition (dao 道); the tradition does not broaden human beings."[97] It is our task to carry the cultural legacy forward, and this is precisely what we do when we interpret and apply li appropriately and creatively, for this kind of "creativity emerges from the interdependence between person and world."[98]

Education as Exhortation and Personal Cultivation

The early Confucians offer us two kinds of teaching method, the verbal and the performative. From the ways in which these are carried out one can see the complementarity and connection between them. By "verbal method" I mean teaching through dialogue. Dialogue in the Chinese tradition is a continuous hermeneutic process in which the teacher is meant to inspire the student to come up with his or her own elaborations of the original ideas. Thus, a "teacher" could also be understood as a text, and the "student," the reader and interpreter of that text. The major part of the *Lunyu*, however, is a particularly conspicuous example of the priority of incitement or exhortation over dictation. At the same time, this accounts for the virtually infinite richness drawn from it by Chinese students of the *Lunyu* for the last two and a half millennia, and, as it happens, for its general failure to leave an impression on Westerners who tend to be disappointed by its lack of theoretical argumentation and "rational" systematization. For the Master, when responding to the questions posed by his disciples, tends to perplex not only his readers but also his own disciples by being extremely laconic and vague. The clear expression of their perplexity in the *Lunyu* is certainly not without significance. Moreover, many of his answers also appear to be mere platitudes or tautologies, and he frequently responds differently to the same question on different occasions. There are some passages, however, where Confucius provides a hint of an explanation, or at least a rationale, for his own method. For example: "If, when showing [the students] one corner and they do not return with the other three, I do not repeat myself."[99]

Confucius's ideal students are those who elaborate on his laconic "hints" and succeed in drawing the whole picture. On one occasion he discusses some sayings with Zigong who subsequently illustrates the Master's answer with an appropriate quote from the *Book of Odes*. Confucius responds to Zigong's performance by praising him for being able to infer what follows from the point he himself made initially.[100] This, however, does not mean that Confucius is fishing for one particular answer, that the "other three corners" are already established and need merely be discovered. Confucius is not just a master of riddles. Nor is it the point, important in Plato's *Meno* and common in contemporary pedagogic theory, that by making the students go through the entire process for realizing the answer one will help them acquire a better and fuller understanding of the issue than if one simply told them the answer. The method of "hinting" certainly serves the purpose of inciting the students to reflect on the issue and develop their own understanding of it. But the key point consists precisely in "their own understanding," or, more appropriately, considering the practical nature of understanding in Chinese thought, "realization."

Confucius's prodigy-student Yan Hui is a good case in point. When Confucius asks Zigong to compare himself with Yan Hui, Zigong responds: "How could I dare comparing myself with Yan Hui! On learning one thing he realizes ten. I myself, on learning one thing, realize the second." Confucius says: "You are not his match. Neither I nor you are his match."[101]

In his translation of this passage, James Legge provides an illuminating elaboration on its fuller meaning. For "ten" also implies completion, and thus Legge translates as Hui "hears one point and knows all about the subject." This is important, because, as François Jullien points out, it means that "the slightest indication bears fruit in" Yan Hui, and he can develop the lesson to the end on his own. However, when Zigong learns something, he can also complete it, but he remains "limited by a successive progress, which is flatly deductive, without rising to universality."[102] This interpretation is further supported by Confucius's comment at the end, that neither he nor Zigong is Yan Hui's match. Confucius perceives Yan Hui's productivity or creativity as being superior to his own.

In the section on learning in the *Liji*, this hinting method is spelled out even more clearly:

> When junzi 君子 have realized the sources for successful teaching [jiao 教], as well as the sources that make it of no effect, they are capable of teaching others. Thus, when junzi teach, they lead and do not herd, they motivate and do not discourage, initiate but do not proceed to the end [da 達]. Leading without herding results in harmony; motivating and not discouraging results in ease; initiating without proceeding to the end results in reflection. Harmony, ease and reflection characterize efficient teaching. . . . Good singers induce people to carry on developing the tunes. Good teachers induce people to carry on developing the ideas. Their words are few but efficient, plain but outstanding, with few illustrations but instructive. Thus they are said to carry on developing the ideas.[103]

The insistence upon the brevity of speech conforms to Confucius's apparent distrust of speech, expressed in his frequent emphasis on xin 信, "to be true to one's words." To this, the notion of zhengming 正名, of "using names appropriately," is closely related. Both zhengming and xin imply that words ought to be properly applied in the right situation at the right time and thus emphasize the conformity between speech and action. There are numerous passages in the *Lunyu* where Confucius underscores the priority of action to speech.[104] To speak of one's intentions is easy. The difficulty consists in accomplishing that which one intends to do. There is, moreover, the obvious possibility of deception through the use of language, probably rampant in the unstable political situation of Confucius's days.[105] For these reasons, he gradually became more wary of what people say, suspending judgment about their character dispositions until their verbally intended actions had been carried out: "The Master said: Initially, in my dealings with others, I listened to their words and believed that they would act accordingly. Now, in my dealings with others, I listen to their words but observe their actions."[106]

That good teachers "initiate but do not proceed to the end" means that they only hint at the path, but do not spell it out in detail. If they proceed to the end, they are dictating, or, indeed, indoctrinating, but not teaching. The nature of the path, moreover, is such that it is necessary that the path unfold for each and every person in a way that is unique for that person: "The Master said: Archery does not consist in penetrating the leather target, because strength differs among the archers. This is the tradition [dao 道] of the ancients."[107]

Zhang Weizhong 張衛中 points out that Confucius, in this passage, is not speaking of warfare archery, but of the kind of artistic archery belonging to the sphere of "ritual and music" (liyue 禮樂).[108] What matters here is not simply to penetrate the leather, but to develop a high skill of archery guided by the aesthetic sensibilities of the tradition and refined by one's own personal endowments. It is certainly important that one ultimately hits the bull's eye, but first one needs to find and develop the style that suits one best, and for this, a concentration on strength, which one may or may not have, can be a serious impediment. Similarly, instead of mindlessly scrambling toward their intended aims, people will have to reflect on, practice, and develop means that accord with the way informed by the tradition, the dao. Although they initially acquire modes of action from within the parameters of the tradition, it is imperative that they be given sufficient leeway to refine and realize their own personalized modes, because the tradition's main evolutionary drive consists precisely in these. Thus, if the teachers also "proceed to the end," they obstruct this evolution and prevent the tradition from growing or, put in another way, the path, instead of continuing, will only lead back to the starting point.

The Confucian philosophy of education is therefore in accordance with the general Confucian concentration on action. In fact, it would be difficult to see how that could not be the case. If the purpose of education is to enhance knowledge and wisdom, and, in turn, knowledge and wisdom are understood principally as the ability to handle affairs efficiently, then education will necessarily revolve largely around ways in which how best to enable the student to develop skills to manage real affairs. A *performative* mode of education, a mode in which the student gains firsthand experience, is therefore emphasized even more than the verbal mode. After all, as quoted in the *Records of Learning* (*Xueji* 學記), a chapter of the *Liji*, "[t]eaching is [only] the half of learning" (*xue xue ban* 學學半).[109] The point of Confucius's vague exhortations is to make his disciples ponder his words, develop their own understanding, and then act on that understanding. Zhi 智 must lead to xing 行.

For this reason, education is to a significant degree left to the students themselves. It is only through self-education or self-cultivation, the kind of education that must never come to an end, as Xunzi says in his opening passage, that we may hope that society keeps developing and adapting to the always unpredictable forces of circumstances as expressed by ming 命 or tianming 天命.

Self-cultivation or personal cultivation (xiushen 修身) could indeed be identified as the crux of the Confucian philosophy. While the notion itself may not be frequently encountered in the classical texts, the idea of cultivating or refining oneself, of analyzing one's own character, stance, and bearing, is pervasive. The meaning of the notion xiushen is suggestive for the importance of ritual propriety for the formation of a noble character, of a junzi, who has the potency, the de, to effect profound changes and improvements wherever he passes through.

Shen 身 has an extremely rich semantic scope and can refer to body, self, life, and/or human character. In the *Shuowen* lexicon, *xiu* 修 is explained through shi 飾, "to decorate" or "to ornament." Judging from this etymological association, xiushen could be understood as "decorating one's character," which comes to expression in the way in which one appears and comports oneself. In the Chinese tradition, the idea of character cannot be isolated from comportment. Just as knowledge (zhi

智) cannot be thought of in abstraction from action (xing 行), there is, as we have seen, no strict border between the internal (*nei* 內) and the external (*wai* 外). There is, therefore, a strong relation between xiushen and the performance of a ritual or ceremony (li). And indeed, Tang Kejing, a modern commentator on the *Shuowen*, takes shi originally to mean *wenshi* 文飾, which can simply mean a ceremonial act.[110] Insofar as "self-cultivation" refers to the body, its relationship with li is further underscored by the latter's cognate relationship with ti 體, or "body," as already mentioned. Hall and Ames suggest that this relationship indicates that "*li* actions are embodiments or formalizations of meaning and value that accumulate to constitute a cultural tradition." They further argue along the following lines:

> Ritual actions, invested with the accumulated meaning of the tradition, are formalized structures upon which the continuity of the tradition depends and through which a person in the tradition pursues cultural refinement. Like a body of literature or a corpus of music, these rituals continue through time as a repository of the ethical and aesthetic insights of those who have gone before. A person engaged in the performance of a particular formal action, taking meaning from it while seeking himself to be appropriate for it, derives meaning and value from this embodiment, and further strengthens it by his contribution of novel meaning and value.[111]

The practice or active embodiment of the li customs is therefore an embodiment of the tradition. Here one may speak with Pierre Bourdieu, who uses the word *hexis* to express the embodiment of the habitus, and thus "to signify deportment, the manner and style in which actors 'carry themselves': stance, gait, gesture, etc."[112] Confucius says quite explicitly that "without studying li 禮, one will be unable to take a stance (li 立)."[113] Bourdieu in fact sees the body as a mnemonic device which absorbs the basics of culture in a process of learning or socializing. It is through the physical experience of bodily action that the habitus, the socially constituted base for practices, is inculcated in a way more effective than through explicit teaching.[114] This insight appears to have been no less clear to Confucius and the first Confucians than it was to Bourdieu.

In the *Zuo Commentary to the Spring and Autumn Annals* (*Zuozhuan* 左傳), it says that "li is the stem of character [*shen* 身]."[115] Gou Chengyi says about this sentence that it is "a concentrated reflection of the *Zuozhuan*'s emphasis on the person's cultivation of the li customs . . . and the first indication of the practical orientation that began in the *Liji* with the words: 'From the son of *tian* 天 to the common people, personal cultivation [xiushen 修身] is the root of all.'"[116] The quotation comes from the *Great Learning* (*Daxue* 大學) chapter of the *Liji*, arguably the most expressive ancient philosophical treatise on the function and importance of xiushen.

The *Daxue* outlines a moral scheme that is as brief in length as it is expansive in scope. It gives the appearance, especially when translated into Western languages, of depicting a step-to-step teleological program beginning with the investigation of things in one's environment, going through personal cultivation, and concluding in the achievement of peace in all under heaven. Universal peace thus begins with the single individual's effort in bettering him- or herself. A typical translation of the part that describes this process is, for instance, that of James Legge:

> The ancients who wished to illustrate illustrious virtue throughout the kingdom, first ordered well their states. Wishing to order well their states, they first regulated their families. Wishing to regulate their families, they first cultivated their persons. Wishing to cultivate their persons, they first rectified their hearts. Wishing to rectify their hearts, they first sought to be sincere in their thoughts. Wishing to be sincere in their thoughts, they first extended to the utmost their knowledge. The extension of knowledge is by the investigation of things.[117]

Then the process is described once again, but now from the beginning to the end, culminating in *tianxia ping* 天下平, or "world peace." The description, as it appears in English translation, is misleading to say the least. It gives the impression that before we can even start thinking of entering the second stage and strive to be sincere in our thoughts, we must first extend to the utmost our knowledge. Such an understanding, however, merely evokes Zeno's paradoxes. In practical terms, therefore, the translation conveys a mere lapse into a purely theoretical orientation toward dedicating one's entire life to the accumulation, or, in this case, extension of knowledge. When have we extended our knowledge to the *utmost*?

The passage certainly expresses, in some sense, a step-to-step process. The problem with the translation is the use of the word "first" followed by a past-tense verb—for example, "wishing to regulate their families, they first cultivated their persons"—suggesting that they had to finish cultivating their persons before they could turn to the task of regulating their families. In classical Chinese, there are no tenses that indicate such a process of moving to the next step only after having concluded the previous one. There is, to be sure, the word *xian* 先, indicating "first," but more in the sense of "first things first," without implying that previous steps have been brought to conclusion. Xian is thus more appropriately translated as "to begin with," upon which the following verb should be in gerundive form to indicate the continuity of the action. The sentence above, then, would be translated as "wishing to regulate their families, they began by cultivating their persons." None of the steps, therefore, will ever be concluded, which amounts to saying that they are all simultaneous. In short, one brings peace to the world by extending one's knowledge to the utmost.[118] However—and this is a decisive point—one does not work on the extension of one's knowledge without also making one's will sincere, without self-cultivation, without regulating one's family, and so on. The stages are certainly consecutive, but they are not isolated, separate processes. The point with the sequence is that if one has not, say, reflected on ways to improve one's own character and attitude, then one will not succeed in bringing accord to one's family. One has to start from the right end. Remember that knowledge in the Chinese context always involves the ability to handle real situations.

Apart from these linguistic arguments, there are more weighty philosophical ones for the present interpretation. In the *Lunyu*, Confucius describes persons of communal humanity (ren 仁) as those who "establish themselves by establishing others and promote themselves by promoting others. To be able to correlate one's conduct with those near at hand could be said to be the method of becoming a person of communal humanity."[119] The following passage, the only one in the *Lunyu* where self-cultivation (xiuji 修己) is explicitly mentioned,[120] is even more illuminating: "Zilu inquired about junzi 君子. The Master replied: 'By cultivating themselves, they are respectful.' 'Is that all?' asked Zilu. The Master replied: 'By cultivating themselves, they bring accord to others.' 'Is that all?' asked Zilu. The Master replied: 'By cultivating themselves, they bring accord to all people. Even a Yao or a Shun would find such a task extremely hard.'"[121]

Confucius is essentially describing the same process as the one depicted in the *Great Learning*. But he is more explicit in pointing out that although the cultivation of oneself requires effort, commitment, determination, persistence, and diligence, abilities that one must nurture in oneself if one wants to become a junzi,[122] it is, at the end of the day, not an individual but a social process, consisting in one's continuously enhanced ability to induce others to contribute to a harmonious communal living: in effect, one educates oneself by educating others. Such a process of education is best realized through the performance of ritual propriety, a performance that is no less social than personal, that demands as much attention to the preestablished patterns of the action as it does to the particular and ever-changing circumstances of the moment, and that is therefore a means of communicating and conveying to others one's understanding of and contribution to tradition and culture.

Without li, the Confucian process of humanization would be unthinkable. For it is precisely li that binds the process into the ordinary reality of human living and enables one to learn how to behave according to the established, though far from being fixed, norm of what constitutes the highest humanity in the form of the junzi. The junzi follows and further clears the path of tradition, dao, through learning and teaching. Clearing this path is no easy matter, and, according to Xunzi, would be impossible without li: "Li is that by which people find footing. When they lose this footing, they are sure to stumble and fall, sink and drown. The negligence of a small matter can result in great disorder. This is what li is all about."[123]

Concluding Remarks

While Confucianism has largely been seen as a peculiarly Chinese ethnocentric ideology during the last two centuries, international scholars are gradually beginning to regard it as a philosophy with a universal appeal. Robert Cummings Neville has called attention to "a profound Confucian tradition of more than two millennia that reflects on the differences between civilized and barbaric rituals, between better norms for personal and social life and worse ones, between better conventions and worse ones."[1] Confucian social values are increasingly being seen as contributing to a healthy, harmonious, and vibrant society. Referring especially to Tu Weiming's "New Confucianism," Neville goes on to say that a "new Confucian theory of ritual convention as constitutive of humanity in both personal and social dimensions provides an even more effective approach to norms in an age of pluralism, social disintegration and conflict."[2] More recently, Neville has argued that "[t]he special contribution of Confucianism to world society is its conception of ritual that unites theory and practice, that provides a sharp tool for moral analysis, and that makes possible the pursuit of such questions as the nature of the good life."[3]

Similarly, A. T. Nuyen, in a provocative essay, has argued that Confucianism has all the resources necessary for claiming universality. Confucianism, he says, is in fact in a better position than a philosophical movement such as liberalism. For the latter makes a claim to universality without admitting to its embeddedness in a culture-specific worldview and metaphysics, whereas Confucianism affirms its own origins as belonging to a distinct culture, while at the same time being "committed to a movement towards universalism."[4] With this "movement," Nuyen means the process presented in the *Daxue*, as discussed in the last section, beginning with self-cultivation and culminating in world peace. However, he also argues that the notion of li is an indispensable element for the validity of the Confucian movement toward universalism:

> [O]nce we focus correctly on what is important in *li*, namely the virtue of orderly conduct aiming at harmony, to be cultivated by a person with *ren* and *yi* who acts towards others with humanity and righteousness, the global significance of *li*, and of Confucianism, becomes clear. A person with *li* must strive to arrive at and abide by rites and rituals that aim at establishing social order. This is surely a necessary virtue if we are to avoid the "clash of civilisations" in the context of globalisation. . . . Far from Confucianism standing in the way of the development of global justice, and far from the universalism of global justice obliterating the culture of Confucianism, it can be said that the idea of global justice is the natural extension of the *li* of Confucianism.[5]

There is certainly much to be said for the views of both Neville and Nuyen. Confucianism may actually turn out to be a much more capable contender on the international arena for bringing about universal consensus than a teaching that purports to base itself on universal rationality while in fact being based on a culture-specific metaphysics. Though li owes its origins to Chinese culture, its emphasis on the adherence to ren 仁 or communal humanity—a notion certainly not restricted to a single community—guiding the practice of doing the right thing at the right time would tend to exclude the possibility of encroaching upon others, whether they be individuals or entire peoples. It can be reasonably assumed that all cultures in the world employ some degree of ritual forms as an explicit method to discipline and socialize its members, especially the younger ones. Among the Confucian thinkers, it is Xunzi who particularly emphasizes this point. But what makes ancient Confucianism particular in this regard is that it also accounts for the creative process that takes over from external disciplining: when the individual is capable of assessing the always unique social circumstances (zhi 知), of figuring out the correct way to deal with them (yi 義), and of ensuring the most productive result for the community (ren 仁). A mastery of li is a prerequisite for being able to lead a creative, fulfilling, and meaningful life in the company of other human beings. Thus, li differs from ritual in the usual Indo-European sense of the notion, as the more the demand for the rigorous invariance of li softens, the more adept the practitioner becomes.

Any society is in possession of some traditional customs, many of which could be compared with the Confucian li. But in mainstream

Western philosophy, such customs have largely been reduced to ethics, an ostensibly "rational" discourse appraised according to the criteria of logic and absolute truth as these came to ascendancy during the post-Renaissance period. Such approaches can in some particular cases be of use to clarify complex situations, but it has become increasingly clear, especially in recent decades, that they are inadequate as an all-embracing criterion for communal human living and can even have harmful consequences. Numerous attempts have been and are fortunately still being made to come up with other approaches, most of which are more inclusive of other important paradigms at play in social living. Nevertheless, the preeminent channel in this respect remains, as of yet, the one of rational ethics. And when rationality, held to be universal, is taken as the single criterion for action, one has stepped on a slippery slope that, despite all good intentions, may lead to narrow and potentially barbaric ethnocentrism.

Where do the li customs come from? They are the most concrete and vivid manifestations of tradition, that which makes up a living tradition as living. The tradition preserves the continuity of the culture in which we become conscious of ourselves as thinking, feeling, and acting individuals and which is the strongest factor in providing us with direction and identity. But the li customs are not unchanging, nor are they meant to be. They are modified, first by individuals, then perhaps by families, groups, and finally by the community as a whole in the wake of all the changes taking place in the human habitat, be these changes due to technological advances, natural occurrences, or some other internal or external factors. No less than other aspects of the Chinese world, li is and always has been regarded, at least by the more sophisticated Chinese thinkers, as being in a process of constant transformation. How could it be otherwise, considering that the li customs are embedded in a cosmology of continuous change? Tradition and culture must be continuously revised and reinterpreted in light of the novel circumstances arising in the ongoing transformation to which we refer as "reality." And this can only be done by their carriers, the real flesh and blood people who embody them. Confucius himself takes it for granted that li has been and will be altered throughout the generations.[6] Indeed, these alterations serve him as a criterion to understand the historical changes of society. Mencius, moreover, is even more explicit in pointing out several times that whether and how li ought to be observed depends in every case on circumstances.[7] Furthermore, in the *Liji*, it says that "time is of greatest importance for li"[8] and that all other considerations are secondary. This remark, according to Jin Jingfang 金景芳, points out that "li transforms by following the times and is not invariable." She then argues that someone who studies the Confucian li and believes that one absolutely must accurately follow every single detail as described in the ancient works is someone who "swallows ancient learning without digesting it, not really understanding the li of Confucius."[9] It is for this reason that I have largely ignored, in this work, the vast ancient Chinese literature describing in detail the enactment of particular li ceremonies, rituals, and customs. As time goes by, these are all bound to become obsolete or inappropriate to the present context and need to be modified accordingly. But this does not mean that li, as customs basing themselves on traditional, formal and even ritualistic action, become obsolete. Indeed, I would say that they are even more urgent now as our contemporary societies have become larger, more individualistic, and increasingly fragmented.

The present work has attempted to draw out the most productive, positive, and creative aspects of li by restricting itself to the philosophical teachings of the early Confucians. At the same time, it is not an attempt to reconstruct the "original" Confucian philosophy of ancient times. The assumption is that such a reconstruction is in any case impossible. Instead, an effort has been made to provide a responsible reading and interpretation of the ancient Confucian philosophy. Additionally, I have sought to enrich the Confucian insights by means of a hermeneutical engagement with a number of Western philosophical sources. This can be seen as a way to "update" or "modernize" these insights, but no less to align them with ideas and points of view more familiar to Western readers in order to facilitate their utilization. The early Confucian thinkers are particularly attractive in that they emphasized the flexible nature of li in its role for both personal education and social order: while a certain structure is maintained, there is considerable room within that structure to personalize and reinterpret li with regard to who is involved and how things are momentarily configured.

As any social philosophy, however, Confucianism is not immune to difficulties, and in actual history, the inherent demands for unceasing creative interpretation and reinterpretation, with all the fuzziness that they entail, were not always met. Whitehead seems to speak to this problem when he says that "[i]n the history of education, the most striking phenomenon is that schools of learning, which at one epoch are alive with a ferment of genius, in a succeeding generation exhibit merely pedantry and routine."[10] Probably the greatest danger for Confucianism consists in political obstacles to its healthy and creative practice, not only deliberate misappropriations but also the formation of social circumstances that restrain the creative elements of li.[11] As Wang Hongyu has pointed out, "the cultural phenomenon of Confucianism has historically led to patterns of moralized governance that are incapable of providing adequate critical regulation of the political system."[12] One reason for the unfortunate formation of such patterns is the temptation to invent a single Confucian tradition with a stable set of ideas, values, and texts. In the political history of Confucianism, such a construction was an important political and ideological strategy employed by Confucians. Today, it is an intellectual strategy of simplification used by some scholars writing about the tradition and its historical development. Already during the Han dynasty, such a scheme aimed at implementing institutionalization, requiring codification of the transmitted teachings.[13]

The emergence of such codification can be seen as early as in the *Lunyu* itself. In book 16, which belongs to another compilation and is written in the state of Qu and not Lu as the others, the open-endedness of Confucius's own philosophy is there sacrificed for, as François Jullien puts it, "flat cataloging (such as the three types of advantageous friends and the three types of injurious friends; the three types of advantageous enjoyment and the three types of injurious enjoyment). In losing its power to indicate, the Confucian proposition becomes catechism." Jullien also points out that under the Han, Confucianism's "success was its downfall." "The Confucian openness is . . . transformed into its opposite: the codification of moralism."[14]

One of the more serious consequences of the codification of li is a collapse of the vital complementarity of the inner and the outer: the *neisheng* 內聖 will eventually be sacrificed for the *waiwang* 外王, although the words remain intact and the *waiwang* still pretends to be *neisheng* on the basis of seemingly impeccable external appearance. Needless to say, this goes immediately against the Confucian philosophy, as exemplified by the *Wuxing* essay as well as by Confucius himself: "When speaking time and again of ritual propriety, how could I just be talking about jade and silk?"[15] It is precisely a defining feature of *xiao ren* 小人, "petty persons," in contrast to junzi 君子, that the former lack the inner potency (*de* 德) emanating from authentic moral worth that enables them to influence and stimulate others through their actions. In their vanity, petty persons aspire to an art of dissimulation but betray their real character through their display of inauthenticity. This is why Confucius laments that "formerly, those who studied did so for the sake of themselves, but nowadays, those who study do so for the sake of others."[16]

To study for the sake of others means to try to win the favor of others by showing off one's smartness, a kind of behavior typical for xiao ren.[17]

A codification of the Confucian teachings, leading to a rupture between external performance and internal significance, eventually results in a "victory" of the former over the latter, of "jade and silk" over *de*. The danger of such a situation arising, where *de* is simply dissimulated through external performance, was far from being unnoticed by the first Confucian thinkers. Confucius says of the "village worthy" (*xiangyuan* 鄉愿), a character similar to the petty person, but one who seems better capable of putting up the appearance of having noble intent, that he "spoils *de*,"[18] in the sense, as Waley comments, of spoiling the market for something. He gives, in other words, *de* a bad name, which might result in people's lack of interest in striving for it. Commenting on Confucius's words, Mencius expresses his fear that the village worthy be "confused with *de*."[19]

In a situation where the distinction between real and false *de* has become blurry, an art of dissimulation would be a tempting art to learn, and there are a number of passages in the Confucian corpus that may be equally tempting to misinterpret. Consider the following passage in the *Mencius*. When Duke Ding of Teng passes away, his son, the crown prince, who enjoys little reputation among the elders and officials in the state, asks Mencius for advice. Mencius tells him to observe the strict three-year mourning period. The elders and the officials, however, are opposed, since it does not accord with tradition in Teng. Mencius still manages to convince the crown prince to go for the three-year period. The crown prince, subsequently, "remained in his hut for five months and gave no commands or precepts. All his officials and kinsmen allowed that he was behaving most wisely. When the time of the funeral arrived, those who came from all over to observe it were greatly pleased with his mournful facial expression and grief of silent tears."[20]

Thus ends the passage, indicating, of course, that the crown prince succeeded in displaying his inner potency or virtue, his *de*, through his gestures. It further suggests his courage and sense of responsibility by changing the received tradition and appropriating—in the sense of personalizing—the proper response to the circumstances at hand. However, in a state in which Confucianism has been institutionalized, and the complementarity of the inner and the outer has been undermined, this passage *could* be seen as a motivation to simply dissimulate a proper response. And if the customs of interaction have been sufficiently codified so that the focus will turn to one's ability to imitate preestablished external patterns, a *xiao ren* might very well get away with such hypocritical mimicry. In such a situation, li ends up being incapable of defending itself to accusations of representing merely "the outer husk rather than the inner kernel."

Another negative consequence of the codification of li is the construction of rigid hierarchies among people based on gender, individual status at birth, or other such contingencies. For instance, Confucianism has frequently been criticized for being a sexist and repressive ideology, designed to maintain the dominance of men over women and of politicians over the common people, often with a reference to Confucius's elaboration on zhengming 正名, namely, that a "prince should be a prince, minister a minister, father a father, and son a son."[21] Allusions are even more frequent to the "Three-Bond Doctrine" (*sangang* 三纲) according to which the wife, the son, and the subject ought to be completely submissive to, respectively, the husband, the father, and the ruler. Many have pointed out that this is an instance of a non-Confucian doctrine that came to be absorbed, most likely for purposes of "convenience," into the institutionalized Confucian state ideology of the Han dynasty, and "is discussed only in *The Hanfeizi*, a legalist text, and not mentioned anywhere in the Confucian classics."[22] While this is certainly true, the practice was nevertheless easily incorporated in the Confucian "system," which suggests that Confucians were susceptible to fixed regulations and reified practices.

The fact of the matter is that as a living, everyday practice, Confucianism is extremely demanding. One does not become a junzi without much effort and persistence. And Confucius, being keenly aware of this, is also a demanding teacher. His teachings require an always active vigilance and entail a consistent insistence upon the application of our informed judgment to interpret and reinterpret the circumstances in which we happen to find ourselves in every moment of our mundane lives. Confucius refuses to tell his disciples what to do, for it is precisely their responsibility to cultivate their abilities to creatively apply the insights gained from their cultural legacy in new situations and thus to carry the tradition forward. For a Confucian, as Roger Ames has remarked, "there is no respite." He goes on to explain that "*li* requires the utmost and relenting attention in every detail of what one does at every moment that one is doing it, from the drama of the high court to the posture one assumes in going to sleep, from the reception of honored guests to the proper way to comport oneself when alone, from how one behaves in formal dining situations to appropriate extemporaneous gestures."²³ Confucius emphasizes persistence in learning and exemplifies this through his own conduct and attitude.²⁴ He also has high expectations of his disciples. Consider the following two sayings from the *Lunyu*:

> I do not open the way for students who are not driven with eagerness; I do not supply a vocabulary for students who are not trying desperately to find the language for their ideas. If, when showing students one corner and they do not return with the other three, I do not repeat myself.
>
> There is nothing I can do for those who are not constantly asking themselves: "What to do? What to do?"²⁵

Who might those be for whom Confucius can do something? Who are capable of constantly asking themselves "What to do? What to do?"? Unquestionably, Confucius's own disciples are eager in their effort to learn. But it is clear that only a few of them seem to have what it takes. After all, Confucius is reluctant to concede that anyone can be said to have obtained the high moral status of ren 仁,²⁶ and he explicitly says that he will never meet a sage, a sheng 聖.²⁷ To be sure, ren, which I have translated here, however unsatisfactorily, as "communal humanity," is not something reached once and for all, but rather describes a steadfast disposition in one's social attitudes and actions that endeavors to take into consideration all the various interests simultaneously at play, and is practiced through the observance of li.²⁸ Thus, he says that his favorite but prematurely deceased student, Yan Hui, "was able to keep his thoughts and feelings (xin 心) bent on ren for three months without departing from it, while ren only appears once in a while in the thoughts and feelings of the others."²⁹

The teachings of Confucius should certainly make our lives better—but, as it would seem at first, not easier. Yet, Confucius seems to have cultivated himself to such an extent that he achieved a spontaneous and rather carefree relationship with his surroundings: "The Master said: 'When I was fifteen, my heart was set on learning; at thirty, I took my stance; at forty, I was no longer perplexed; at fifty, I had realized the heavenly forces of circumstance; at sixty, my ear was attuned; at seventy, I could give my thoughts and feelings free rein without overstepping the boundaries.'"³⁰ By seventy, then, the Master had apparently acquired such a profound sense of his social environment and circumstances that this sense had become, as it were, his second nature, and no deliberation, no conscious thought of established li customs, was required. This seems very desirable indeed. But it took a long time and undoubtedly much persistence. After all, he was seventy! And yet, he still refuses to acknowledge his own sagacity or communal humanity.[31] How many people have the endurance to strive in every moment of their lives toward a goal that still falls short of the stated ideals? Could this perhaps be Confucianism's Achilles' heel—that it is unrealistically demanding?

Certainly, Confucius himself is aware of just how demanding his teachings are. He sometimes alludes to individuals who are incapable of following the way, who seek to appear sophisticated in their actions while actually only imitating external, mechanized forms that dissimulate genuine sophistication.[32] Ranyou, for instance, Confucius's somewhat mediocre disciple, appears not to have the required strength to travel the way.[33]

On closer inspection, however, there is more to the case of Ranyou. While motivated and wanting to learn, he appears to lag behind in comparison with his fellow disciples. But he still continues. Ranyou may not be as talented and creative as the others, but he clearly feels that his studies are doing something for him. It is of course the case, as Neville has observed, that "most of us are good people with very murky characters, extremely imperfect love, little steady connection with excellence, and with lazy habits that turn rituals to stultifying repetition rather than creativity."[34] Despite our many flaws, we all enjoy improvement, however slight it may be. Motivation may therefore turn out to be the most vital factor. By insisting that anyone can become a sage, Mencius seeks to provide such a psychological motivation. And Confucius strongly indicates that a well-traveled journey will be both pleasant and rewarding. Time and again, Confucius describes "fondness of learning" (*hao xue* 好學) as a sort of necessary prerequisite for the journey. And it is surely no coincidence that the initial passage of the *Lunyu* should express the profound pleasure found in the combination of learning and applying what one has learned. It precisely sets the tone for the task at hand. Thus, the task of cultivating oneself certainly requires effort, but it is simultaneously an enjoyable process that provides significance and direction to our lives. One should certainly worry about one's progress during the process, but this worry is a cultivated habit of alertness to one's role and responsibility in every situation rather than some kind of oppressive sensation of dread. Fondness of learning leads to such alertness, and, if adequate, the likelihood is that the learning will be well applied in one's responses, again leading to the pleasure of which Confucius speaks in the initial passage of the *Lunyu*. Moreover, as Confucius says, "exemplary persons are calm and unperturbed, while petty persons are always agitated and anxious."[35] Persistently practicing li in order to figure out and deal with one's social environment will, after all, eventually make one's life "easier" in some sense of that word. Thus, what matters is not the ultimate goal, but the journey itself. In any case, an ultimate goal seems logically excluded in a world of constant change, and, importantly, we are not, in the practice of li, vying for a ticket to "Heaven," but trying to lead better and more meaningful lives here and now.

Confucius's insistence that he will never meet a sage, his refusal to point out a ren 仁 in real life, his denial that he himself is either sage or ren—all these should therefore be understood as performative pedagogical assertions. One the one hand, of course, modesty is a necessary condition for successful self-cultivation; but on the other, Confucius believes in inspirational exemplary behavior to be emulated, not imitated. If li, the matrix for self-cultivation, are to be appropriate and instructive, they must be creative and sincere exertions on behalf of the practitioners themselves. Having at one's disposal an acknowledged living sage or person of communal humanity, however, entails the temptation to superficially imitate that person's behavior and thus reify the li customs. Sheng 聖 and ren 仁 are therefore more aptly understood as some sort of regulative ideals that may guide us along the way but are eventually beyond reach. Indeed, the following passages from the *Lunyu* are strongly indicative of such thinking:

> The Master said: "Engage in learning as though you cannot reach it and as though you fear you are going to lose it."
>
> Yan Hui said with a deep sigh: The more I look up at it, the higher it soars; the more I penetrate into it, the harder it becomes. While looking at it in front of me, it is suddenly behind me. The Master succeeds in leading me forward, step by step at a time; he broadens me with culture and disciplines me through li 禮. Should I want to quit, I could not. And when I have depleted my abilities, it is as though something rises up right in front of me. But even though I want to follow it, there is no path to take."[36]

There is no end to the process of learning. Indeed, Xunzi states this quite explicitly in the very first sentence of the voluminous work bearing his name. The human being's cultivation and refinement is an ongoing process that demands that we always "do our utmost" (*zhong* 忠).

It follows then that Confucianism should be so demanding that it virtually requires, to borrow and reconstrue a Maoist term, a "continuous revolution" in the individual can hardly be considered an argument against it. It is true, however, as Confucius himself admits, that there are those that will opt for dissimulation and thus contribute to a codification of its practices. But neither does this simple fact devalue its teachings. We live in a world that is increasingly overpopulated, in which our scarce resources are unequally distributed, and in which egotism and greed are perhaps the main sources of our ills. It is but natural that citizens of a global community should make more demands of each other—and that each should make more demands of him- or herself.

As a mode of respectful interpersonal action, li is meant to ensure that disputes arising between people remain and can be mediated on a personal level. This is why Confucius prefers the application of li to the application of law or governmental decrees, for human life revolves predominantly around social issues involving other persons, and thus a maximally harmonious society requires that its citizens preside over a capacity to communicate effectively with one another. In this respect, li contains a profound critical element that can be aimed at modern, and perhaps in particular, Western, societies. The heavy reliance upon law as absolute principles in the West is one of the consequences of the rationalization of modernity. To a Confucian thinker, such a principle may easily become a sort of dogma and thus has a negative effect on personal edification, which demands the continuous effort of evaluation and reevaluation of the ever new situations at hand. It is tempting to understand one of Confucius's sayings as an implicit criticism of an overly principled mode of thinking: instead of producing a society of junzi, who seek harmony, we produce one of xiao ren, who seek sameness.[37] Such thinking leads to a disregard for the situational and the particular, and results in the general inability to act "appropriately" (yi 義) and according to circumstances.

Advocating thus for li is of course not to suggest that we abandon the idea of principles or laws and leave the question of appropriate behavior to the whims of each and everyone. But we may have let our principles "spoil" us, in the pedagogical sense of that term, such that we leave too much of the social interaction that comes with communal living up to impersonal bureaucratic processes. When a conflict arises on a personal level, we tend to seek, not a *solution* through personal engagement, but *resolution* through professional representation within the frame of law. As everyone knows, there is another important reason for such behavior, and, interestingly, Confucius seems to speak to it directly when he says that "[a] junzi understands what is appropriate; a xiao ren understands what is of personal advantage."[38]

Hence, an overly firm reliance upon law and principles constitutes a part of the development that has produced the impersonal, tension-ridden societies of today. However, an antagonism to inviolable principles is not without its problems. The tendency to aim above all at collective harmony and peace can result in gross injustice against individuals, whereby the sacrifice of the few is justified for the sake of the well-being of the many. Moreover, as Albert H. Y. Chen has pointed out, a nonprincipled mediation through li instead of a principled litigation through law may be ineffective in situations where the disputing parties are hierarchically unequal, such that the less powerful party is compelled to accept the compromise reached through the mediation, and may in the end obtain less than his or her due.[39] In such a case, justice based on flexible li morality instead of on fixed law appears to fail, and the more powerful are able to exploit the less powerful by taking advantage of the flexibility of the "system." To this a Confucian could of course respond that such persons would be xiao ren and that a junzi should simply avoid them. But if the junzi allow xiao ren to obtain the important offices and the larger material wealth of society, then what hope can they have of exerting a significant edifying influence on the people?

We face many dilemmas and, for all our advances in science and technology, find no simple solutions. There is, in any case, no simple blueprint for the perfect society. Any blueprint is self-refuting through its stagnant nature. A good society requires constant nurture and hard work to remain good. This was quite clear to the early Confucians, and this is what makes their sophisticated treatment of ritual and social values still relevant to our contemporary societies, which have undergone vast changes in the last few centuries and are certainly much more complex than they used to be. Science, technology, global capitalism, and mass media and communication have radically transformed our ways of valuing, living, and coexisting. And yet human life has not necessarily become inherently different as a result. Now as before, a well-functioning society requires a meaningful level of cohesion and cooperation, but also deference and intrahuman respect. And, perhaps even more important, a well-functioning society also requires the will to personal cultivation. Without the motivation to improve oneself, to become "better" at living with others, one will hardly be capable of envisioning a "good life" as consisting in anything beyond the simple accumulation of material goods. This acquisitive disposition in the "last human being" is probably the most dangerous threat to human civilization at present.

The present work has been composed by an "outsider," but one who has learned to greatly admire the Confucian approach to the world and its edifying philosophy of humanization. It was written in the twofold hope that, first, the Confucian philosophy can function, if not as a direct source of transformation in the West, then at least as an inspiration for Westerners to revisit and rethink their own rich humanist tradition, one which encourages the development of the human being's finest sensibilities of which the world is presently in much need; and that second, in the growing *anomie* of Chinese society at present, it may remind people of the virtually inexhaustible heritage of wisdom contained in and constituting Chinese culture—a wisdom, if productively interpreted and applied, which can no doubt enable the Chinese people to realize, in these disorientating times, "where they should place their hands and feet."

Notes

Introduction

1. Camus (1966), p. 44.
2. Gadamer (1990), p. 301.
3. Cf. Warnke (1987), p. 114.
4. Gadamer (1990), p. 302.
5. Warnke (1987), pp. 114–15.
6. Nietzsche (1967–1977), §3.12.
7. Cf. an illuminating discussion of Nietzsche's perspectivism in Parkes (1994), esp. pp. 289ff.
8. Whitehead (1938), pp. 9–10.
9. Ibid., p. 11.
10. Weber (1988a), p. 175.
11. Ibid., pp. 175ff.
12. Whitehead (1938), p. 11.
13. Ibid., p. 2.
14. This tendency is of course subject to some qualifications. First, the consensus will hardly be complete. There is always room for some disagreement, but this disagreement will mostly be about details that have no major impact on the understanding of the ideas in general. Second, there may occur, at some point, radical changes in a culture's ideology that completely transform its attitude to the ideas, and a new "orthodox" understanding of them emerges. This second possibility, however, is more of an exception and may even be a mere temporary state of affairs after which the previous attitude will be restored in a slightly modified form.
15. *Zhuangzi* 60/22/78. Unless otherwise specified—for example, by reference to existing English translations—all translations of non-English sources are my own.
16. Cited in Legge (1967), vol. 1, p. 11.
17. Ames (2011), p. 173.
18. Cf. Hall and Ames (1987), p. 85; Zou Changlin (2000), p. 329.
19. Hall and Ames (1987), p. 87.
20. Vandermeersch (1994), p. 144.

21. Cited in Vandermeersch (1994), p. 145.

22. In fact, this is also the sense that li evokes in the People's Republic of China. Zou Changlin (2000), p. 329, notes that due to political and social events in the twentieth century, especially during the May fourth movement and the cultural revolution, the notion of li is not only considered with suspicion, but as downright "reactionary." This may also account for the relative lack of consideration given to it by contemporary Chinese philosophers. It suffices to take a couple of fairly recent examples. In an otherwise ambitious explication of the categories of Chinese philosophy by Ge Rongjin (2001), li does not receive a separate discussion and is only considered briefly in its relation with zhongyong 中庸 (p. 566) and ren 仁 (p. 703). In a similar study by Zhang Dainian, li is omitted altogether. The translator notes in his preface that while this may be "the most obvious omission," Zhang is of the firm opinion that li "is not a philosophical term" (Zhang Dainian 2002a, p. xvii).

23. That Weber's oeuvre has generally been misunderstood as an attempt to trace back the "progress" and "success" of Western capitalism to the "rationalized" modes of Protestantism exemplifies the rather dogmatic belief in progress of this period. Though this misconstrual of Weber's thesis still lingers among academics, it should be evident that he was mainly concerned with—and even more concerned *about*—the cultural consequences of the religiously inspired rational capitalism and in particular, the (rather unattractive) kind of humanity produced in the process. See Weber's own clarifying remarks in Winckelmann (1978), p. 303. A thorough consideration of this perspective in Weber's work would call for a complete rereading of his studies of Confucianism and Daoism, but it can obviously not be undertaken here.

24. Cited in Bell (1997), p. 254.

25. Bell (1997), p. 254.

26. Herbert Fingarette, in his well-known analysis of the Confucian li, is a good example in point. He argues that despite all appearances, our allegedly informal Western societies are in fact permeated by ceremonial behavior and that it is precisely "in the medium of ceremony that the peculiarly human part of our life is lived" (Fingarette 1972, p. 14).

27. Bell (1997), pp. 254–55.

28. I am thinking especially of philosophers such as Jürgen Habermas and John Rawls, both of whom argue for the importance of retaining and developing further the Enlightenment notion of reason. There are, however, others who emphasize the importance of finding a synthesis between reason and tradition—for example, Alasdair MacIntyre and Hans-Georg Gadamer, though the former still tends toward a rather fixed notion of reason. There are in any case few if any philosophers who would deny that reason plays an enormously important role in improving the human condition.

29. Some commentators and translators appear to attempt to downplay the ritual aspect of li. Thus, for example, Ames (2011), as already mentioned, speaks

of "propriety through one's roles and relations"; Liu Shu-hsien (1998) calls it simply "propriety"; and Chen Jingpan (1990), p. 249, uses "the rules of proper conduct," though with the important caveat that "the Chinese moral concept of the term *Li* like that of *Jen* [ren] has really no exact equivalent in English."

30. Cf. Bell (1997), p. 150. Frits Staal, focusing on the subjective aspect of ritual performance, claims that ritual is essentially a formalized sequence of movements and utterances that has no meaning external to itself: "The performers are totally immersed in the proper execution of their complex tasks. Isolated in their sacred enclosure, they concentrate on correctness of act, recitation, and chant. The primary concern, if not obsession, is with rules. There are no symbolic meanings going through their minds when they are engaged in performing ritual" (Staal 1979, p. 3). "Ritual," Staal says elsewhere (1989), p. 433, "may be defined, in approximate terms, as a system of acts and sounds, related to each other in accordance with rules without meaning." Similarly, Roy A. Rappaport (1999), p. 24, takes "'ritual' to denote *the performance of more or less invariant sequences of formal acts and utterances not entirely encoded by the performers*" (italics in original). It is significant, I believe, that neither Staal nor Rappaport includes a discussion of the Confucian li in their treatment of ritual.

31. See Tu Weiming, Hejtmanek, and Wachman (1992), p. 5.

32. On this latter point, cf. Gay Garland Reed, who argues that Lei Feng, the working hero presented by the Communist regime to the Chinese people for emulation in the 1960s, "represented a proletarianized version of earlier Confucian prototypes" (Reed 1998, p. 360).

Chapter One. First Assemblage: Tradition and Timeliness

1. According to numerous scholars, this applies even still to contemporary Chinese society. See for instance Bell (1997), p. 148; Tu Weiming, Hejtmanek, and Wachman (1992), pp. 95–96. Hui Jixing (1996), p. 58, says, "Li is the crux of the formation and preservation of the unique type and nature of Chinese culture; it is Chinese culture's unifying and conserving spirit." The same view would seem to be at least strongly implied by Zou Changlin (2000), pp. 15ff., in his claim that li is the foundation of Chinese culture.

2. Kant (1923), p. 35.

3. Marx (1965), pp. 9–10.

4. In 1958, Lu Dingyi, then a member of the Chinese Communist Politburo, wrote that carrying a "combination of education with productive labour into effect means a fight with the old traditions that have persisted for thousands of years.... Today, in our educational work, vigorous efforts are being made to pull down the out-dated and set up the new" (cited in Solomon, 1979, p. 159. It is worth noting, though, in this context, that the seeds of suspicion toward tradition had already been sown in China before a Marxist-based ideology became

dominant with the founding of the People's Republic. The extreme reverence for tradition among the Qing emperors is generally seen to be the main reason for China's scientific and economic stagnation during the "modern" period, resulting in catastrophic and humiliating defeats against the more modernized "sea-barbarians" of the West and Japan in the nineteenth century. After the overthrow of the Qing dynasty and the founding of the Republic of China, the protagonists of modern China were generally antagonistic to anything traditional. Tran Van Doan (Chen Wentuan) (1994), pp. 129–30, writes that these early twentieth-century intellectuals, and, in fact, "most . . . reform-minded Chinese up to recent times [held that] tradition was nothing but corruption, decadence, obsolescence. . . and this tradition was nothing other than Confucianism." The mentality fostered in such an atmosphere, especially after the catastrophe of World War I, an event which tended to be attributed to "liberal" decadence, was clearly favorable for a "progressive" philosophy such as Marxism to gain a foothold in Chinese culture.

5. On this issue, see for example Weber (1988a), p. 152; MacIntyre (1984), pp. 51ff.; Gadamer (1990), pp. 283–84.

6. My frequent use of the word "tradition" in its singular form in this work is an abstraction for the purposes of simplification. I use it in a sense close to its etymological meaning (or to the German *Überlieferung*) to refer to that which is handed down from generation to generation. It therefore does not carry the implication that a tradition can be clearly demarcated by an exclusive identification or "ownership" of its practices and customs. I think there are few, if any such traditions, and that any fairly complex combination of behaviors and practices to which we may assign the label "tradition" is always constituted by a multiplicity of traditions.

7. Dewey (1922), p. 16.

8. Aristotle (1941), 1253a.

9. MacIntyre (1984), p. 222.

10. Gadamer (1990), p. 284.

11. Ibid., p. 285. Eliot Deutsch underscores the relationship between ritual and tradition, whereby, as he says, the former is sustained by the latter. He then offers an insight similar to Gadamer's regarding the mode of authority enjoyed by tradition, but with a specific reference to ritual: "An orthopraxy becomes its rule, so that more often than not the answer to why one does a particular ceremonial/ritual act is, 'That is the way it is done'" (Deutsch 1991, pp. 16–17).

12. Perhaps a good exemplification of the historical misapprehension of the concept of tradition is that it has been rediscovered by left-wing political thinkers who have incorporated it in their political philosophy. Andrej Grubacic (2003), for example, an outspoken anarchist, emphasizes the productive import of tradition as something "handed down" or "transmitted." This meaning of tradition, he says, "relates to the new and creative way of reviving the experience of tradition. Such a, let us say immediately, positive way of conveying, has been put into effect of the other side of the general human nature, provisionally deemed revolutionary, along the lines of paradoxically expressed

truth: a wish for a change and, at the same time, a healthy need to remain the same." Grubacic's reevalued anarchistic position would seem to have much in common with Deutsch's notion of "creative anarchism" in his "Community as Ritual Participation."

13. Cf. MacIntyre (1984), p. 221.
14. Gadamer (1990), p. 286.
15. *Lunyu* 2.15.
16. Cf. Hall and Ames (1987), pp. 44–45. See also Waley's (1997) note to his translation of this passage, p. 19.
17. *Lunyu zhijie* (1997), p. 12.
18. MacIntyre (1984), p. 223.
19. *Lunyu* 3.14. The modern belief in the "holy trinity" of philosophy, reason, and progress, combined with the widespread tendency to classify all kinds of traditionalism as obscurantism has resulted in the all too commonly held view that there is little philosophical substance in the thought of Confucius and thus, as argued by Chad Hansen, that "we may eventually be forced into acquiescing in the growing consensus that Confucius was an apologist for a feudal code of ethics" (Hansen 1976, pp. 203–4).
20. Schwartz (1996), p. 51.
21. In his celebrated novel, *Frøken Smillas fornemmelse for sne* (*Smilla's Sense of Snow*), the Danish writer Peter Høeg plays with the abundance of words for various kinds of snow and ice in one of Greenland's dialects, all of which, however, can only be translated into Danish, and, for that matter, most other Western languages, by adding one or more qualifying adjectives to the noun "snow" or "ice."
22. Cf., for example, Hall and Ames (1987), p. 294; Bauer (2001), p. 31.
23. François Jullien maintains that "the commentaries have not set themselves up as hermeneutics. Instead of *interpreting*, they elucidate" (Jullien 2000, p. 274). While our points certainly converge, I think that Jullien nonetheless goes too far in contrasting interpretation and elucidation. Interpretation always implies elucidation. The problem, I suspect, is that among Westerners the term "interpretation" is automatically associated with a quest for the "objective" or the "one and only true" meaning. As discussed in the introduction, however, such an understanding fails to grasp the nature of interpretation, which requires creativity, elucidation, and adaptability. Perhaps the most explicit expression of the Chinese hermeneutic tradition is found in the statement by the Song dynasty philosopher Lu Jiuyuan 陸九淵 (Xiangshan 象山, 1139–1193) that just as "the six classics interpret me, I interpret the six classics [六經注我，我注六經]" (Lu Jiuyuan 2000, p. 24). Cf. also Chun-chieh Huang who says, speaking of the neo-Confucians' reading of the *Mencius*: "During the prolonged dialogues back and forth among [Zhu Xi] and his disciples we never find them regarding the *Mencius* as an objective text unrelated to their personal lives. They all blended their life experiences into their various readings of the *Mencius*" (Huang 2001, p. 258).

24. The discourse can then of course be further developed externally, which has been, and, moreover, is taking place in these very pages.

25. Hall and Ames (1987), pp. 294–95.

26. It is illuminating, in this particular case, that zheng 政, "to govern," is explained in the *Shuowen jiezi* with its homonym zheng 正, "proper" or "to make proper." Xunzi also emphasizes this prescriptive root of the word "to govern." Cf. Knoblock (1994), vol. 3, p. 149.

27. *Lunyu* 13.3.

28. Ren Jiyu (1966), vol. 1, p. 68.

29. Ge Rongjin (2001), p. 386.

30. Knoblock (1994), vol. 3, pp. 116–18.

31. Ge Rongjin (2001), p. 386. This "consequences-intentions" confusion seems in fact rather common. Mao Chen (1995, p. 3), in his otherwise rather careful and sophisticated study of the May fourth movement, states, without further elaboration, that "Confucius, the traditional authority in pre-modern China, imposed rigidities upon Chinese culture [sic] and had an influence that extended well into the modern period."

32. Jullien (1995), p. 260.

33. Ames and Hall (2003), p. 57; cf. also Ames and Hall (2001), p. 63, and Ames and Rosemont Jr. (1998), p. 45, where similar explanations are provided. In fact, Ames and Rosemont (1998), p. 45, come close to my suggestion by saying that "to realize the *dao* is to experience, to interpret, and to influence the world in such a way as to reinforce and extend the way of life inherited from one's cultural predecessors." Ames and Hall (2003), pp. 57ff., in their translation of the *Daodejing*, seem indeed to elaborate on this idea by translating dao as "way-making."

34. *Lunyu* 7.1.

35. *Lunyu zhijie* (1997), p. 12.

36. *Liji* 32.28/146/26–27; *Liji zhijie* (2000), p. 448.

37. *Lunyu* 2.11.

38. Cf. Lin Li (2002), p. 321.

39. The root of the word "appropriate" is the Latin *proprius*, meaning "one's own." In Confucian thought, it is the character yi 義 that expresses this complex thought of appropriateness. See Hall and Ames (1987), esp. p. 105.

40. MacIntyre (1984), p. 222.

41. The conventional English translation of junzi 君子 is "gentleman," which, however, due to its unfortunate sexism, is unacceptable. As the characters for junzi imply, it signifies a lord and is in fact synonymous with "lord" or "nobleman." But it is a prescriptive term indicating the moral, cognitive, and affective qualities that a true lord *ought to* possess. The junzi is thus Confucius's consummate person, someone who has become noble and refined through self-cultivation and learning. In recent years, a multitude of translations have been proposed for this difficult term, none of which, in my opinion, catches the original junzi. I shall therefore leave it untranslated in the following. Cf. also an illuminating discussion of junzi by Antonio S. Cua (2003), pp. 329ff.

42. Bell (1997), p. 256.
43. Bourdieu (1990), p. 25.
44. Ibid., pp. 80–81.
45. Ibid., p. 81.
46. Tang Junyi (1988), pp. 111–12.
47. Cf. Deutsch (1992), p. 117.
48. Tang Junyi (1988), p. 112.

49. As Tang himself points out (1988), p. 112, his interpretation of these characters can be further supported by the *Shuowen jiezi*, which explains the two characters through their mutual reference.

50. Another way of explaining the Chinese cosmology of process is through the notion of *qi* 氣, the psychophysical energy of which the world is made according to the classical Chinese worldview. Not only does qi exclude the possibility of a matter-spirit dualism by being the source of both the material and the spiritual aspects of reality, but it also incorporates, so to speak, the notion of time by virtue of being its own source of constant motion and change.

51. Tang Junyi (1988), p. 122.
52. Jullien (1995), p. 15.
53. This will be explored further in chapter 3.
54. *Lunyu* 9.17.

55. In his *Yuanshi rujia daojia zhexue* 原始儒家道家哲學. Cited in Tang Yinan (2000), p. 280.

56. Cited in Tang Yinan (2000), p. 280.

57. Zhang Xianglong (1999), p. 55, refers to the *Yijing* as "the 'gene' of Chinese culture [that] shaped it in every respect, from calendar, medicine, military arts, architecture, literary, and graphic arts, to morality and socio-political thought."

58. Cf. Hall and Ames (1987), pp. 238–39.
59. Chen Lai (2001), pp. 107–8.

60. Cf. Tang Yinan (2000), p. 278; Ren Junhua (2001), pp. 30–31. While Confucius may not be the author of the *Yizhuan*, there is much to indicate that he knew the *Yijing* and studied it. In the *Lunyu*, there are, in fact, two references to the text. First, in 7.17, Confucius asks that he be given a few more years so that he will have had fifty years to study the *Yijing*, and thereby be able to avoid serious mistakes. Admittedly, the authenticity of this passage is not beyond question, as some versions of the *Lunyu* do not contain such a reference. See for example Ames and Rosemont (1998), p. 241n108. Second, in 13.22, though not mentioning the *Yijing* by name, Confucius quotes the exact words of the commentary to hexagram 32, heng 恆, or constancy.

61. Graham (1989), p. 368.

62. Tu Weiming (1985), p. 39. It is not uncommon to portray time in Chinese thought as proceeding according to the forms of either a cycle or a spiral. For example, Tang Yinan (2000), pp. 284–85, argues for the former, while Tang Junyi (1988), pp. 118–120, argues for the latter. There is some truth in all of these formulations, but it depends of the aspect on which one focuses.

Ancient Chinese views of history in a broader sense often emphasize the order of recurrent events (e.g., the seasons) and can thus be termed "cyclic" from that point of view. On the other hand, the order can be seen as "spiral" in the sense that novel phenomena also emerge along with the recurrent ones. However, Tu Weiming's point, as I take it, is that these accounts imply an order ascribed to reality that is too rigorous and can therefore be misleading. While there is certainly some order in the process of reality, it is nevertheless ultimately indeterminate.

63. Zhang Dainian (2002b), p. 105.

64. Ge Rongjin (2001), p. 556.

65. These two clusters of meaning of the same character are in fact distinguished verbally in modern Chinese through a difference in tones. The former is pronounced in the first tone while the latter in the fourth. This tonal differentiation had its equivalence also in classical Chinese.

66. *Lunyu* 13.3.

67. Cf. Zhang Xianglong (1999), pp. 50–51.

68. Cf. Tang Yinan (2000), pp. 285–86. In the language of Zhang Xianglong (1999), p. 55, "'following Time' is not 'opportunism' but 'opportunity-making.'"

69. *Yizhuan* interpretation of the hexagram Meng 蒙. *Zhouyi. A Concordance to Yi Ching*, 5/4. Cf. also Tang Mingbang (1997), p. 13; Ge Rongjin (2001), p. 559.

70. Tang Mingbang (1997), p. 12.

71. Tang Yinan (2000), p. 286. Chung-ying Cheng (1991), p. 25, also touches upon the Confucian adaptation of the notion of *shizhong* from the *Yizhuan* and its implication for creativity in human action. Cheng renders *shizhong* as "timeliness," which appears to accord with my understanding.

72. Cited in Tang Yinan (2000), p. 286. The passage is from Hui Dong's *Yishang shizhong shuo* 易尚時中說. The quotations are from the *Zhongyong*, 2, and the *Mencius* 5B.1, respectively. In the latter case, I follow the translation of D. C. Lau (1970). Zhao Zhentao et al. (1993) translate the sentence in a corresponding manner as "Confucius was the one who knew when to do what to do," and Legge (1998–2000) somewhat abstrusely, as "Confucius was the timeous one." Jullien (2000), p. 404n7, comments on the Mencius passage as follows: Confucius "is defined not by a (specific) quality but by the 'moment' (that is, what was required of him in each situation during the course of things)."

73. Ge Rongjin (2001), p. 559.

74. *Lunyu* 18.8.

75. Ge Rongjin (2001), p. 559. Cf. Jullien (1995), pp. 198–99, where he speaks of the temporally embedded situation in Chinese thought as a moral way or strategy: "Learn how to make the most of the tendency at work in the course of things; allow the setup represented by the situation simply to develop according to its tendency. Every historical situation, even the most unfavorable, is always rich in the possibility of change, since a positive development over the

more-or-less long term is always a possibility: if not now, then later. Only one has to count on the one factor that is the most influential: the factor of time."

76. Legge later changed the title radically to *The State of Equilibrium and Harmony*, presumably after having realized that *The Doctrine of the Mean* would be highly misleading.

77. The term "rational" is ambiguous, carrying a heavy cultural and historical baggage, but refers here to the notion of *logos*. *Logos* can also be understood as "discursive thought," which may be a more appropriate interpretation in this case. Tiles (2000), pp. 206–7, points out that with regard to determining the mean, Aristotle "avoids connotations of abstract calculation while keeping the association that '*logos*' has with articulate speech."

78. Thus Gadamer (1990), p. 45, says that "Greek ethics—the Pythagorean and Platonic ethics of moderation, the ethics of mesotes that Aristotle constructed—is in a profound and extensive sense an ethics of good taste." See also Tiles's (2000) lucid explication of Aristotle's notion of the mean, also including a discussion of what comes across as a similar idea in the Confucian literature, pp. 205ff.

79. *Lunyu* 11.16.

80. *Lunyu* 13.21. *Mencius* 7B.37 comments extensively on this passage. Mencius, however, speaks of zhongdao 中道 instead of zhongxing 中行, which, although practically interchangeable, supports my interpretation of "staying right on path," or following the wisdom and norms of tradition, as I will argue.

81. *Lunyu* 2.18.

82. *Mencius* 7A.26.

83. Zhang Dainian (2002a), p. 358.

84. Cf. Jullien (2000), p. 265: "[T]he golden mean has nothing in common with the half measure (aurea mediocritas: what is needed is not too much); depending on the situation, it can correspond to one extreme or another (it can mean to 'become resolutely engaged' as well as to 'withdraw,' according to the terms of the Chinese alternative, but it cannot waver)."

85. *Mencius* 7A.41.

86. *Lunyu* 19.7.

87. It is interesting, in this case, that as before, Zixia comes across as too one-dimensional in his overemphasis on learning, unless of course he means that the junzi's "shop" is the social sphere. One may speculate whether the later emphasis on "ordinary practices," as in the *Zhongyong*, is an attempt to ensure that the Confucian philosophy does not develop into a mere scholastic tradition of passive learning.

88. *Liji* 32.2/142/27–29.

89. *Liji* 32.4/143/1–2. Cf. *Lunyu* 14.28, where Confucius describes three characteristics of the way of the junzi (junzi zhi dao 君子之道), one of which consists in the wise not being "misled." The implication is comparable to the *Zhongyong* passage. "Wise" applies to someone who will generally not be

misled—this is precisely what it means to be wise. Otherwise, Confucius might say, in line with his idea of "using names correctly" (zhengming), we begin valuing things and people inappropriately by assigning wrong terms to them, and confusion reigns in society.

90. *Liji* 32.23/146/5. The *Shuowen jiezi* defines zhi 知 through its components, the "mouth" (kou 口), implying communication, and "implementing" (shi 矢), both of which constitute the semantics of the character. Thus, "know-how" is already implicit in the Chinese notion of knowing. In ancient Chinese thought, moreover, there was always a close relationship between knowledge (zhi 知) and action (xing 行). See Ge Rongjin (2001), pp. 413ff. The intimacy of this relationship found its culmination in the philosophy of Wang Yangming 王陽明 (1472–1529), who explicitly maintained "the continuity of knowledge and action" (zhixing heyi 知行合一). In his *Instructions for Practical Living* (*Chuan xi lu* 傳習錄), he says that "[k]nowledge is the design of action, action is the workmanship of knowledge. Knowledge is the beginning of action, action is the completion of knowledge. In a particular point of time, although one only speaks of knowledge, it already has action contained in it, and although one only speaks of action, it already has knowledge contained in it." Cited in Chen Lai (2001), p. 414.

91. *Lunyu* 6.22. See also a discussion by Ames and Hall (2001) of the strong practical emphasis contained in the notion of zhi, pp. 84–85.

92. Cf. *Lunyu* 17.8: "The flaw in being fond of acting wisely (zhi 知) without being fond of learning (xue 學) is that it leads to recklessness (*dang* 蕩)."

93. *Lunyu* 11.12. Cf. *Lunyu* 2.16, 7.21 and *Liji* 32.8/143/19–20.

94. The verb "to savor" derives from the Latin *sapere*, meaning "to be sensible," thus, "to taste," from which also the word "sagacity" is derived. This wordplay, I believe, does reflect the implications contained in the *Zhongyong* passage: one whose knowledge "oversteps" ordinary reality, who is unable to know things belonging to the routine of everyday life, is not really knowledgeable.

95. Ge Rongjin (2001), p. 556 [中庸即是用中之常道，要求人們常行之。].

96. Most recent interpretations of *zhongyong* tend toward positions corroborating the one I am proposing here. Tu Weiming (1976, p. 27) translates *zhongyong* as "centrality and commonality," whereby "centrality" refers to a "state of mind wherein one is absolutely unperturbed by outside forces." Ames and Hall (2001), p. 43, translate it as "focusing the familiar affairs of the day." I agree with the latter that understanding *zhongyong* as "the doctrine of the mean," in the way in which it is normally understood, is a most unfortunate interpretation that fails to make sense of the work bearing the same title. Ren Junhua (2001), pp. 130ff., also rejects any association between *zhongyong* and the Aristotelian notion of mesotes and argues that the former involves the attainment of inner and outer harmony through learning and practice: "To master '*zhongyong*' requires both learning and practice; learning brings knowledge, practice brings completion"

(p. 132). He also says that the source of this learning, as emphasized by the *Zhongyong*, is our immediate environment, "emanating from the trivial matters of our everyday life" (p. 130).

97. Cf. Chen Chaoqun (1999), p. 18, who argues, mostly on the basis of the remarks on *guo* and *bu ji*, that "the meaning of '*zhong*' in *Zhongyong* is far from being 'middle' [*zhongjian* 中間], but behavior according to a certain standard."

98. *Daodejing* 47. I follow Ames and Hall (2003), p. 217n126, in interpreting the passage on the basis of the Mawangdui edition, according to which the last line has the *fu* 弗 instead of the *bu* 不 negative. This causes the verb *wei* 為, "to do," to become transitive and to require an object, possibly referring to the author's disapproval in the first lines of seeking the distant at the expense of the near. In lines 4 and 5, I have followed the interpretation in *Laozi Zhuangzi zhijie* (1998), p. 28.

99. *Lunyu* 6.30.

100. *Lunyu* 7.29.

101. Cf. the "Confucius at Home at Leisure" ("Zhongni yanju" 仲尼燕居) chapter in the *Liji* 29.2/136/27: "Li is that by which one acquires the ability to hit the mark [zhong]."

102. *Lunyu* 15.29.

103. *Xunzi* 20/8/23–24.

Chapter Two. Second Assemblage: From Reason to Intelligence

1. In a casual conversation I once had with a Chinese train conductor in Hunan Province, he adamantly denied that Confucius was a philosopher (*zhexuejia* 哲學家) and insisted that he was "merely" a thinker (*sixiangjia* 思想家) and an educator (*jiaoyuxuejia* 教育學家). This view seems in fact to be fairly representative for modern China. Leng Chengjin, a well-known scholar in the fields of literature and aesthetics, states that "Confucius was a great educator," but is vague on the issue of whether he was a philosopher and only says that he was a part of the "philosophical breakthrough" during the pre-Qin era (Leng Chengjin 1999, p. 32). Chen Jingpan (2000), pp. 26ff., refers to important intellectuals during the political and intellectual turmoil in China after the foundation of the Republic in 1911, such as Hu Shi, Feng Youlan, and Lin Yutang, who all emphasize the status of Confucius as an important educator.

2. Gou Chengyi (2002), p. 364.

3. Ibid., p. 365. Cf. Ge Rongjin's (2001) rather curious gloss on Confucius's notion of zhengming, where he strongly implies that Confucius's intention was to restore the old feudalistic social order (p. 386).

4. Cf. Chen Chaoqun (1999), p. 29, who explicitly expresses this view. He, however, balances it by pointing out that there is also an important

"individualist" dimension in Confucius's philosophy. As will be discussed, these two aspects are really two sides of the same issue.

5. Cf. Snook (1972), p. 29.

6. One thinks also of the Chinese word for "propaganda," or *xuanchuan* 宣傳. In a modern Chinese dictionary, *xuanchuan* is explained in two ways: first, "to illustrate or explain something to the masses," and second, "to make the masses believe something and thereby cause them to act accordingly." The second of these explications seems to correspond to our modern pejorative notions of propaganda or indoctrination. The first, however, is value-neutral, and refers to the act of (officially) disseminating information to the people. This is, admittedly, not a word for "education," but it partially implies education in the narrower sense of providing information.

7. Nagai (1976), p. 14. Snook (1972), p. 27, points out that "whereas American writers stress method, philosophers of education in Great Britain typically argue that it is the content taught which determines whether indoctrination is taking place." Nagai's formulation therefore represents the most typical Western conceptualizations.

8. Cf. Snook (1972), p. 31.

9. From the 1932 pamphlet *Dare the School Build a New Social Order*, cited in Garrison (1986), p. 265.

10. Dewey and Childs (1933a), p. 72.

11. Ibid., p. 288.

12. Weber (1972), p. 726.

13. Weber (1988b), p. 604ff. Being a "personal choice," however, does not mean that values originate in the individual *only*. The cultural environment certainly effects value relations between the people living within it. Weber speaks in this respect of "elective affinities" (*Wahlverwandtschaften*), a tendency among culturally related people to assign similar meanings—and thus values—to similar kinds of action. Although the cultural environment will impose some limits on the possible meanings of an action, this is not a relation of necessity or determinism, but one of tendency or probability reigning between people of the same cultural group that will then find more subtle variances among people of different classes and subcultures within the larger group. What Weber means by "personal choice" is that the values, independent of their adoption, are *ultimately* that person's endorsement, which, as he stressed on several occasions, also means that they are the person's responsibility. See for example Weber (1982).

14. Weber (1972) p. 544.

15. Weber (1988a), p. 204; Weber (1988b), p. 598.

16. Nietzsche (1967–1977), vol. 4, "Zarathustras Vorrede," §5.

17. Martin Barker formulates this in such a way that "rationality itself disappears in the process, to be replaced by a *rationale per person*. . . . Who educates the educator? No one. But domination makes it appear to everyone that everyone does. Education is domination" (Barker 1980, p. 242).

18. Macmillan (1983), p. 370.

19. Snook (1972), p. 27.

20. This identification rests further upon the analytic distinction between theoretical and practical reason, distinguished merely on the basis of application and not nature. We notice this identification, or, rather, desire for identification, in the tendency in modern ethical discourse to seek a parallel between the precision of the natural sciences and a model of strategic human action in practical matters. The problem here is not merely that the methods of the natural sciences are too narrow to account adequately for human action, but also, which is actually a consequence thereof, that such a parallel will end up restricting human behavior to a culturally specific model of means-end rational deliberation in which a fixed hierarchy of values is taken for granted.

21. In modern Chinese, reason or rationality is conveyed as *lixing* 理性 or *lizhi* 理智. Interestingly, a reason for something is composed of the two: *daoli* 道理.

22. An illuminating example is Richard Wilhelm's 1910 translation of the *Daodejing*, in which he renders dao as *Sinn*. Due to the original meaning of *Sinn* as "way" or "direction," in comparison to its more recent meanings of "sense," "meaning," and "mind" or "consciousness," this translation is in many ways intriguing. However, Wilhelm justifies this choice by saying that he came upon the idea from reading Johann Wolfgang Goethe's *Faust I*, in which Faust "attempts to render the opening words of the Gospel of John . . . as: 'In the beginning there was the sense/meaning [Im Anfang war der Sinn],'" and then adds in a footnote, as if providing a perfectly self-evident justification, that "in the Chinese Bible-translations, λόγος is rendered as dao almost throughout" (Wilhelm 1976, pp. 24f).

23. This applies in particular to a rendering of dao as "reason" in early Confucian philosophy, such as by James Legge—for example, in his translation of the *Mencius* 2A.2 where qi 氣 is said to be "the mate and assistant of righteousness [yi 義] and reason [dao 道]" (Legge 1998–2000, vol. 2, p. 190).

24. Li 理 played an important role among Mohist, Daoist, Legalist, and Buddhist thinkers, but, with the exception of Xunzi, received relatively little attention from Confucian thinkers until Zhang Zai 張載 and especially the brothers Cheng Hao 程顥 and Cheng Yi 程頤 made it the central concept of Song Confucianism in the eleventh century. See Chan (1969), pp. 45ff. From there, it was fused with qi 氣 in a conceptual pair that purported to provide the key to understanding the cosmos in its operations. I shall not consider the neo-Confucian treatment here. Instead, I shall turn to Xunzi once again, who, as it happens, was deliberately ignored by the Song-Ming thinkers, but who provides the most elaborate discussion of li 理 in the classical period.

25. Cf. Weber (1988a), p. 152, who points out that the methods of the natural sciences and even mathematics are products of culture and consensus and have no claim to universal objectivity in the strict sense of the word.

26. Cf. Hall and Ames (1995), esp. pp. 11ff.

27. Aristotle (1941), for instance, uses *logos* in both of these senses. See for instance his *Politics*, 1332a, or *Ethica Nicomachea* 1134a, where he clearly intends it to mean an ethical sense of rationality. In *Metaphysics* 991b, however, he understands it as mathematical proportion or ratio.

28. Nonetheless, there are certainly differences between the Kantian *Vernunft* and classic conceptions of reason, at least as these have been usually understood. In my view, one of the main attractions of the Kantian *Vernunft* is the priority he gives to practical reason. Thus, human moral action, in a wide sense of the notion, is presented as conditioning, in a complex manner, our understanding and appraisal of the "objective" (or intersubjective) structures of reality. I believe, however, that this vital aspect of Kant's philosophy has gradually been neglected, probably due to the ultimate supremacy of the natural sciences in Western industrialized culture, so that, first, the unity of theoretical and practical reason is often ignored, and second, priority is given to its theoretical or epistemological aspect.

29. Xu Fuguan (2001), p. 290.

30. Tang Junyi (1988), pp. 125–26.

31. Tu Weiming (1985), p. 43.

32. *Liji* 32.1/142/21.

33. Cf. *Lunyu* 15.29, and p. 46 above. There are, moreover, sections in the *Mencius* that reiterate this connection; see, for example, 7A.14: "Those who are junzi [君子] transform where they pass by and work wonders where they abide. They belong to the same stream as heaven above and earth beneath."

34. John Dewey (1922), p. 196.

35. Nietzsche (1967–1977), vol. 3, §333. Perhaps an even more striking passage is the following from his unpublished manuscripts 1887–1888: "The misjudgment of passion and *reason* [*Vernunft*], as if the latter were an essence in itself and not rather a state of relation between the various passions and desires; and as if any passion did not contain a quantum of reason" (Nietzsche 1967–1977, vol. 13, §11 [310]).

36. Bourdieu (1990), p. 47.

37. Ibid., pp. 49–50.

38. Ibid., pp. 50–51. Note that by "mechanical reaction," Bourdieu refers to attempts to locate conduct in a wholly objectified and determining environment, such as in the case of "mechanized ritual" as discussed in the first section. The attribution of calculative reason to the subject as an abstract entity thus constitutes the other side of the unfortunate objectivist-subjectivist dichotomy with which he claims that the social sciences have been left.

39. Cf. also Dewey (1994), p. 246: "Scientific men, philosophers, literary persons, are not men and women who have so broken the bonds of habits that pure reason and emotion undefiled by use and wont speak through them. They are persons of a specialized infrequent habit. Hence the idea that men are moved by an intelligent and calculated regard for their own good is pure mythology.

Even if the principle of self-love actuated behavior, it would still be true that the *objects* in which men find their love manifested, the objects which they take as constituting their peculiar interests, are set by habits reflecting social customs."

40. Dewey (1944), p. 343. In this sense, in fact, Dewey's ideas present themselves as a potential response to Weber's paradox. For if reason is no longer seen as distinct from, let alone opposed to, passions and desires, then values cannot be seen in separation from reason either. Reason is in effect reinterpreted to incorporate the ability to valuate.

41. Cf. Dewey (1934) where "reason" is used only when referring to the discussion of other thinkers, but "intelligence" when Dewey elaborates on his own philosophy. Cf. also James Gouinlock's "Introduction" in Dewey (1994), p. xliv: "The faculty psychology and the epistemology upon which the conception of *reason* rested have been widely discredited. The conception of intelligence as a function of behavior is replacing the notion of an innate faculty inherently possessed of power to know."

42. "Habits" of course bring to mind the Greek *hexis* and, in this discussion, certainly have a relation with Aristotle's understanding of the term as one of the three states of the soul, in which case it probably comes closer to the modern notion of "character." See *Ethica Nicomachea* 1105b, in Aristotle (1941). For the purposes of focus, however, and because Bourdieu uses *hexis* to indicate the individual embodiment of the more socially constituted habitus, I shall avoid a potentially confusing discussion of Aristotle's account of *hexis*.

43. Dewey (1922), pp. 14ff.

44. Ibid., p. 16. To attribute behavior to an isolated self or innate instincts, Dewey says, is to take "social products for psychological originals" (Dewey 1922, p. 142).

45. Dewey (1922), p. 172.

46. Ibid., p. 176.

47. Ibid., p. 90.

48. Dewey (1993), p. 9.

49. Cf. Dewey (1934), p. 33.

50. Dewey (1944), p. 343.

51. Bourdieu (1990), p. 52.

52. Ibid., p. 56.

53. Ibid., pp. 55f.

54. Hence the English translation of the monograph's title, in the French original *Le sens pratique*, which could also be rendered as "Practical Sense."

55. I give in to the temptation here to quote a few words from J. Krishnamurti that echo the Confucian sensibility: "The moment you come to a conclusion as to what intelligence is, you cease to be intelligent. That is what most of the older people have done: they have come to conclusions. Therefore they have ceased to be intelligent. So you have found out one thing right off: that an intelligent mind is one which is constantly learning, never concluding" (Krishnamurti 1964, pp. 21–22).

56. This mode of thinking is what some have described as "correlative," as distinct from "analytic" or "causal" thinking—for example, Graham (1989), pp. 319ff. Hall and Ames (1995), pp. 124–25, write that "[f]rom the perspective of correlative thinking, to explain an item or an event is, first, to place it within a scheme organized in terms of analogical relations among the items selected for the scheme, and then to reflect, and act in terms of, the suggestiveness of these relations. Correlative thinking involves the association of image- or concept-clusters related by meaningful disposition rather than physical causation. Such thinking is a species of imagination grounded in necessarily informal and hence ad hoc analogical procedures presupposing both association and differentiation." In other words, things will be explained through their perceived or, perhaps more appropriately, constructed association with other things in their shared field. Instead of seeking to discover essence, ancient Chinese thinkers construct relations. In this way, the explained is never wholly independent of the explainer; a subject-object dichotomy never arises.

57. *Lunyu* 1.1. There is an additional line that reads: "To be unknown by others and yet to be free from frustration—is this not a junzi?"

58. Dewey (1944), pp. 10, 321.

59. *Mencius* 7A.21.

60. A good example is Irene Bloom, who claims that Mencius's arguments about xing 性 are "unfailingly inclusive and which always emphasize what human beings *in general* are like" (Bloom 1997, p. 23). She is, however, not arguing for some kind of fixed or unchangeable human nature, as she also holds that "the Mencian concept of xing is best understood as dynamic and developmental rather than static" (Bloom 1997, p. 31).

61. *Mencius* 6A.6.

62. Cf. commentary in *Mengzi zhenyi*, *Zhuzi jicheng*, vol. 1, p. 443.

63. In *Mencius* 2A.6. One could of course argue, on an etymological basis, that "emotion" implies "motion" and therefore refers both to internal and external processes. However, there is a tendency to think of emotions in an essentialist manner similarly to "feelings." We speak, for instance, of people who "don't express their emotions." Brian Bruya suggests an interpretation of qing 情 that comes close to mine, at least as it occurs in the *Lunyu* 13.4, where he explains it as "reacting (not just acting) sincerely to circumstances without duplicity" (Bruya 2003, p. 82). When discussing its use in the *Mencius*, however, Bruya opts for "spontaneous emotions" (p. 88) in an attempt to establish the absence of a semantic divide between Mencius and Xunzi in terms of qing. In my view, the terms "emotions" and "spontaneous emotions" still lack the implication of real action that I see present in Mencius's use of qing. This implication is clearer yet in the well-known saying (*chengyu* 成語), admittedly owing its origin to a much later date, or the sixth century CE: *qing bu zi jin* 情不自禁, which expresses the inability not to act (and thus react) in a certain way.

64. *Mencius* 6A.6.

65. Lau (1970), p. 11.
66. *Lunyu* 17.2.
67. Chen Jingpan (1990), p. 76.
68. Following Ames and Rosemont (1998), p. 214.
69. *Lunyu* 18.6.
70. *Lunyu* 18.6.
71. *Lunyu* 18.8. Some of the persons mentioned occur in other passages and are described there as being "worthy" (*xian* 賢)—for example, Bo Yi and Shu Qi in 7.15 and Liu Xiahui in 15.14. There are also frequent references to these as sages (shengren 聖人) in the *Mencius*. Moreover, in the *Lunyu* 14.37, Confucius speaks of different kinds of "worthy persons [*xian zhe* 賢者] [having] resigned from the world" and then adds at the end that "those who have done this are seven persons." In *Lunyu zhengyi* (*Zhuzi jicheng*, vol. 1, p. 324) these persons are said to be the above-mentioned Jie Ni and his recluse companion Chang Ju (*Lunyu*, 18.6); the old man, or *Zhang ren* (18.7); Shi Men (14.38), whose name is usually and possibly mistakenly taken to refer to a place called Stone Gate; He Kui (14.39), most likely also a name but usually translated as someone carrying a basket; the border official at Yi, or *Yi feng ren* (3.24); and the madman of Chu (18.5). The Han dynasty commentator Zheng Xuan (127–200) argues that the number 7 is an error and that there were actually ten persons, namely, Bo Yi, Shu Qi, Yu Zhong, Liu Xiahui, and Shao Lian (five of the seven mentioned in 18.8); Jie Ni and Chang Ju (18.6); the madman of Chu; the basket carrier, or He Kui; and last, another referred to in 18.7 as He Diao, also normally translated as "basket carrier." Cf. *Lunyu zhengyi*, *Zhuzi jicheng*, vol. 1, p. 324. It is further tempting to think of the seven persons as those mentioned in 18.8.
72. *Lunyu* 7.19. I follow Chen Jingpan (1990), p. 79, in understanding *le* 樂 as "optimism."
73. *Lunyu* 7.20.
74. *Lunyu* 7.7. Cf. also 7.8 where Confucius stresses the importance of his students' sharing the eagerness (fen 憤) that he ascribes to himself in 7.19 as quoted above.
75. *Mencius* 4A.2.
76. *Mencius* 6A.7. See also 4B.32 where he says, "Yao and Shun were the same as other people," and 6B.2 where he affirms that anyone is able to become a Yao or a Shun.
77. Following Hall and Ames (1987), pp. 208ff.
78. *Mencius* 7B.24. I follow *Mengzi zhengyi* (*Zhuzi jicheng*, vol. 1, pp. 582–83) in understanding the dispositions of the human senses as toward good or pleasant tastes, smells, and so on.
79. Xu Fuguan (2001), p. 145.
80. *Mencius* 7A.3.
81. *Mencius* 3A.3.

82. *Mencius* 4B.12.

83. Perhaps a good indicator of the Chinese conception of life as a process of dynamic interaction between one's natural makeup and external occurrences is that in modern Chinese the word *xingming* 性命 means "life."

84. *Mencius* 6A.7.

85. Most likely such a perception of Xunzi as a pessimist was the most important factor in his being regarded by Han Yu 韓愈 (768–824), and, in fact, all the subsequent neo-Confucians, as unworthy of belonging to the "correct transmission" of the Confucian tradition. Han Yu and later Cheng Yi (1033–1107) both attacked Xunzi for his claims about renxing and established Mencius's notion as the "orthodox" Confucian doctrine. See Chan (1963), pp. 450ff., 567.

86. Hagen (2007), p. 122. Cua (2003), p. 821, has also noted that "Xunzi's remark that 'human nature is bad' . . . is quite inadequate as it stands for distinguishing his view from that of Mencius."

87. Cited in Hagen (2007), p. 124. Knoblock (1994), vol. 3, p. 139, also notes that "later scholars have, from time to time, suggested that [Mencius's and Xunzi's] views are compatible."

88. Cf. a similarly expounded thesis by Eno (1990), pp. 149–50.

89. *Xunzi* 88/23/45–46.

90. *Xunzi* 1.1.1.

91. *Xunzi* 73/19/74–77.

92. *Xunzi* 86/23/3–4. However, this does not mean that the possibility of becoming a junzi or even a sage is reserved only for the select few. Xunzi is quite explicit on this (21/8/39–40): "Being base-born wishing to be noble; being ignorant wishing to be wise; being poor wishing to be rich—is this possible? I say that it can only be done through learning. One who presides over such learning and puts it into practice is called a "scholar-apprentice" (shi 士); one who ardently strives within it is a junzi; one who has realized it is a sage [sheng 聖]." Such a comment can hardly be counted as pessimistic.

93. Graham (1989), p. 255; cf. also p. 129. Note that I have converted the non-*pinyin* romanization to *pinyin*.

94. *Xunzi* 28–9/9/69–70.

95. See pp. 46–47 above.

96. *Xunzi* e.g., 64/17/42–43.

97. Eno (1990), p. 152. Hagen (2007) argues, most convincingly, for an interpretation of Xunzi as a "constructivist"; that is to say, that Xunzi takes the categories of society mainly as social constructions for practical purposes rather than discovered analogies with the cosmic realm, as many interpreters have maintained.

98. Hall and Ames (1999), p. 157. In the "Confucius at Home at Leisure" ("Zhongni yanju" 仲尼燕居) chapter in the *Liji* 29.4/137/18, it is stated quite explicitly that li is a kind of li: "*li ye zhe li ye* 禮也者理也." Peng Lirong (2003), p. 80, comments on this sentence by saying that "according to Confucius, li

禮 is the reason [lixing 理性] in things and affairs, the lawfulness that must be followed; a violation of li results in chaos." The common understanding of the ancient Chinese li 理 as "reason," or lixing, in contemporary Chinese discourse is certainly subject to some qualification, but it seems acceptable as long as it is understood more flexibly, as Peng does, as the opposite of chaos (luan 亂).

99. Yi 義, on the basis of its etymological relation to a "self" or an "I," could also be taken to mean "signification" or "personalization." Cf. Hall and Ames (1987), pp. 89ff. It is worth noting that Ge Rongjin (2001), pp. 203–4, argues that during the pre-Qin era, li 理 tended to be interpreted or mediated through li 禮 and yi 義.

100. *Xunzi* 96/27/20.

101. *Xunzi* 64/17/46–47.

102. Knoblock (1994), vol. 1, pp. 302f.n69.

103. See *Xunzi*, for example chapter 9. Cf. also Hagen (2007), p. 56: "As times change and as the cultural tradition develops greater understanding, li [禮] may be modified, but this is not something outside the *li yi* scope just described. Modification of *li* is a special case of using one's developed sense of appropriateness in the application of *li*."

104. Some thinkers have somewhat provocatively identified the Confucian li 禮 with rationality. For instance, de Miribel and Vandermeersch (2001), p. 100, write that "[i]n order to guarantee that each person's social behavior coheres with [the] nature of things, behavioral patterns were developed according to which one is supposed to orient oneself: the rites. To follow the rites means to ensure that one does not stray from the way of reason. The ritual and the rational concurs in classical Chinese thought, just as, conversely, the irrational concurs with that which violates the rites." While not explicit on this point, de Miribel and Vandermeersch probably mean li 理 when referring to the "nature of things." In this case, their statement would more or less correspond to my interpretation, though failing to account for the important mediation of yi 義.

105. Gou Chengyi (2002), p. 381, seems to expound an interpretation of the differences between Mencius and Xunzi that corroborates mine:

> Mencius's theory that the natural dispositions are good pointed out the possibility for all human beings to become sages [shengxian 聖賢] by following li 禮 and yi 義, and therefore expressed a certain optimism with regard to the study of li [lixue 禮學]. This embodied a particular kind of encouragement that was also decisive for Mencius's overall passionate attitude to the human study of li. Xunzi's theory of *xing e* 性惡, however, while far from denying the possibilities inherent in the human being's accomplished study of li, laid particular stress on the necessity of pursuing personal cultivation through exertion, precisely because he was deeply aware of the difficulty attached to such a task. Thus, he was obviously not as optimistic [leguan 樂觀] as Mencius but insisted on an attitude of tranquility bordering on

graveness. With the presupposition of the *xing e* thesis, the restrictive particularity of li receives ample emphasis. Thus, to bring the meaning of the study of li to expression, there is no conflict between the theses of *xing e* and *xing shan*; their differences consist in their stressing different points: *Xing shan* stresses the possibilities inherent in li, while *xing e* stresses the necessity of li for pursuing personal cultivation through exertion.

Chapter Three. Third Assemblage: Education as Humanization

1. In a very similar manner, Dewey (1994), p. 17, also speaks of philosophy as a "critique of prejudices."
2. Gadamer (1990), p. 16.
3. Ames and Hall (2001), p. 51.
4. Cf. Warnke (1987), pp. 157ff.
5. Gadamer (1990), pp. 22–23. I have opted for the translation "generality" and "general" for the German "Allgemeinheit" and "allgemein" instead of "universality" and "universal" as Gadamer speaks elsewhere of "Universalität" when referring to epistemological claims that are clearly more sweeping than his own. See for instance his critical discussions of Schleiermacher on p. 200 and Husserl on p. 251.
6. Gadamer (1990), p. 30. Italics and English in original.
7. Ibid., p. 26.
8. Schmidt (2000), p. 166.
9. Gadamer (1990), p. 22. This is not to say that these two kinds of consciousness are identical, rather that they describe dimensions of the edified consciousness that are derived directly from the experience of its life-world, and thus both relate to the human senses. Gadamer (1990), p. 22, goes on to say that the edified consciousness, be it aesthetic or historical, relates to "the senses in their immediacy, that is to say, it knows in single cases how surely to distinguish [between things] and to evaluate, even without being able to provide its reasons. In this way, someone who has aesthetic sense knows how to tell apart the beautiful and the ugly, good or bad quality, and someone who has historical sense knows what is and what is not possible for an era, and has sense for the differentness [*Andersartigkeit*] of the past compared with the present."
10. Warnke (1987), p. 28.
11. Ibid., p. 29.
12. Hegel (1970b), p. 78. Italics in original.
13. Gadamer (1990), p. 360.
14. One of Hegel's innovations was to emphasize the "intentional" element of experience (though that particular notion had to wait for Franz Brentano to be coined). In contrast to Aristotle, John Locke, and Kant, who

explain experience as a process in which objects independent of consciousness affect our senses and produce concepts in them, Hegel argued that the difference between consciousness and its object is itself determined by consciousness and therefore that experience proceeds actively from within. Cf. Schnädelbach (1999), p. 56. Hegel himself says that "[t]he principle of *experience* includes the infinitely important qualification that for receiving and establishing the content [of experience] the human being must himself *be present*, or, more accurately, his apprehension of this content must be such that it is in agreement and unified with *the certainty that he has of himself*. He must himself be present, whether only with his external senses or with his profounder spirit, his essential self-consciousness" (Hegel 1970a, §7, pp. 49–50).

15. Gadamer (1990), p. 361.
16. Ibid., p. 361.
17. Ibid., p. 366.
18. Ibid., p. 364.
19. Ibid., p. 367.
20. Ibid., p. 363.
21. This statement, however, is subject to the qualification that despite the apparent abstractions of his philosophy, Hegel himself saw his project as immediately practical. He perceived his own era as being characterized by a lack of edification (*Unbildung*), as being stuck in a contradiction between the past and the present, and maintained that the alienation resulting from this contradiction opened an opportunity to turn the human (or the European) consciousness towards the path of *Bildung*. See Pöggler (1980), p. 253. See also Schmidt (2000), p. 166, who maintains that the "process of *Bildung* . . . , as Hegel informs us, is not merely a theoretical process but also a practical one—and the path of this process is the path of philosophy."
22. Dewey (1938), p. 17.
23. Ibid., p. 33.
24. Dewey (1938), p. 35. Insofar as the development of the individual is regarded as being dependent upon that individual's interaction with his or her environment, there is certainly a behaviorist tone in this. Dewey emphasized, however, that human beings are not merely passive recipients of stimuli from the environment, but actively select stimuli and respond to them in accordance with their own purposes or aims. For further discussion on this, see Noddings (1998), p. 28.
25. Dewey (1934), p. 244. Cf. Dewey (1993), p. 89: "The existence of communication is so disparate to our physical separation from one another and to the inner mental lives of individuals that it is not surprising that supernatural force has been ascribed to language and that communication has been given sacramental value."
26. Cf. Dewey (1934), p. 44.
27. Dewey (1934), p. 22.
28. Dewey (1922), p. 90.

29. Dewey (1938), p. 44.

30. Dewey (1934), p. 24.

31. Dewey's notion of continuity or progress is undeniably Hegelian in the sense of the "enrichment" of the past as opposed to its "overcoming." But there is nothing in Dewey's philosophy that implies anything close to a deterministic vision of history as an unfolding progress—successful continuity depends largely on human effort.

32. Cf. Noddings (1998), pp. 26–27, who, while herself defending Dewey's philosophy of education, discusses some of the criticisms that it has received from others.

33. Hegel, explaining his idealist epistemology, writes that when seeking knowledge, we compare the knowledge we have of an object with our perception of it. Therefore, the criterion as to whether our knowledge coheres with the object lies in us—that is, in our consciousness. If the comparison yields the result that our knowledge does not cohere with our perception of it, then consciousness changes its knowledge in order to cohere with the object: "but in the transformation of knowledge, the object itself also really changes, because the available knowledge was essentially a knowledge of the object; along with the knowledge it itself becomes different, because it essentially belonged to that knowledge" (Hegel 1970b, p. 78). I wish to distinguish my own formulation from Hegel's, however, in that I am not concerned with an epistemological criterion. Rather, and in a more Deweyan fashion, I am interested in the continuous change that I undergo through having experiences, which then leads to a qualitative transformation of that which I experience. This may sound idealist, but the formulation does not assume anything about the nature of the "things" that we experience, but accepts that the only access we have to them is through experience, where "experience," however, can be of many different kinds.

34. In his novel *The Captive* (*La Prisonnière*), part five of *In Search of Lost Times* (À la recherche de temps perdu).

35. Warnke (1987), p. 60, writes that "on Gadamer's view, unless the audience attempts to guard itself from the confrontation with their own lives that art provokes, the experience of art is one in which the audience is necessarily taken up into the work, experiences it as authoritative and learns to view its own world in light of the work of art. Aesthetic experience is thus itself a form of knowledge."

36. Although Kant was revolutionary in that he seemingly granted the aesthetic an independent realm, the criterion of taste was, ultimately, subjected to the strict domination of reason. An insightful discussion of Kant's rationalization of artistic taste may be found in Land (1991).

37. Hall and Ames (1987), p. 134. Cf. also Hall and Ames (1995), pp. 116ff. The distinction that Hall and Ames introduce between "logical" and "aesthetic" order is very close to the distinction between "correlative" and "analytic" thinking made by Graham (1989), esp. pp. 320ff.

38. Whitehead (1967), pp. 29ff.

39. Ibid., p. 31.
40. Bell (1997), p. 152.
41. Ibid.
42. Jennings (1982), p. 113.
43. Ibid., p. 114.
44. Ibid., pp. 113–14.
45. In the words of Jennings (1982), p. 114, "[i]t would still be possible to argue that the transition from not-knowing to knowing is extrinsic to the ritual itself were it not for the groundbreaking work of Victor Turner who has located the transitional or liminal state within the ritual itself. This liminality, Turner has shown, is not accidental to, but is constitutive of, the ritual process. The generative mode of ritual knowledge is inscribed in the ritual process through this liminal and transitional moment."
46. Jennings (1982), p. 115.
47. Ibid., pp. 118–19. In an intriguingly similar manner, Pierre Bourdieu speaks of the "logic of the transposable character of dispositions," which a Bourdieu commentator explains as a "capacity of basic dispositions . . . to structure and create relevance in social contexts and fields other than those in which they were originally acquired and to which they are generatively most appropriate. . . . The dispositions appropriate to one field are translated according to the logic of another field. . . . This is how diverse social settings and practices exhibit a stylistic coherence or thematic unity" (Jenkins 2002, p. 78).
48. Ames (2011), p. 109.
49. Ekstrom and Hecht (2007), p. 261.
50. Cited in Jennings (1982), p. 115.
51. Andersen (2001), p. 173.
52. Eno (1990), p. 177.
53. *Xunzi* 23/8/87.
54. Williams and Boyd (1993), p. 93.
55. Ibid., p. 140.
56. Ibid., pp. 68ff.
57. Ibid., pp. 75–76. This sentence was originally italicized for emphasis, but it is unnecessary here.
58. Williams and Boyd (1993), pp. 93–98, provide an interesting discussion of these aspects of the artwork and the ritual insofar as they contain metaphorical elements. Their understanding of the pedagogical function of art closely resembles that of Gadamer in his discussion of the "aesthetic consciousness."
59. *Xunzi* 77–8/20/39–40. I follow Andersen (2001), p. 173, in understanding yi 意 as "meaning"; otherwise, I follow, for the most part, the outstanding translation of this passage by Knoblock (1994), vol. 3, p. 85.
60. Williams and Boyd (1993), pp. 123, 129.
61. Ames (2011), for example, p. 109, though he uses variations of this formulation throughout in his work.
62. Cf. Ames (2011), p. 178.

63. Ames and Rosemont (1998), p. 52.
64. Goncharov (1954), p. 219.
65. *Lunyu* 1.12 and 3.26 respectively. Cf. Peng Lirong (2003), p. 82.
66. *Zhuangzi* 91/33/14.
67. *Liji* 32.23/146/5–6. Cf. also an interesting discussion of *neisheng waiwang* by Geldsetzer and Hong (1998), pp. 26–41. The authors tie it to Confucianism and the general line of thought in Chinese philosophy.
68. "Records of Music" ("Yueji" 樂記) chapter of the *Liji* 19.26/104/10–11.
69. "Records of Music" ("Yueji" 樂記) chapter of the *Liji* 19.1/98/17–18.
70. *Lunyu* 2.3.
71. *Lunyu* 13.3.
72. Jin Shangli (2002), pp. 124–25.
73. *Lunyu* 17.11.
74. Li Ling (2003), p. 78 §1.
75. *Mencius* 7A.21.
76. Pang Pu (2000), p. 30.
77. Cf. Li Ling (2002), p. 78 §1.
78. Cf. Cook (2000), pp. 119–20.
79. Li Ling (2002), p. 78, §2.
80. Ames and Hall (2001), pp. 64–65.
81. Ames and Hall (2003), pp. 59–60.
82. Li Ling (2002), p. 79, §17.
83. Ibid., p. 79, §§10–11.
84. See for example Xing Wen (2000), p. 77.
85. Following Cook (2000), p. 128.
86. *Mencius* 5B.1.
87. *Lunyu*, 12.19.
88. Knoblock (1994), vol. 2, 304f. n43. Cf. Cook (2000), p. 129: "The qualities of the sage are . . . jade-like in both luster and resonance—manifest forms of external evidence that cannot fail to influence those who gaze upon their radiance or become captivated by the harmonious melody of virtue embodied."
89. Cf. *Mencius*, 7A.13.
90. Li Ling (2002), p. 78, §2.
91. François Jullien, for instance, seems to give too much weight to "efficacy" and the "logic of manipulation" in Chinese thought, claiming, as I have already cited, that "[a]rt, or wisdom, as conceived by the Chinese, . . . lies in strategically exploiting the propensity emanating from that particular configuration of reality, to the maximum effect possible" (Jullien 1995, p. 15). Though this is certainly an important aspect of the ancient Chinese world orientation, Jullien makes it sound as if there is a kind of value-ignoring means-end rationality at play, however different it may be from the kind detected by Weber in Western culture.
92. *Lunyu* 14.6.

93. *Lunyu* 3.3.
94. Deutsch (1996), p. 86.
95. Wu and Hu (2010), p. 108.
96. Ibid., p. 108.
97. *Lunyu* 15.29.
98. Wang (2007), p. 282.
99. *Lunyu* 7.8.
100. *Lunyu* 1.15.
101. *Lunyu* 5.9.
102. Jullien (2000), p. 202.
103. "Records of Learning" ("Xueji" 學記) chapter of the *Liji* 18.6–7/97/10–12 and 15–17.
104. Cf. *Lunyu* 4.22, 4.24, 12.3; *Liji* 32.8/143/23.
105. Cf. *Lunyu* 17.18.
106. *Lunyu* 5.10.
107. *Lunyu* 3.16.
108. Zhang Weizhong (1997), p. 20.
109. Following Ren Pingzhi (2000), p. 288; Legge (1967), vol. 2, p. 83.
110. *Shuowen jiezi jinshi*, p. 1220.
111. Hall and Ames (1987), p. 88.
112. Cf. Jenkins (2002), p. 75.
113. *Lunyu* 16.13.
114. Cf. Jenkins (2002), pp. 75–76. He further explains that "[i]t is in bodily hexis that the idiosyncratic (the personal) combines with the systematic (the social). It is the mediating link between individuals' subjective worlds and the cultural world into which they are born and which they share with each other" (Jenkins 2002, p. 75).
115. *Zuozhuan*, Duke Cheng, year 13; Legge (1998–2000), vol. 5, pp. 379/381.
116. Gou Chengyi (2002), p. 193; for the *Liji* quotation, see 43.1/164/29.
117. Legge (1967), vol. 2, pp. 411–12. What I have referred to as "all under heaven" (*tianxia* 天下), and certainly could be understood as "the whole world," as it is, in fact, by He Baihua and He Youling (1992), is translated by Legge as "throughout the kingdom."
118. Cf. *Mencius* 7B.32, where this idea of fulfilling the ultimate task by beginning with the first is explicitly expressed, though, as is often the case in the Confucian literature, xiushen 修身, and not zhizhi 知至, is taken as the first: "A junzi adheres to [the process of] bringing peace to the world by cultivating himself [君子之守修其身而天下平]."
119. *Lunyu* 6.30.
120. Xiushen 修身 and xiuji 修己 can be considered synonymous in this context. *Shen* 身, as body, would seem to emphasize human comportment, but, in accordance with the vague *nei/wai* distinction as discussed above, considerations of one's *shen* regard just as much one's *ji* 己.

121. *Lunyu* 14.42. Above, I translated yi 以 as "by" in the sense of "doing x by doing y." But in this passage, the yi plays with its own ambiguity and thereby underscores the two-way individual-social relationship in the process. Hence, it is not merely such that I bring accord to people *in order to* cultivate myself: I also cultivate myself *and am thereby* able to bring accord to people. This ambiguity leads Fingarette (1979), p. 130, to argue that "the word 'cultivate' in 'cultivate oneself' does not really seem to have 'oneself' as the object, but has instead a more specific aim such as 'one's capacity to pacify the people.' Waley's translation is suggestive of this: 'Cultivate in himself the capacity to ease the lot of other people.'" Fingarette's overall thesis is that a junzi defers his self and will to the dao and thus that Confucius "shares in the pan-Asian ideal of selflessness as crucial to salvation" (Fingarette 1979, p. 137).

While this interpretation is intriguing, I believe that it is misguided and leads us away from trying to understand the consistent but complex correlative or "dialectical" self-others relationship in Confucian thought. On this issue, see also Ames (1991).

122. Cf. Fingarette (1979), p. 129.
123. *Xunzi* 97/27/41.

Concluding Remarks

1. Neville (2000), p. 187.
2. Ibid., p. 190.
3. Neville (2008), p. 24.
4. Nuyen (2003), p. 81.
5. Ibid., p. 83.
6. *Lunyu* 2.23.
7. *Mencius*, e.g., 1A.7, 4A.17, 6B.1, 7A.19.
8. "How Li Form Vessels" ("Li Qi" 禮器) chapter of the *Liji* 10.4/64/29.
9. Jin Jingfang (1998), p. 6.
10. Whitehead (1967), p. 1.
11. See on this, for example, Zhu's (1990) description of the unfortunate circumstances in which Ming and Qing scholars found themselves, leading to the tendency to a reification of the Confucian practices, in particular of the li customs. In my view, however, political or social oppression is not the only danger. Excessive individualism, downplaying tradition and the importance of the social sphere, and consumerism, with its ensuing lethargy, are also likely to undermine social creativity.
12. Wang (2007), p. 296n3.
13. Cf. Chow, Ng, and Henderson (1999). This collection of essays focuses on Confucianism as a temporal-specific, nonessentializable system of thinking, which, through human intervention and creative interpretation, was in a process

of constant change and adaptation to its particular historical circumstances. As Ng and Chow point out in their "Introduction: Fluidity of the Confucian Canon and Discursive Strategies," the continuous hermeneutic transformation of the Confucian texts and doctrines generated "the constant need to canonize and legitimize texts and ideas, that is, to fix a boundary to establish a sense of stable authority. This imposed finality is, of course, fictive, and all canonical traditions are ephemeral" (Chow, Ng and Henderson 1999, p. 2).

14. Jullien (2000), pp. 212–13.
15. *Lunyu* 17.11.
16. *Lunyu* 14.24.
17. Xunzi 2/1/32 quotes this passage from the *Lunyu* and then attributes it directly to the difference between the junzi and the xiao ren. He continues (2/1/32–3) thus: "The learning of the junzi serves to refine his person; the learning of the xiao ren serves the same purpose as offerings of poultry and calves." Wang Yunlu (*Xunzi zhijie*, 2000), p. 7, explains that while "the ancients often offered each other presents of poultry and calves, the indication here is that petty persons study for the sake of showing off, to be obsequious to others."
18. *Lunyu* 17.13.
19. *Mencius* 7B.37.
20. *Mencius* 3A.2.
21. *Lunyu* 12.11.
22. Nuyen (2003), p. 80. Nuyen also mentions (p. 80) that "the only thing close enough to the 'Three-Bond Doctrine' we can find is the discussion of the 'five relationships' in The Mencius [3A.4], which stresses, not the hierarchical structure, but the reciprocal nature of the relationship between friends, the young and the old, husband and wife, children and their parents, and subjects and their sovereign."
23. Ames (2011), p. 174.
24. For example, *Analects* 7.2 and 7.20.
25. *Analects* 7.8, and 15.16 respectively.
26. For example, *Analects* 5.5, 5.8 and 5.19.
27. *Analects* 7.26.
28. See *Analects* 12.1. Cf. also *Xunzi* 75/19/121, who says that only the sage understands the observance of li, and that li is the way of ren when practiced by junzi.
29. *Analects* 6.7.
30. *Analects* 2.4.
31. *Analects* 7.34.
32. Some examples are *Analects* 2.24, 3.12, and 3.18. See also, on the potential degeneration of li, Tan (2011), p. 479.
33. *Analects* 6.12.
34. Neville (2008), p. 24.
35. *Analects* 7.37. Cf. also 9.29.

36. *Analects* 8.17, 9.11.
37. *Lunyu* 13.23.
38. *Lunyu* 4.16. Cf. Albert H. Y. Chen (2003), pp. 260–61, who emphasizes that "in traditional China . . . the pursuit of material self-interest that underlies civil litigation was perceived to be inconsistent with the Confucian ideal of self-cultivation, character formation and personal growth."
39. Ibid., pp. 270ff.

Literature Cited

Ames, Roger T. 1991. "Reflections on the Confucian Self: A Response to Fingarette." In *Rules, Rituals, and Responsibility: Essays Dedicated to Herbert Fingarette*, edited by Mary I. Bockover. La Salle: Open Court.
———. 2011. *Confucian Role Ethics: A Vocabulary*. Hong Kong: The Chinese University Press.
———, and David L. Hall. 2001. *Focusing the Familiar: A Translation and Philosophical Interpretation of the Zhongyong*. Honolulu: University of Hawai'i Press.
———, and David L. Hall. 2003. *Dao De Jing*. "Making This Life Significant." *A Philosophical Translation*. New York: Ballantine Books.
———, and Henry Rosemont Jr. 1998. *The Analects of Confucius: A Philosophical Translation*. New York: Ballantine Books.
Andersen, Poul. 2001. "Concepts of Meaning in Chinese Ritual." *Cahiers d'Extrême-Asie* 12, pp. 155–183.
Aristotle. 1941. *The Basic Works of Aristotle*. Edited by Richard McKeon. New York: Random House.
Barker, Martin. 1980. "Kant as a Problem for Weber." *The British Journal of Sociology* 31, pp. 224–244.
Bauer, Wolfgang. 2001. *Geschichte der chinesischen Philosophie. Konfuzianismus, Daoismus, Buddhismus*. München: Verlag C. H. Beck.
Bell, Catherine. 1997. *Ritual. Perspectives and Dimensions*. Oxford: Oxford University Press.
Bloom, Irene. 1997. "Human Nature and Biological Nature in Mencius." *Philosophy East and West* 47, no. 1, pp. 21–32.
Bourdieu, Pierre. 1990. *The Logic of Practice*. Translated by Richard Nice. Stanford: Stanford University Press.
Bruya, Brian. 2003. "*Qing* (情) and Emotion in Early Chinese Thought." In *Chinese Philosophy and the Trends of the 21st Century Civilization* / 中國哲學和21世紀文明走向, edited by Fang Keli 方克立. Di 12 jie guoji Zhongguo zhexue dahui lunwenji 4 第12屆國際中國哲學大會論文集. Beijing: Commercial Press.
Camus, Albert. 1966. *Carnets 1942–1951*. Translated with a preface and notes by Philip Thody. London: Hamish Hamilton Ltd.

Chan, Wing-tsit. 1963. *A Source Book in Chinese Philosophy*. Princeton: Princeton University Press.
———. 1969. *Neo-Confucianism, Etc.: Essays by Wing-tsit Chan*. Hanover, NH: Oriental Society.
Chen Chaoqun 陳超群. 1999. *Zhongguo jiaoyu zhexue shi* 中國教育哲學史. Vol. 1. Jinan: Shandong jiaoyu chubanshe.
Chen Jingpan. 1990. *Confucius as a Teacher—Philosophy of Confucius with Special Reference to Its Educational Implications*. Beijing: Foreign Languages Press.
Chen Lai 陳來 et al. 2001. *Zhongguo zhexue shi* 中國哲學史. Beijing: Beijing daxue chubanshe.
Chen Wentuan. See Tran Van Doan
Chen, Albert H. Y. 2003. "Mediation, Litigation, and Justice: Confucian Reflections in a Modern Liberal Society." In *Confucianism for the Modern World*, edited by Daniel A. Bell and Hahm Chaibong. Cambridge: Cambridge University Press.
Chen, Mao. 1997. *Between Tradition and Change. The Hermeneutics of May Fourth Literature*. Lanham/New York/London: University Press of America.
Cheng Chung-ying. 1991. *New Dimensions of Confucian and Neo-Confucian Philosophy*. Albany: State University of New York Press.
Chow, Kai-wing, On-cho Ng, and John B. Henderson, eds. 1999. *Imagining Boundaries. Changing Confucian Doctrines, Texts, and Hermeneutics*. Albany: State University of New York Press.
Cook, Scott. 2000. "Consummate Artistry and Moral Virtuosity: The "Wu xing 五行" Essay and Its Aesthetic Implications." *Chinese Literature: Essays, Articles, Reviews* 22, pp. 113–146.
Cua, Antonio S., ed. 2003. *Encyclopedia of Chinese Philosophy*. New York: Routledge.
de Miribel, Jean, and Léon Vandermeersch. 2001. *Chinesische Philosophie*. Translated by Thomas Laugstien. Bergisch Gladbach: BLT.
Deutsch, Eliot. 1991. "Community as Ritual Participation." In *On Community*, edited by Leroy S. Rouner. Notre Dame: University of Notre Dame Press.
———. 1992. *Creative Being: The Crafting of Person and World*. Honolulu: University of Hawai'i Press.
———. 1996. *Essays on the Nature of Art*. Albany: State University of New York Press.
Dewey, John. 1922. *Human Nature and Conduct*. New York: Henry Holt and Company.
———. 1934. *Art as Experience*. New York: Perigee Books.
———. 1944. *Democracy and Education: An Introduction to the Philosophy of Education*. New York: The Free Press.
———. 1938. *Experience and Education*. New York: Simon and Schuster.
———. 1993. *The Political Writings*. Edited by Debra Morris and Ian Shapiro. Indianapolis: Hackett.
———. 1994. *The Moral Writings of John Dewey*. Revised Edition. Edited by James Gouinlock. New York: Prometheus Books.

———, and John L. Childs 1933a. "The Social-Economic Situation and Education." In *The Educational Frontier*, edited by William H. Kilpatrick. New York: D. Appleton-Century.

———1933b. "The Underlying Philosophy of Education." In *The Educational Frontier*, edited by William H. Kilpatrick. New York: D. Appleton-Century.

Eno, Robert. 1990. *The Confucian Creation of Heaven: Philosophy and the Defense of Ritual Mastery.* Albany: State University of New York Press.

Fingarette, Herbert. 1972. *Confucius:The Secular as Sacred.* New York: Harper and Row.

———. 1979. "The Problem of the Self in the Analects." *Philosophy East and West* 29, no. 2, pp. 129–140.

Gadamer, Hans-Georg. 1990. *Wahrheit und Methode. Grundzüge einer philosophischen Hermeneutik.* 6th ed. Tübingen: J. C. B. Mohr (Paul Siebeck).

Garrison, James W. 1986. "The Paradox of Indoctrination: A Solution." *Synthese* 68, pp. 261–273.

Ge Rongjin 葛榮晉. 2001. *Zhongguo zhexue fanchou tonglun* 中國哲學範疇通論. Beijing: Shoudu shifan daxue chubanshe.

Geldsetzer, Lutz and Hong Han-ding. 1998. *Grundlagen der chinesischen Philosophie.* Stuttgart: Reclam.

Goncharov. 1954. *Oblomov.* Translated by David Magarshack. Harmondsworth: Penguin.

Gou Chengyi 勾承益. 2002. *Xianqin Lixue* 先秦禮學. Chengdu: Bashu shuhui chuban faxing.

Graham, A. C. 1989. *Disputers of the Tao Philosophical Argument in Ancient China.* Chicago/La Salle: Open Court.

Grubacic, Andrej. "Towards an Another Anarchism." ZNET. 7 February 2003. <http://www.zcommunications.org/towards-another-anarchism-by-andrej-grubacic> (retrieved 1 March 2012).

Hagen, Kurtis. 2007). *The Philosophy of Xunzi A Reconstruction.* Chicago and La Salle: Open Court.

Hall, David L., and Roger T. Ames. 1995. *Anticipating China: Thinking Through the Narratives of Chinese and Western Culture.* Albany: State University of New York.

———. 1999. *The Democracy of the Dead: Dewey, Confucius, and the Hope for Democracy in China.* La Salle: Open Court.

———. 1987. *Thinking Through Confucius.* Albany: State University of New York.

Hansen, Chad. 1976. Review of *Confucius: The Secular as Sacred*, by Herbert Fingarette. *Journal of Chinese Philosophy* 3, pp. 197–204.

Hawkins, John N., Zhou Nanzhao, and Julie Lee. 2001. "China: Balancing the Collective and the Individual." In *Values Education for Dynamic Societies: Individualism or Collectivism*, edited by William K. Cummings, Maria Teresa Tatto, and John Hawkins. Hong Kong: Comparative Education Research Centre, The University of Hong Kong.

Hayhoe, Ruth. 2001. "Lessons from the Chinese Academy." In *Knowledge across Cultures: A Contribution to Dialogue among Civilizations*, edited by Ruth Hayhoe and Julia Pan. Hong Kong: Comparative Education Research Centre, The University of Hong Kong.

He Baihua and He Youling. 1992. *The Great Learning / Daxue* 大學: *A Chinese-English Bilingual Edition*. Jinan: Shandong youyi chubanshe.

Hegel, Georg Wilhelm Friedrich. 1970a. *Enzyklopädie der philosophischen Wissenschaften I*. Vol. 8 of *Theorie-Werkausgabe*. Frankfurt am Main: Suhrkamp.

———. 1970b. *Phänomenologie des Geistes*. Vol. 3 of *Theorie-Werkausgabe*. Frankfurt am Main: Suhrkamp.

Huang, Chun-chieh. 2001. *Mencian Hermeneutics: A History of Interpretations in China*. New Brunswick: Transaction Publishers.

Hui Jixing 惠吉星. 1996. *Xunzi yu Zhongguo wenhua* 荀子與中國文化. Guiyang: Guizhou renmin chubanshe.

Høeg, Peter. 1999. *Frøken Smillas Fornemmelse for Sne*. København: Rosinante Forlag.

Jenkins, Richard. 2002. *Pierre Bourdieu*. Revised edition. Routledge: London/New York.

Jennings, Theodore W. 1982. "On Ritual Knowledge." *The Journal of Religion* 26, pp. 111–127.

Jin Jingfang 金景芳. 1998. "Tan li 談禮." In *Ershi shiji zhongguo lixue yanjiu lunji* 二十世紀中國禮學研究論集, edited by Chen Qitai 陳其泰, Guo Weichuan 郭偉川, and Zhou Shaochuan 周少川. Beijing: Xueyuan chubanshe.

Jin Shangli 金尚理. 2002. *Li yi yue he de wenhua lixiang* 禮宜樂和的文化理想. Chengdu: Bashu shushe.

Jullien, François. 2000. *Detour and Access: Strategies of Meaning in China and Greece*. Translated by Sophie Hawkes. New York: Zone Books.

Jullien, François. 1995. *The Propensity of Things: Toward a History of Efficacy in China*. Translated by Janet Lloyd. New York: Zone Books.

Kant, Immanuel. 1923. "Beantwortung der Frage: Was ist Aufklärung?" In *Abhandlungen nach 1781*. Vol. 8 of *Kant's Werke*. Berlin: Walter de Gruyter and Co.

Knoblock, John. 1994. *Xunzi: A Translation and Study of the Complete Works*. 3 vols. Stanford: Stanford University Press.

Krishnamurti, J. 1964. *Think on These Things*. New York: Harper and Row.

Land, Nick. 1991. "Delighted to Death." *Pli (Formerly Warwick Journal of Philosophy)* 3, no. 2, pp. 76–88.

Laozi Zhuangzi zhijie 老子莊子直解. 1998. Annotated by Chen Qinghui 陳慶惠. Hangzhou: Zhejiang wenyi chubanshe.

Lau, D. C. 1970. *Mencius*. Harmondsworth: Penguin Books.

Legge, James. 1967. *Li Chi: Book of Rites*. 2 vols. New York: University Books Inc.

———. 1998–2000. *The Chinese Classics*. 5 vols. Taibei: SMC Publishing, Inc.

Leng Chengjin 冷成金. 1999. *Zhongguo wenxue de lishi yu shenmei* 中國文學的歷史與審美. Beijing: Zhongguo renmin daxue chubanshe.

Li Ling 李零. 2002. *Guodian Chu jian jiao du ji* 郭店楚簡校讀記. Beijing: Beijing daxue chubanshe.

Liji 禮記. 1992. *A Concordance to the Liji*. Edited by D. C. Lau and Chen Fong Ching. Hong Kong: Commercial Press.

Liji zhijie 禮記直解. 2000. Annotated by Ren Pingzhi 任平直. Hangzhou: Zhejiang wenyi chubanshe.

Lin Li. 2002. "The Difficulties of Importing the Western Idea of Human Rights into China—A Jurisprudential Approach." In *Chinese Ethics in a Global Context: Moral Bases of Contemporary Societies*, edited by Karl-Heinz Pohl and Anselm W. Müller. Leiden: Brill.

Liu Shu-hsien. 1998. *Understanding Confucian Philosophy: Classical and Sung-Ming*. Westport: Praeger Publishers.

Lu Jiuyuan 陸九淵. 2000. *Xiangshan yulu* 象山語錄. Jinan: Shandong youyi chubanshe.

Lunyu 論語. 1966. *A Concordance to the Analects of Confucius*. Harvard-Yenching Institute Sinological Index Series. Supplement no. 16. Taibei: Chinese Materials and Research Aids Service Center, Inc.

Lunyu zhijie 論語直解. 1997. Annotated by Zhang Weizhong 張衛中. Hangzhou: Zhejiang wenyi chubanshe.

MacIntyre, Alasdair. 1984. *After Virtue: A Study in Moral Theory*. 2nd ed. Notre Dame: University of Notre Dame Press.

Macmillan, C. J. B. 1983. "On Certainty and Indoctrination." *Synthese* 56, pp. 363–372.

Marx, Karl. 1965. *Der 18. Brumaire des Louis Bonaparte*. Frankfurt am Main: Insel-Verlag.

Mencius 孟子. 1966. *A Concordance to the Meng Tzu*. Harvard-Yenching Institute Sinological Index Series. Supplement no. 17. Taibei: Chinese Materials and Research Aids Service Center, Inc.

Nagai, Michio. 1976. *Education and Indoctrination: The Sociological and Philosophical Bases*. Tokyo: University of Tokyo Press.

Neville, Robert Cummings. 2000. "Tu Wei-ming's Neo-Confucianism." *The International Review of Chinese Philosophy and Religion* 5, pp. 163–194.

———. 2008. *Ritual and Deference: Extending Chinese Philosophy in a Comparative Context*. Albany: State University of New York Press.

Nietzsche, Friedrich. 1967–1977. *Sämtliche Werke. Kritische Studienausgabe in 15 Bänden*. Edited by Giorgio Colli and Mazzino Montinari. Berlin: de Gruyter Verlag.

Noddings, Nel. 1998. *Philosophy of Education*. Boulder: Westview Press.

Nuyen, A. T. 2003. "Confucianism, Globalisation and the Idea of Universalism." *Asian Philosophy* 13, nos. 2/3, pp. 75–86.

Pang Pu 龐樸. 2000. *Zhubo «Wuxing» pian jiaozhu ji yanzhou* 竹帛《五行》篇校注及研究. Taibei: Wanjuanlou tushu.

Parkes, Graham. 1994. *Composing the Soul: Reaches of Nietzsche's Psychology.* Chicago: University of Chicago Press.
Peng Lirong 彭立榮. 2003. *Ru wenhua shehuixue* 儒文化社會學. Beijing: Renmin chubanshe.
Pöggler, Otto. 1980. "Hegels Bildungskonzeption im geschichtlichen Zusammenhang." *Hegel-Studien* 15, pp. 241–269.
Rappaport, Roy A. 1999. *Ritual and Religion in the Making of Humanity.* Cambridge: Cambridge University Press.
Reed, Gay Garland. 1998. "Is Lei Feng Finally Dead? The Search for Values in a Time of Reform and Transition." In *Education in Post-Mao China*, edited by Michael Agelasto and Bob Adamson. Hong Kong: Hong Kong University Press.
Ren Jiyu 任繼愈, ed. 1966. *Zhongguo zhexue shi* 中國哲學史. 3 vols. Beijing: Renmin chubanshe.
Ren Junhua 任俊華. 2001. *Yixue yu ruxue* 易學與儒學. Beijing: Zhongguo shudian.
Schmidt, Dennis J. 2000. "'Was wir nicht sagen können...'" In *Hermeneutische Wege. Hans-Georg Gadamer zum Hundertsten*, edited by Günter Figal, Jean Grondin, and Dennis J. Schmidt. Tübingen: J. C. B. Mohr (Paul Siebeck).
Schnädelbach, Herbert. 1999. *Hegel zur Einführung.* Hamburg: Junius Verlag.
Schwartz, Benjamin I. 1996. *China and Other Matters.* Cambridge: Harvard University Press.
Shuowen jiezi jinshi 說文解字今釋. 2001. Originally compiled by Xu Shen 許慎. Annotated by Tang Kejing 湯可敬. Changsha: Yuelu shushe.
Snook, I. A. 1972. *Indoctrination and Education.* London/Boston: Routledge and Kegan Paul.
Solomon, Richard H. 1979. "Educational Themes in China's Changing Culture." In *Education in Comparative and International Perspectives*, edited by Kalil I. Gezi. New York: Holt, Rinehart, and Winston, Inc.
Staal, Frits. 1979. "The Meaninglessness of Ritual." *Numen* 26/1, pp. 2–22.
———. 1989. *Rules without Meaning, Ritual, Mantras, and the Human Sciences.* New York: Peter Lang.
Tan, Sor-hoon. 2011. "The *Dao* of Politics: *Li* (Rituals/Rites) and Laws as Pragmatic Tools of Government." *Philosophy East and West* 61(3), pp. 468–491.
Tang Junyi 唐君毅. 1988. "Zhongguo zhexue zhong ziran yuzhou guan zhi tezhi 中國哲學中自然宇宙觀之特質." In *Zhongxi zhexue sixiang zhi bijiao* 中西哲學思想之比較. Taibei: Xuesheng shuju.
Tang Mingbang 唐明邦, ed. 1997. *Zhouyi pingzhu* 周易評注. Beijing: Zhonghua Shuju.
Tang Yinan 唐亦男. 2000. "Cong rudao dui shijian de kanfa lun «Yizhuan» "shi zhong" yi gainian zhi yiyi 從儒道對時間的看法倫«易傳»"時中"一概念之意義." In *Rujia yu 21 shiji Zhongguo—goujian, fazhang "dangdai xin rujia"* 儒家與21世紀中國—構建，發展"當代新儒家," edited by Zhu Ruikai 祝瑞開. Shanghai: Xuelin chubanshe.

Tiles, J. E. 2000. *Moral Measures: An Introduction to Ethics East and West*. London: Routledge.
Tran Van Doan [Chen Wentuan 陳文團]. 1994. "The Dialectic of Tradition and Modernity." *Taida zhexue lunping* 台大哲學論平17, pp. 129–162.
Tu Weiming. 1976. *Centrality and Commonality: An Essay on Chung-yung*. Monographs of the Society for Asian and Comparative Philosophy, no. 3. Honolulu: The University Press of Hawaii.
———. 1985. *Confucian Thought: Selfhood as Creative Transformation*. Albany: State University of New York Press.
———. 1999. "The Confucian World." Colorado College. 5 February 1999. <http://coloradocollege.edu/academics/anniversary/Transcripts/TuTXT.htm> (retrieved 28 June 2012).
———, Milan Hejtmanek, and Alan Wachman. 1992. *The Confucian World Observed: A Contemporary Discussion of Confucian Humanism in East Asia*. Honolulu: The East West Center.
Vandermeersch, Léon. 1994. *Etudes sinologiques*. Paris: Presses Universitaires de France.
Waley, Arthur. 1997. *Confucius: The Analects*. Beijing: Waiyu jiaoxue yu yanzhou chubanshe.
Wang, Hongyu 2007. "Interconnections Within and Without: The Double Duty of Creative Educational Leadership." *Changing Education—Leadership, Innovation and Development in a Globalizing Asia Pacific*. Edited by Peter D. Hershock, Mark Mason and John N. Hawkins. Hong Kong: Comparative Education Research Centre, pp. 273–296.
Warnke, Georgia. 1987. *Gadamer. Hermeneutics, Tradition, and Reason*. Stanford: Stanford University Press.
Weber, Max. 1972. *Wirtschaft und Gesellschaft*. Tübingen: Verlag von J. C. B. Mohr.
———. 1982. *Politik als Beruf*. Berlin: Duncker und Humblot.
———. 1988a. "Die 'Objektivität' sozialwissenschaftlicher und sozialpolitischer Erkenntnis." In *Gesammelte Aufsätze zur Wissenschaftslehre*. Tübingen: Verlag von J. C. B. Mohr.
———. 1988b. "Wissenschaft als Beruf." In *Gesammelte Aufsätze zur Wissenschaftslehre*. Tübingen: Verlag von J. C. B. Mohr.
Whitehead, Alfred North. 1938. *Modes of Thought*. New York: The Free Press.
———. 1967. *The Aims of Education and Other Essays*. New York: The Free Press.
Wilhelm, Richard. 1976. *Laotse. Tao te king. Das Buch des Alten vom Sinn und Leben*. Zürich: Buchklub Ex Libris.
Williams, Ron G., and James W. Boyd. 1993. *Ritual Art and Knowledge: Aesthetic Theory and Zoroastrian Ritual*. Columbia: University of South Carolina Press.
Winckelmann, Johannes, ed. 1978. *Die protestantische Ethik II.—Kritiken und Antikritiken*. Gütersloh: Gütersloher Verlagshaus Gerd Mohn.

Wu, Zongjie, and Meixin Hu 2010. "Ritual Hermeneutics as the Source of Meaning: Interpreting the Fabric of Chinese Culture." *China Media Research* 6(2), pp. 104–113.

Xing Wen. 2000. "The 'Wanzhang' Chapter in the Mencius and the Bamboo Slip *Wu Xing*." *Contemporary Chinese Thought* 32, no. 1, pp. 63–78.

Xu Fuguan 徐復觀. 2001. *Zhongguo renxinglun shi. Xianqinpian* 中國人性論史。先秦篇. Shanghai: Sanlian shudian.

Xunzi 荀子. 1966. *A Concordance to Hsun Tzu*. Harvard-Yenching Institute Sinological Index Series. Supplement no. 22. Taibei: Chinese Materials and Research Aids Service Center, Inc.

Xunzi zhijie 荀子直解. 2000. Annotated by Wang Yunlu 王雲路. Hangzhou: Zhejiang wenyi chubanshe.

Zhang Dainian 2002a. *Key Concepts in Chinese Philosophy*. Translated by Edmund Ryden. Beijing: Foreign Languages Press/New Haven: Yale University Press, 2002.

———. 2002b. *Wan si ji: Zhang Dainian zixuan ji* 晚思集：張岱年自選記. Beijing: Xin shijie chubanshe, 2002.

Zhang Xianglong. 1999. "The Time of Heaven in Chinese Ancient Philosophy." *Contemporary Chinese Thought* 30, no. 4, pp. 44–61.

Zhao Zhentai, et al. 1993. *Mencius/Mengzi* 孟子: *A Chinese-English Bilingual Edition*. Jinan: Shandong youyi chubanshe.

Zhouyi 周易. 1966. *A Concordance to the Yi Ching*. Harvard-Yenching Institute Sinological Index Series. Supplement no. 10. Taibei: Chinese Materials and Research Aids Service Center, Inc.

Zhu, Weizheng 1990. *Coming out of the Middle Ages*. Translated by Ruth Hayhoe. Armonk and London: M. E. Sharpe, Inc.

Zhuangzi 莊子. 1956. *A Concordance to Chuang Tzu*. Harvard-Yenching Institute Sinological Index Series. Supplement no. 20. Cambridge: Harvard University Press.

Zhuzi jicheng 諸子集成. 1986–1996. 8 Vols. Shanghai: Shanghai shudian chubanshe.

Zou Changlin 鄒昌林. 2000. *Zhongguo li wenhua* 中國禮文化. Beijing: Shehui kexue wenxian chubanshe.

Index

Ames, Roger T., 12, 27, 29, 41, 94, 138n33, 142n96, 143n98; on correlative thinking, 148n56, 154n37; on de 德 (excellence), 105; on education, 83; on li 禮 (ritual propriety) 12–13, 29, 100, 115, 125, 134n29; on reason, 59–60, 79
Analects of Confucius. See *Lunyu* 論語
Andersen, Poul, 97, 155n59
anomie, 26, 28, 103, 131
Aristotle, 152n14; on habit (hexis), 147n42; on the human being, 23; on the mean (mesotes), 40, 141nn77–78; on reason, 61, 146n27
art, 106, 109, 139n57; of dissimulation, 123–24; of divination, 36; martial, 97; pedagogical function of, 93, 99, 154n35, 155n58; ritual performance as, 97–98, 101, 113; as wisdom, 34–35

Barker, Martin, 144n17
Barthes, Roland, 4
Bell, Catherine, 14, 95
Bildung. *See* edification
Bloom, Irene, 148n60
Bo Yi 伯夷, 106, 149n71
body, 109; as mnemonic device, 115; role in ritual, 96; as ti 體 and shen 身, 96, 114, 115, 157n120

Bol, Peter, 16
Book of Documents. See *Shujing* 書經
Book of Odes. See *Shijing* 詩經
Book of Rites. See *Liji* 禮記
Bourdieu, Pierre, 50, 60, 65, 98; on habitus, 68–69, 115, 147n42, 155n47; on practice 31–33; on reason, 64–65, 68–69, 80, 146n38; on ritual, 32–33, 146n38; on time, 32–33, 69
Boyd, James W., 97–99, 109, 155n58
Brentano, Franz, 152n14
Bruya, Brian, 148n63
Burke, Peter, 14

Callery, J. M., 11
Camus, Albert, 1
capitalism, 13, 21, 65, 130, 134n23
ceremony. *See* li (ritual propriety)
Chen Chaoqun 陳超群, 143n97, 143n4
Chen Jingpan 陈景磐, 73, 135n29, 143n1, 149n72
Chen, Albert H.Y., 130, 160n38
Cheng Chung-ying 成中英, 140n71
Cheng Hao 程顥, 145n24
Cheng Yi 程頤, 145n24, 150n85
Childs, John L., 55
Chow, Kai-wing, 158n13
Christianity, 13, 22, 53, 63
communication, 88, 130; John Dewey on, 90, 153n25
Confucianism 儒家, 4, 11, 16–17, 50, 51, 71, 75, 81–82, 119–31,

Confucianism 儒家 *(continued)*
134n23, 156n67, 158n13; on authenticity, 104–5, 108–9; contemporary relevance of, 119–22, 129–31; cosmological visions of, 35–36; on education, 86, 89, 100, 114; li 理 (pattern) and, 145n24, 151n104; li 禮 (ritual propriety) and, 12–13, 15, 17, 46, 82, 99, 118, 134n26; modern antagonism to, 136n4; problems of, 122–25, 141n87; on reason, 69–70, 77, 79–80, 145n23, 151n104; on time and circumstances, 38–41, 45; tradition and, 27–29, 60, 62, 79; on zhi 智/知 (understanding, realization, wisdom), 43, 73

Confucius 孔子, 49, 79, 80, 82, 106, 138n41, 139n60, 143n1, 144n4, 149n71, 158n121; considered reactionary, 51–52, 137n19, 138n31, 143n3; on cosmic change, 35–36; on de 德 (excellence), 107–8, 124; on junzi 君子 (exemplary/edified person), 117–18, 125, 129, 141n89, 148n57; on li 禮 (ritual propriety), 12, 15–16, 100–1, 103–4, 115, 121–23, 150n98; optimistic stance of, 73–75, 77; on sheng 聖 (sagacity), 126–27; on teaching and learning, 111–15, 117; 125–30; on tradition, 26–30, 46, 110; on zhi 智/知 (understanding, realization, wisdom), 102, 142n91; zhong 中 (focus, hitting the mark) and, 38–41, 43–44

consciousness, 86–87, 145n22; aesthetic, 87, 93, 109, 152n9, 155n58; edified, 85, 152n9; false, 52; G.W.F. Hegel on, 152n14, 153n21, 154n33; historical 86–88, 152n9

Counts, George, 54–55

Cua, Antonio S., 138n41, 150n86

dance, 97–98, 104; Xunzi on, 98–99
dao 道 (way, tradition), 29–31, 42–44, 46–47, 59–62, 74, 79, 97, 102, 110, 113, 118, 138n33, 141n89, 145nn22–23, 158n121
Daodejing 道德經, 45, 59, 61, 138n33, 145n22
Daoism 道家, 10–11, 78, 134n23, 145n24; compared with Confucianism, 35–36; on dao 道 (way, tradition), 29, 59–60, 62
Daxue 大學 (*Great Learning*), 116, 119
de Miribel, Jean, 151n104
de 德 (excellence), 59–60, 79 105–8, 114, 124; David L. Hall and Roger T. Ames on, 105
democracy, 13, 56
Deutsch, Eliot, 109, 136n11, 137n12
Dewey, John, 50, 60, 71, 81, 109, 147n44, 153n24, 154n31; on communication, 90, 153n25; educational philosophy of, 88–91, 147n41, 154n32; on habit and reason, 23–24, 50, 63–69, 80, 88–91, 146–47nn39–41; on indoctrination, 55; on the reasonable, 65, 68, 69, 90
Dilthey, Wilhelm, 86–87
Ding of Teng, Duke 騰定公, 124
doing and undergoing, 90
dongli 動理 (dynamic patternings), 62, 91
Duan Yucai 段玉裁, 13

edification (Bildung), 81, 85–86, 88, 129, 153n21
education, 15, 56, 58, 62, 70–71, 80–81, 83–84, 86, 94, 108, 122, 135n4; David L. Hall and Roger T. Ames on, 83; experience and, 88–91, 114; and indoctrination

49, 50–55, 144n6; philosophy of, 17, 82, 88, 89, 114, 154n32; ritual and, 95–100, 110, 118; 'traditional' and 'progressive,' 88–89. *See also* edification (Bildung); jiao 教 (education, teaching); teaching; xue 學 (learning)
effective history (Wirkungsgeschichte), 5
Ekstrom, Linda, 97
emotion, 16, 40, 49, 68, 72, 86, 90, 103–4, 146n39, 148n63
Enlightenment, 13, 14, 21–22, 24–25, 49, 52, 55–59, 63, 83, 84, 134n28
Eno, Robert, 79, 97
Erya 爾雅, 44
experience, 10, 32, 65, 67–69, 71, 81–82, 86–94, 97, 105, 136, 138n33, 152n9, 152n14, 154n33; aesthetic, 108–9, 154n35; as Erfahrung, 81, 86–87, 89; as Erlebnis, 86–87; of ritual, 96–98
experiential continuum, 89–91

family, 100, 117
Feng Youlan 馮友蘭, 143n1
Fingarette, Herbert, 134n26, 158n121
freedom, 25, 50, 56, 58, 86, 94

Gadamer, Hans-Georg, 2–3, 5–6, 9, 81–82; on edification (Bildung), 84–89; on experience, 86–89, 91, 109, 154n35; on reason, 24–25; on sense (Sinn), 93, 99, 141n78, 152n9; 155n58; on tradition, 3, 5, 24–25, 62, 81, 84–85, 87–88, 134n28, 136n11
Ge Rongjin 葛榮晉, 28–29, 38–40, 44, 134n22, 143n3, 151n99
Goethe, Johann Wolfgang, 145n22
Goncharov, Ivan, 101
Gongsun Chou 公孫丑, 42
Gou Chengyi 勾承益, 51, 115–16, 151n105

Graham, A. C., 37, 78
Great Learning. See *Daxue* 大學 (*Great Learning*)
growth, 89, 91, 98, 160n38
Grubacic, Andrej, 136n12
Guodian 郭店, 16, 104

Habermas, Jürgen, 134n28
habit, 45, 69, 127; Confucius on, 73; and hexis, 147n42; John Dewey on, 23, 50, 63, 65–68, 89–91, 146n39; as li 禮 (ritual propriety), 80
habitus, 50; Pierre Bourdieu on, 68–69, 115, 147n
Hagen, Kurtis, 150n97, 151n103
Hall, David L., 27, 29, 94, 138n33, 142n96, 143n98; on de 德 (excellence), 105; on education, 83; on li 禮 (ritual propriety) 13, 115; on reason, 60, 79
Han Yu 韓愈, 150n85
Han 漢 (dynasty), 16, 36, 40, 123, 125, 149n71
Hanfeizi 韓非子, 125
Hansen, Chad, 137n19
harmony, 11, 62–63, 74, 102, 105, 112, 120, 129–30, 142n96
He Baihua 何百華, 157n117
He Youling 賀友齡, 157n117
Hecht, Richard D., 97
Hegel, G. W. F., 5, 14, 81, 88, 91; on edification (Bildung), 83–84, 86, 153n21; on experience (Erfahrung), 86–87, 89, 92–93, 152n14, 154n33; on reason, 84
Herder, Johann Gottfried, 83
hermeneutics, 2, 5, 24, 27, 81, 84, 86, 88, 110–11, 122, 137
hexis, 115, 147n42. *See also* habit
Høeg, Peter, 137n21
Hu Meixin, 110
Hu Shi 胡适, 143n1
Huang Chun-chieh 黃俊傑, 137n23

Hui Dong 惠棟, 39, 140n71
Hui Jixing 惠吉星, 135n1
humanization, 13, 17, 82, 84, 118, 131
Husserl, Edmund, 152n5

individualism, 13, 158n11
indoctrination, 49–50, 51–55, 57–58, 82, 144n6
inner and outer (neiwai 內外), 101, 102–3, 109, 123–25, 142n96
intelligence, 65–66, 68, 77, 80, 147n41, 147n55. *See also* reason

Jenkins, Richard, 157n114
Jennings, Theodore W., 95–97, 99, 109, 155n45
jiao 教 (education, teaching), 62, 86, 112. *See also* teaching
Jie Ni 桀溺, 73–74, 149n71
Jin Jingfang 金景芳, 122
Jixia Academy 稷下學宮, 29
Jullien, François, 29, 34, 112, 123, 137, 140n75, 141n84
junzi 君子 (exemplary/edified person), 39, 41, 74–76, 97, 114, 129, 138n41, 141n87, 158n121; Confucius on, 117–18, 125, 129, 141n89, 148n57; contrasted with xiao ren 小人 (petty person), 108, 123, 129, 130, 159n17; dao 道 (way, tradition) of, 31, 62; de 德 inspired, 107–8; Mencius on, 42, 71, 76, 105, 146n33, 157n118; on successful teaching, 112; Xunzi on, 47, 79, 150n92, 159n17, 159n28

Kant, Immanuel, 14, 21, 25, 26, 56–57, 61, 93, 146n28, 154n36
Knoblock, John, 28, 80, 107, 150n87
Kongzi 孔子. *See* Confucius 孔子
Kotwal, Dastur, 99

Krishnamurti, J., 147n55

language, 2–3, 29, 86, 92, 103, 113, 153n25; Chinese 20, 26–27, 29, 33–34, 45, 117, 140n65, 144n6; Indo-European 27, 83–84, 116, 137n21; Inuit 27–28, 137n21; private, 20
Lau, D.C., 73
le 樂 (joy, optimism), 71, 74, 104, 107, 149n72, 151n105
learning. *See* xue 學 (learning)
Legalism 法家, 73, 125, 145n24
Legge, James, 11, 40–41, 112, 116, 145n23, 157n117
Lei Feng 雷鋒, 135n32
Leng Chengjin 冷成金, 143n1
li 理 (patternings), 79–80, 91, 106, 150–51nn98–99, 151n104; combined with qi 氣 (vital energy), 145n24; in dongli 動理, 61–62, 91; Mencius on, 77; as reason, 59–61, 69, 145n21; Xunzi on, 79–80
li 禮 (ritual propriety), 11–13, 19, 22, 69, 81–82, 94, 95, 99, 119–23, 126, 128, 135nn29–30; Confucius on, 12, 15–16, 100–1, 103–4, 115, 121–23, 150n98; as cognate of ti 體 (body), 96; combined with yue 樂 (music), 16, 102–4, 109, 113; as embodiment of (Chinese) tradition, 115–16, 135n1; flexibility of, 122; interplay with li 理 and yi 義, 71, 76, 78–80, 150–51nn98–99, 151nn103–5; law and, 129–30; meaning and, 79, 82, 115, 120; Mencius on, 71–72, 75–76; personalization of, 99–103, 109–10; reification of, 51, 123–25, 128, 134n22, 158n11; time and, 97–98, 120–22; Roger T. Ames on, 12–13, 29, 100, 115, 125, 134n29;

universal application of, 119–21; Xunzi on, 46–47, 79–80, 118, 120, 151n103, 159n28; zhong 中 (focus, hitting the mark) and, 46–47, 143n101; in *Wuxing* essay, 104–5, 108

Liji 禮記 (*Book of Rites*), 16, 40, 51, 95, 102, 112, 114, 116, 121

Lin Yutang 林語堂, 143n1

Liu Shu-hsien 劉述先, 135n29

Liu Xiahui 柳下惠, 106, 149n71

Locke, John, 152n14

logos, 60, 141n77, 145n22, 146n27

Lu Dingyi 陸定一, 135n4

Lu Jiuyuan 陸九淵 (Lu Xiangshan 陸象山), 137n23

Lunyu 論語 (*Analects of Confucius*), 15–16, 26, 27, 30, 35, 39, 41, 42–43, 46, 62, 70, 71, 73, 103, 107, 111, 113, 117, 126, 127–28, 139n60, 148n63; describing comportment of Confucius, 100–2; dogmatism of, 51, 123

MacIntyre, Alasdair, 23–24, 26, 31, 134n28

Macmillan, C. J. B., 58

Madman of Chu 楚狂, 74, 149n71

Mao, Chen, 138n31

Maoism, 17, 129

Marx, Karl, 4, 21

Marxism, 21, 31, 51, 52, 54, 135n4

Mawangdui 馬王堆, 16, 36, 143n98

meaning, 27, 44, 88, 90–91, 128, 155n59; *dao* 道 (way, tradition) as, 145n22; education and, 91–93; habit and, 67–68, 90–91; of human action, practice, 19, 20, 23, 30, 33, 56, 66, 69, 90; lack of, 26, 66, 90, 109, 135n30; *li* 禮 (ritual propriety) and, 79, 82, 115, 120; personal construction of, 7–8, 44, 56, 71, 79, 90–92, 109–10, 115; role of culture and tradition in, 7–8, 14, 24, 71, 79, 97, 98–99, 109–10

Mencius 孟子, 15, 50, 104, 121, 124; on Confucius, 39; optimistic stance of, 75–76, 127; on *junzi* 君子 (exemplary/edified person), 42, 71, 76, 105, 146n33, 157n118; on *li* 禮 (ritual propriety), 71–72, 75–76; on *renxing* 人性 (natural human dispositions), 73; 75–80, 148n61, 148n63, 150n85, 150n87, 151n105; on rhythm, 106; on *sheng* 聖 (sagacity), 106, 149n71, 151n105; on *xin* 心 (heart-mind, sense, feelings), 71–72, 75–76, 77, 105; on *zhong* 中 (focus, hitting the mark), 41–42, 141n80; on *yi* 義 (appropriateness), 71–72, 77–78, 151n105; on *zhi* 智/知 (understanding, realization, wisdom), 71–72, 76, 105, 106

Mengzi 孟子. *See* Mencius

ming 命 (forces of circumstances), 75–77, 114

Ming 明 (dynasty), 145n24, 158n11

Mohism 墨家, 29, 145n24

Molière, 64

music, 33; Confucian discussion of, 15–16, 81, 102–4, 106–8, 113, 115. *See also le* 樂 (joy, optimism)

Nagai, Michio, 53–54, 58, 144n7

Nagel, Thomas, 2

Neo-Confucianism 宋明儒家, 137n23, 145n24, 150n85

Neville, Robert Cummings, 119–20, 127

New Confucianism 新儒家, 119

Ng, On-Cho, 158n13

Nietzsche, Friedrich, 4, 7, 8; on last human beings, 57; on perspectivism, 5–6, 68; on reason, 63–64, 146n35

Noddings, Nel, 154n32
Nuyen, A. T., 119–20, 159n22

objectivity, 9, 34, 84, 137n23, 146n28; Alfred North Whitehead on, 8; Friedrich Nietzsche on, 5–6, 64; Hans-Georg Gadamer on, 5, 9, 85; Max Weber on, 145n25; scientific claim to, 31, 53–54, 145n25
Ōmuro Mikio, 77
optimism, 73–75, 77, 80, 104, 107–8, 149n72, 151n105. See also le 樂 (joy, optimism)

Pang Pu 龐樸, 105
Peng Lirong 彭立榮, 102, 150n98
personal cultivation. See xiushen 修身
personalization, 81, 101, 151n99; as creative act, 92, 100; of ritual performance, 94, 100, 109–10, 122; of tradition, 30, 62, 94, 114, 124
petty persons. See xiao ren 小人.
Plato, 21, 111, 141n78; on reason, 57, 61, 63
power, 52, 103, 130; as de (excellence), 105, 107–8; Max Weber on, 50, 56–57; of reason, 14; of tradition, 25
prejudgement (Vorurteil), 2, 6, 8, 11, 82
Proust, Marcel, 92
Pythagoreans, 61, 141n78

qi 氣 (vital energy), 139n50, 145nn23–24
qing 情 (spontaneous (re)actions), 72, 148n63. See also emotion
Qing 清 (dynasty), 39, 136, 158n11

Ranyou 冉有, 127
Rappaport, Roy A., 135n30
rationality. See reason
Rawls, John, 134n28
reason, 59, 60–61, 63, 82, 85, 120–21, 137n19, 144n17, 145n20, 146nn27–28, 154n36; Chinese candidates for, 26, 59–63, 69–70, 77–79, 145n21, 145n23, 150n98, 151n104; contrasted with impulses, 63–63; contrasted with ritual and tradition, 14, 19, 21–22, 52–53, 82–83; David L. Hall and Roger T. Ames on, 59–60; as dongli 動理 (dynamic patternings), 62; Enlightenment notion of, 21–22, 24–25, 49–50, 55–58, 82–83, 134n28; Friedrich Nietzsche on, 64, 146n35; G.W.F. Hegel on, 84; Hans-Georg Gadamer on, 24–25; as instrumental or means-end rationality (Zweckrationalität), 14, 56, 59, 65, 108, 145n20, 156n91; John Dewey on, 63–64, 65–66, 68, 80, 88, 90–91, 146–47nn39–41; Max Weber on, 55–59; Pierre Bourdieu, 64–65, 68–69, 80, 146n38; as Vernunft, 61, 146n28, 146n35; as value-rationality (Wertrationalität), 56, 57. See also dongli 動理 (dynamic patternings); intelligence; reasonable, the
reasonable, the, 50, 63, 80; John Dewey on, 65, 68, 69, 90; Pierre Bourdieu on, 65, 69
Reed, Gay Garland, 135n32
Reformation, 14
Ren Jiyu 任繼愈, 28–29
Ren Junhua 任俊華, 142n96
ren 仁 (communal humanity), 105, 120, 126, 128, 159n28; implying social sense, 108–9
renxing 人性 (natural human dispositions), 50, 72–73, 75, 77–78, 150n85. See also xing 性 (natural dispositions).

rhythm, 33, 94, 97; Xunzi on, 99; Mencius on, 106
ritual, 11–13, 15, 16, 19, 20, 22, 28, 31, 35, 46, 51, 69, 71, 72, 76, 77, 79–80, 81, 102–4, 108, 109, 113, 119, 122, 123, 127, 130, 134nn29–30, 136n11, 151n104; educational value of, 94–99, 110, 114–15, 118, 120, 155n45, 155n58; modern distaste for, 13–14, 21, 31; Pierre Bourdieu on, 32–33, 146n38. See also li 禮 (ritual propriety)
romanticism, 22, 24–25
Rosemont, Jr., Henry, 41, 138n33; on li 禮 (ritual propriety), 100
Rousseau, Jean-Jacques, 72
Rujia 儒家. See Confucianism 儒家

sagacity. See sheng 聖
sangang 三綱 (Three Bond Doctrine), 125
Schleiermacher, Friedrich, 152n5
Schmidt, Dennis J., 153n21
Schwartz, Benjamin, 26
self-cultivation. See xiushen 修身 (personal cultivation)
sense, 46, 126, 145n22, 146n27, 147n54; aesthetic, 109, 152n9; of appropriateness, 69, 71, 76, 78, 79, 81, 96–97, 151n103; common, 26, 69; general and communal (Sinn), 81, 84–87, 99, 101, 108, 145n22; of shame, 72, 103; for situation, 33, 40; of values, 51; as xin 心 (heart-mind, sense, feelings), 72, 77
Shaftesbury, Earl of, 85
shan 善 (goodness), 72, 73, 75, 107, 152n105
Shang 商 (dynasty), 12, 15, 26, 36
shen 身 (body, self). See body
sheng 聖 (sagacity), 75, 76, 108, 128, 142n94; Confucius on, 126–27; inner sage and outer king 内聖

外王, 102, 123, 156n67; Mencius on, 106, 149n71, 151n105; Wuxing essay on, 104–6; Xunzi on, 150n92
Shiji 史記 (Historical Records), 36
Shijing 詩經 (Book of Odes), 15, 107, 111
Shujing 書經 (Book of Documents), 15
Shun 舜 (sage-king), 39, 75, 117, 149n76
Shuowen jiezi 說文解字, 12–13, 38, 44, 114–15, 138n26, 139n49, 142n90
Sima Qian 司馬遷, 36
Snook, I. A., 58, 144n7
Song 宋 (dynasty), 137n23, 145n24
space, 33–35
Spencer, Herbert, 13
Staal, Frits, 135n30

Tang Junyi 唐君毅, 33, 35, 62, 139n49, 139n62
Tang Kejing 湯可敬, 115
teaching, 52–53, 82, 111–13, 115, 118, 125. See also jiao (teaching)
tianming 天命. See ming 命
Tiles, J. E., 141n77, 141n78
time, 32, 88, 91, 100; conception in Chinese thought, 19, 33–35, 37, 42–43, 45, 70, 106, 142n75; li 禮 (ritual propriety) and, 97–98, 120–22; Pierre Bourdieu on, 32–33, 69; zhong 中 (focus, hitting the mark) and, 38–39, 140nn71–72
tradition, 1, 9, 19–22, 26–31, 42, 45–47, 49–50, 61–63, 79–80, 91, 93, 94, 96, 109, 121, 124–25, 134n28, 136n6, 136n12, 151n103, 158n11; Alasdair MacIntyre on, 23; as dao 道 (way, tradition), 29, 44, 46, 60, 62, 79, 97, 111, 113, 118, 141n80; modern opposition to, 21, 52, 55, 56, 82–83, 135n4; Confucian and Chinese, 12–13, 15, 19–20, 26, 35, 37, 39, 43–45,

tradition (*continued*)
51, 75, 81, 102, 104, 108, 110–11, 114, 119, 123, 137n23, 150n85, 159n13; David L. Hall and Roger T. Ames on, 115; Eliot Deutsch on, 136n11; G.W.F. Hegel on, 84; Hans-Georg Gadamer on, 3, 5, 24–25, 62, 81, 84–85, 87–88; Karl Marx on, 21; practice and, 20; reason embedded in, 70; romantic glorification of, 22

Tran Van Doan (Chen Wentuan 陳文團), 135n4

truth, 58, 137n12; absolute, 121; Alfred North Whitehead on, 7; Hans-Georg Gadamer on, 87, 93; as meaningfulness, 93; objective, 34, 53; reason and, 53, 63, 91; transcendent, 46; universal, 86

Tu Weiming 杜維明, 37, 62, 119, 139n62, 142n96

Turner, Victor, 96, 99, 155n45

values, 2, 5, 22, 50, 53–55, 65, 89, 145n20, 147n40; Confucian, 17, 119, 123; cultural tradition and, 45–46, 95–96, 115; feudal, 49, 51–52; Max Weber on, 55–59, 144n13, 156n91; moral and social, 13, 22, 130; perspective and, 6–8; practices and, 24, 30; true, 56

van der Leeuw, Gerardus, 97

Vandermeersch, Léon, 13, 154n104

Vico, Giambattista, 85

virtue. *See* de 德 (excellence)

von Landwagen, Baron, 101

Waley, Arthur, 41, 124, 158n121

Wang Hongyu, 123

Wang Yangming 王陽明, 142n90

Wang Yunlu 王雲路, 159n17

Warnke, Georgia, 5, 86, 154n35

Warring States period, 2, 16, 17, 36, 38

Weber, Max, 7, 14, 134n23, 145n25, 147n40; on power, 50, 56–57; on reason and values, 55–59, 63, 65, 144n13, 156n91

Whitehead, Alfred North, 94–95, 122; on objectivity, 8; on perspective, 6–7; on truth, 7

Wilhelm, Richard, 145n22

Williams, Ron G., 97–99, 109, 155n58

wisdom. *See* zhi 智/知 (understanding, realization, wisdom)

Wittgenstein, Ludwig, 20, 58

Wu Zongjie, 110

Wuxing essay 五行篇, 82, 104–9, 123

Xia 夏 (alleged dynasty), 12, 26

xiao ren 小人 (petty persons), 107, 108, 123–24, 128, 159n17

xin 信 (being true to one's words), 113

xin 心 (heart-mind, sense, feelings), 103, 126; Mencius on, 71–72, 75–76, 77, 105

xing 性 (natural dispositions), 62, 102, 150n83; Mencius on, 71–77, 151n105, 148n60; Xunzi on, 77–78, 150nn85–86, 151n105

xiushen 修身 (personal cultivation), 15, 71, 73, 76, 82, 83, 100, 105, 114–17, 119, 128, 130, 138n41, 151n105, 160n38; music and, 16; Xunzi on, 78

Xu Fuguan 徐復觀, 61, 76

Xu Shen 許慎, 12

xue 學 (learning), 26, 41, 114, 142n92. *See also* edification (Bildung); education; jiao 教 (education, teaching)

Xunzi 荀子, 28, 69, 97, 98, 114, 128, 138n26, 145n24, 148n63; compatibility with Mencius, 50, 77, 150nn86–87, 151n105; as constructivist, 150n97; on dance,

98–99; on junzi 君子 (exemplary/edified person), 47, 79, 150n92, 159n17, 159n28; on li 禮 (ritual propriety), 46–47, 79–80, 118, 120, 151n103, 159n28; on sheng 聖 (sagacity), 150n92; on xing 性 (natural dispositions), 77–78, 150nn85–86, 151n105; on xiushen 修身 (personal cultivation), 78; on yi 義 (appropriateness), 46–47, 78–80, 120, 151n103; on zhong 中 (focus, hitting the mark), 46–47, 79

Yan Hui 顏回, 112, 126, 128
Yao 堯 (sage-king), 39, 75, 117, 149n76
Yi Ya 易牙, 75
Yi Yin 伊尹, 106
yi 義 (appropriateness), 69, 108, 120, 129, 138n39, 145n23, 151n99, 151nn103–4; Mencius on, 71–72, 77–78, 151n105; in *Wuxing* essay, 104–6; Xunzi on, 46–47, 78–80, 120, 151n103
Yijing 易經 (*Classic of Changes*), 36–37, 39, 139n57, 139n60
Yili 儀禮, 51
yin & yang 陰陽, 36–37, 39
Yizhuan 易傳, 36, 38–39, 139n60, 140n71
yue 樂. *See* music; le 樂 (joy, optimism)

Zeno from Elea, 116
Zhang Dainian 張岱年, 37–38, 42, 134n22
Zhang Weizhong 張衛中, 26, 30, 113
Zhang Xianglong, 139n57, 140n68

Zhang Zai 張載, 145n24
Zhao Zhentao 趙甄陶, 140n72
Zheng Xuan 鄭玄, 149n71
zhengming 正名 (using names appropriately), 28–29, 38, 103, 113, 125, 141n89, 143n3
zhi 智/知 (understanding, realization, wisdom), 43, 44, 71, 73, 108, 120, 142n91, 157n118; action and, 114, 142n90; Confucius on, 102, 142n91; Mencius on, 71–72, 76, 105, 106; in *Wuxing* essay, 104–7; Xunzi on, 78; Zhongyong on, 102
zhong 中 (focus, hitting the mark), 19, 38–42, 143n101; as moderation, 41–42; in shizhong 時中, 38–40, 140nn71–72; Xunzi on, 46–47, 79; in zhongdao 中道 and zhongxing 中行, 42, 141n80; in zhongyong 中庸, 43–45, 142nn96–97
Zhongyong 中庸, 143n97; notion, 40, 43–45, 134n22, 142n96; text, 30, 38–40, 43, 46, 62, 72, 79, 86, 102, 141n87,
Zhou 周 (dynasty), 12, 15, 26, 28–29, 36, 43, 46, 51, 73, 80
Zhu Xi 朱熹, 137n23
Zhuangzi 莊子, 10, 35, 78, 102
Zigong 子貢, 41, 111–12
Zilu 子路, 43–44, 73–74, 103, 117
Zisizi 子思子, 15, 39, 40, 104
Zixia 子夏, 41–43, 141n87
Zizhang 子張, 41, 43
Zoroastrianism, 97, 99
Zou Changlin 鄒昌林, 135n1
Zuozhuan 左轉 (*Zuo Commentary to the Spring and Autumn Annals*), 115–16